HOUSING RESEARCH AND DEVELOPMENT

UNIVERSITY OF ILLINOIS
1204 WEST NEVADA
URBANA, ILLINOIS 61801

THE FUTURE OF COUNCIL HOUSING

THE FUTURE OF COUNCIL HOUSING

Edited by John English

CROOM HELM
London & Canberra

© 1982 John English
Croom Helm Ltd, 2-10 St John's Road, London SW11

British Library Cataloguing in Publication Data

The Future of council housing.
 1. Public housing - Great Britain
 I. Title II. English, John, 1944
 363.5   HD7333.A3

ISBN: 0-7099-0900-4

Printed and bound in Great Britain by
Biddles Ltd, Guildford and King's Lynn

Contents

Preface

Council housing has developed since the 1920s until it is now one
of the two dominant tenures in Britain, catering for nearly a third
of households. It is thus far removed from, for instance, American
public housing which accommodates only the poorest in society. In
recent years, however, under the combined influences of a sharp
reduction in the level of investment and of a growing number of
sales, there has been increasing uncertainty about the future of
council housing. Both trends have been heightened by the policies
of the Conservative government elected in 1979, whose cuts in
public expenditure are concentrated on council housing and which
has introduced the tenants' statutory right to buy at a substantial
discount on market value. Looking into the future it is possible to
envisage, and this is certainly the government's objective, a much
smaller and radically altered council sector which will be confined
to the residual role of meeting the 'real needs' of those who are
unable to achieve owner occupation.

Discussion of policy towards council housing - and particularly
towards sales - has been bedevilled by crude assertions and lack
of analysis. The aim of this book is to examine the present state
of council housing, to clarify the implications of government policies (especially its emphasis on sales), and to look at prospects
for the future. The council sector cannot be examined in isolation
from the rest of the housing system: for example, almost any significant change affecting it is likely to have repercussions on
owner occupation. Furthermore, housing policy has implications
for the economy as a whole. The book thus seeks to take a wide-
ranging view of council housing. If one future for the council
sector is implicit in the policies of the present government, none
of the other main parties has a coherent alternative. Certainly
the position before the present government took office does not
represent such an alternative; the attractions which are conferred on owner occupation by subsidy and taxation policy
ensured that the drift towards residual council housing was
already well-established. Some of the requirements for the
continued existence of a large council sector catering for a wide
range of households are outlined in the final chapter. Choices
about policy are quite properly political decisions, but it is
desirable that they should be made in the light of a realistic view
of likely costs and benefits. This book may make some contribution to more informed debate about housing policy.

Two final points should be made. First, although the book is
specifically concerned with council housing, owned and managed

by local authorities, most of the analysis is equally applicable to the (small) remainder of the public sector in Britain – mainly housing provided by the new towns and the Scottish Special Housing Association. Terms such as 'the public sector' are generally used interchangeably with 'council housing'. Secondly, housing is a field where policy statements, research findings and so forth appear fairly continuously so that no book can be absolutely up to date when it is published, but as far as possible account has been taken of developments up to mid-1981. There is an appendix on the final report of the House of Commons Environment Committee on council house sales which was published after the main text of the book had been completed.

1 The First Sixty Years of Council Housing

David Whitham

The building of council housing on a substantial scale in Britain
began with the introduction of exchequer subsidies at the end of
the First World War, though its origins go back to the nineteenth
century. An understanding of the 60 years of the history of public sector housing, and of the events which led up to the subsidy
legislation of 1919, is important because changing policies and
attitudes have profoundly affected the quality and character of
the stock which exists today. Discussion of the present and future
roles of council housing must take account of this inheritance. The
development of housing policy in Britain has been covered several
times before and in far greater detail than is possible here,[1] but
this chapter attempts to outline the evolving role, size and form
of the public sector. Statistics have generally been avoided,
though tables are included showing numbers of dwellings built and,
for more recent years, the breakdown between houses and flats.

TOWARDS COUNCIL HOUSING

British housing at the end of the First World War presented a
crisis both of quantity and quality. Advancing byelaw standards
and the products of the housing reform movement in the private,
co-operative and public sectors, though far from numerous, had
shown that high standards were achievable for working-class
housing. Those standards had become expectations but they were
at the margin of affordability, victim to increasing costs, dearer
money, higher rates and new taxation. These threats apart, other
outlets for investment had diverted savings from private house
building which had come to a virtual standstill about 1908.

Wartime experience had shown that both supply and quality of
available housing impeded mobility of labour. To ease these obstacles
the Admiralty and the War Office together with the Ministry of
Munitions had supplied, directly or indirectly, more than 7,000
houses between 1914 and 1918 in England and Wales, and 4,000 in
Scotland.[2] Social initiatives by the Ministry of Munitions had been
numerous, but nothing was done that was not seen to be necessary
to fighting the war. The crisis of quality had already bitten hard
in 1911, when Admiralty torpedo workers transferred from Woolwich rejected the tenement 'houses' offered to them in Greenock.[3]
The decision to house government workers involved in such moves
at 'garden-city' standards, in generously planned cottages at
twelve to the acre, had been made before the war began and it was

accepted that such provision would have to be subsidised. In
August 1914 a new housing act was rushed on to the statute book
and under it was built the first state-subsidised housing, at
Rosyth in Scotland and the Well Hall estate near Woolwich Arsenal.

The war experience showed, not surprisingly, that housing conditions were worst in the older industrial areas dominated by heavy
industry, and, as the torpedo workers had realised, they were
nowhere worse than in Scotland. In Scotland, too, the crisis of
supply broke most dramatically in the Glasgow rent strikes of
1915,[4] leading directly to rent control, a 'temporary' measure that
was not easily to be relinquished.

As early as 1911 concern about Scottish housing had caused the
appointment of a royal commission which eventually reported in
1917.[5] The commission had shown great interest in the provision
of houses by local authorities and took evidence from authorities in
England, notably Liverpool and the London County Council (LCC),
which had special experience of council housing. In accordance
with the terms of their appointment, the commissioners studiously
ignored the effects of rent control, but could not ignore the pressures of the war. But even discounting these special circumstances,
the majority report found the failure of the private supply of
working-class housing proven.

> Doubtless the climax came with the war; the failure however had
> become manifest long before then. But whatever its causes, the
> disorganisation flowing from the war makes an immediate revival
> of uncontrolled private enterprise on an adequate scale
> impossible.
> There is, in our view, only one alternative: the State itself,
> through the local authorities, is alone in a position to assume
> responsibility... the local authorities must be placed under
> an unmistakable obligation to maintain a continuous and sys-
> tematic survey of their housing accommodation [and] - failing
> provision by any other agencies - to undertake themselves -
> with financial assistance from the State - the necessary
> building schemes.[6]

A minority of the commissioners dissented: while not denying the
need for some state provision, they would have limited it to a
clearly residual role. They doubted the capacity of local authorities
to do the job, they feared the effects of subsidised housing on the
market as a whole and, not least, were concerned about 'the voting
power of the municipal tenant'.[7]

NEEDS, STANDARDS AND SUBSIDY

The controversy that had accompanied its production, and the
forceful arguments employed, if anything increased the persuasive
power of the Scottish royal commission's report. Earlier in 1917 the
Local Government Board had sent a circular letter to local authorities asking for estimates of housing need, and had appointed a

committee under the chairmanship of Sir John Tudor Walters to
consider practical questions of constructing and planning working-
class houses, a remit extended to cover Scotland early in 1918.
The resulting document, [8] called for convenience the Tudor Walters
Report, is justly famous as possibly the most comprehensive housing manual ever written.

The whole report clearly bears the stamp of Raymond Unwin,
who had been appointed architectural advisor to the Local Government Board in August 1914, and seconded to the Ministry of
Munitions, where he had been influential in establishing the
garden-city model for wartime housing.

In the Tudor Walters Report garden-city (or, more accurately,
garden-suburb) standards were codified and presented as a system, in which a consistent approach to house design, construction,
layout and circulation was set out: a revolutionary standard of
residential environment, previously open only to a privileged or
fortunate minority, was prescribed as an attainable norm for new
working-class housing. In internal layout and equipment, density
and planning, the recommendations went far beyond even the best
municipal housing that had been provided before the war.

Local authority replies to the circular letter of 1917 had suggested that about 300,000 houses were needed to make good the
shortage of working-class houses in England and Wales, and about
100,000 in Scotland. Tudor Walters suggested that if the low
standard that had been applied was only slightly raised it would
probably add another 200,000, so that the need in Great Britain
was about 500,000 houses, in addition to an estimated 'ordinary
demand' of 100,000 houses each year. [9]

The line of argument then proceeded to consider standards and
here took a firmly radical turn. The shortage was of all kinds of
houses, not merely those for the badly paid; standards had been
rising and would continue to do so; the number of houses needed
was so large that meeting it would profoundly affect the standard
of housing as a whole; many existing houses fell below accepted
minimum standards and more would soon become outdated: the
shortage was of good homes, not of barely acceptable ones. Therefore,

> it is only wise economy to build dwellings which, so far as may
> be judged, will continue to be above the accepted minimum, at
> least for the whole period of the loan... say 60 years; to add
> to the already large supply of houses on the margin line might
> prove anything but economical in the long run. [10]

The arguments about the nature and level of government subsidy
have been recounted elsewhere, [11] but Addison's Housing and
Town Planning, Etc. Act, 1919, was generous in the extreme, con-
ceding to the demand of the local authorities that their own expenditure should be limited to the product of a penny rate (four-
fifths of a penny in the corresponding Scottish act) for schemes
approved in the first three years. The duties placed upon councils

were almost exactly those recommended by the Scottish Royal Commission; they were required to survey the needs of their areas
and to make and carry out plans for providing the necessary
houses. Building schemes required the consent of the Ministry of
Health, which had succeeded the Local Government Board in June
1919. Rents, related to controlled rents of similar (privately
rented) houses built before the war and to tenants' ability to pay,
were also to be agreed by the ministry.

IMPLEMENTING THE POLICY

The handbook issued to guide councils in planning their housing
schemes implemented Tudor Walters's recommendations to the full
and in certain respects prescribed standards that were somewhat
higher. Densities were restricted to not more than twelve houses
to the acre in urban districts and eight in rural areas, with houses
built in semi-detached pairs or rows of four. Every house was to
have a bath (though not necessarily in a bathroom) or space to
provide one if, initially, no proper water supply was available.
The garden-city repertoire of north- and south-aspect houses,
small crescents and culs-de-sac, and special house types for corner
sites were all employed. Schemes were usually designed by architects from local panels, selected by a competition organised jointly
by the Ministry of Health and the Royal Institute of British Architects, so that regional variations were encouraged. What was consistent was the generous layout, with curving tree-lined roads,
wide verges and large gardens, and careful detail and variety of
house design that have secured these earliest schemes a place
among the most popular estates in many a council's housing stock.
    The first requirement under the 1919 Act was the housing sur-
vey. Housing authorities were sent a 'Form of Survey of Housing
Needs' for completion and return to the ministry within three
months. The form was surprisingly comprehensive, closely resemb-
ling those prescribed for the Housing Strategy and Investment
Programme returns of the late 1970s, and like them was subject to
a degree of interpretive and imaginative latitude. [12]
    The total returns from local authorities in England and Wales
showed an estimated housing need until July 1922 of 824,700 dwellings, and the 1919 total of all adopted schemes (which were still
subject to approval by the ministry) was for 633,758 council
houses. [13] By the Spring of 1920 councils had made firm proposals
for building 162,000 houses, sanctioned by the Ministry of Health.
For local authorities inexperienced in building on such a scale and
operating within an entirely new administrative structure, the rate
of building achieved was remarkable, rising to over 86,000 houses
completed in 1922. This was in spite of the abolition of building
licensing in December 1918 which had put local authorities at a
disadvantage in practically every respect compared with other
customers in a great building boom. [14] Tender prices rocketed, to
about three times pre-war prices in 1920, but after that fell rapidly

in the slump that followed. The 1919 Act programme, 'the first
experiment' as Bowley called it,[15] was first cut back, then abandoned by government on grounds of high costs and profligate
spending by the councils. But by that time costs were past their
peak[16] and there really could have been no better investment
than to pursue resolutely the adopted programme. Merrett argues
that the reasons were political[17] and that the cabinet, reluctant
from the start to be committed to a full-scale state housing programme with open-ended subsidy, took advantage of disarray
within the Labour movement to rid themselves of an expensive
palliative. This adds strength to the thesis that the 1919 Act,
triumph for the housing movement though it was, had been
regarded by the Lloyd George coalition government primarily as
an insurance against industrial unrest, if not revolution.[18]

Early in 1921 the ministry had produced 'revised' survey figures,
on the basis of their own new and much more drastic definition of
'need', reducing at a stroke the total 'need' in England and Wales
from 824,700 to 457,450.[19] Scottish needs were similarly reduced
by about 50 per cent. These figures were further eroded under
Treasury pressure and reappeared in government statements as a
round 300,000, after which Addison left his ministry. His successor, Sir Alfred Mond, repeated that the total need was 300,000, of
which 50,000 would be provided by the private sector - subsidised
under the Housing (Additional Powers) Act, 1919 - and the remainder by local authorities and housing associations. Later in
1921 even those targets were abandoned; the total number of
dwellings to be provided by local authorities was to be 170,000,
which effectively meant completing only those houses for which
contracts had already been agreed.

Building under the Addison Act ended entirely in 1923. In all,
213,821 houses were built, 170,090 by local authorities, 4,545 by
housing associations and 39,186 by private builders with the subsidy.[20] Allowing for formation of new households - and Tudor
Walters's estimate of 100,000 a year was probably not far wrong -
the shortage at the end of the Addison experiment was worse than
it had been at the end of the war. Nevertheless, the achievement
was tremendous. Up to 1914 few local authorities had built houses
at all; the total number of dwellings built in England and Wales
was about 23,000.[21] Most of them were in London or other large
towns and, because of their usual function as vessels of rescue
from the slums, most of them provided accommodation of a lower
standard than contemporary byelaw housing. But Sayle in 1924
was able to describe

> in any town in England... the new 'Council Houses'. If they
> are in a small group they will certainly be newer and more
> attractive than their neighbours: if they are in a large group
> they will be found on the outskirts of the town, often pleas-
> antly situated on high ground, the whole estate bearing a
> close resemblance to a 'Garden Suburb'. Whatever else these
> houses may be, they are at least different - different

externally, differently planned and giving different accommodation from prewar 'working-class houses', the best of
which were built at least ten years earlier.[22]

The success of the Tudor Walters Report and the Addison Act had
been remarkable. In just three years of building, the model of a
new and attainable working-class life style had been disseminated
through the whole country, and the smallest rural district council
had proved its ability to build and manage houses for its people.
Housing expectations and the politics of housing could never be
the same again.

THE CHAMBERLAIN AND WHEATLEY ACTS

Despite the lack of enthusiasm evident in the cabinet, and the
Treasury's reaction to the open-ended Addison subsidy in opposing subsidy of any kind, the Ministry of Health remained convinced of a continuing need. Mond proposed a local authority
programme of 80,000 dwellings over the years 1923-4 with a fixed
annual subsidy of £3 per house. A general election in November
1922 confirmed in office the new Conservative administration which
was inclined to greater confidence in the revival of private enterprise if builders were given adequate aid. The Housing Act, 1923,
introduced by Neville Chamberlain and generally referred to as
the Chamberlain Act, was actually drafted under his predecessor,
Griffith-Boscowen, who had been minister following the fall of the
Coalition government and who was a veteran Unionist housing
reformer.[23]

The 1923 Act introduced fixed-rate subsidies of £6 per year for
20 years for each house. There was a bias in favour of private
building; the local authority would pass on the subsidy, usually
capitalised at £70, to the builder of a house to the required standards, whether for letting or for sale. Authorities were given extra
powers to grant mortgages to purchasers, but could build houses
themselves only if they could show that private builders could not
meet local needs. To qualify for subsidy, space standards markedly less generous than those of 1919 had to be met: a minimum of
620 and a maximum of 950 sq ft and it was obligatory to provide a
bath. The government's belief was that the problem was temporary and that assistance was needed only to restore normal supply;
the subsidies were therefore payable only for houses completed
before October 1925.

The really important innovation of the 1923 Act was the introduction of a fixed-rate subsidy, and the effects of this will be
discussed below. In fact the act was never tested as the sole
source of housing finance because the Conservatives were replaced
by the first Labour government in January 1924. Labour's ten
months in office would now be only an historical curiosity but for
the performance of John Wheatley as Minister of Health who, in the
Housing (Financial Provisions) Act, 1924, created its abiding mem-
orial.

Wheatley was a Clydesider, a great polemicist and a veteran of
housing politics in that worst-housed and most politicised area.
He set himself the task of committing local authorities and the
building industry to a long-term programme of building subsidised
housing to rent, intended eventually to replace the extinct private
supply.[24] The 1924 Act retained and extended the Chamberlain
subsidy, but overlaid it with a new and more generous subsidy
structure for houses to rent. An exchequer contribution of £9 per
house for 40 years was to be supplemented by a local authority
rate contribution of £4 10s. There was provision for a review of
the subsidy every two years. The 1924 Act contained something
for everyone. Besides extended subsidies, a 15-year building programme was planned up to 1939 and agreement was reached with
the building trade unions to increase the number of apprentice-
ships so as to expand the capacity of the industry.

The Wheatley Act established the role of the local authorities in
providing housing to let that has never since seriously been
questioned. Building programmes have been attacked, finance has
been attacked, access to public sector housing has been attacked,
but John Wheatley's proposition remains.

It is worth looking now at the effects of the fixed-rate subsidy,
that is so much per house for so many years, introduced in 1923,
established by Wheatley and, with variations, to remain as the
standard form of housing subsidy until the late 1960s. Clearly it
is a good arrangement for central government; open-ended subsidies like that of 1919 must be anathema to the Treasury. If there
has to be subsidy, a fixed sum per house, easily multiplied by
production, is the recipe for good budgeting. Detailed scrutiny of
proposals is not nearly so necessary; if a council chooses to gold-
plate its bath taps (a commonly alleged extravagance difficult to
find in practice) then it is on their own heads and must be paid
for either out of rents or rates. But, while the fixed-rate subsidy
provides a safeguard against extravagance, it does nothing to
improve housing standards or defend them from attrition at the
hands of careless or indifferent authorities.

With the reduction of space standards in 1923 went a reduction
in layout and environmental standards. The architects' panels
were abandoned and the care and enthusiasm that had produced
the earlier schemes, giving every town its own garden suburb, in
most areas gave way to mechanical repetition of a limited range of
standard house types. Council houses were still better built and,
because constructed in large contracts, better laid out than the
products of private builders; but we can see, during the late
1920s and early 1930s a tendency for the styles and standards of
design and layout in public and private housing sectors to con-
verge to a suburban mediocrity. This was not true everywhere:
the inner suburbs of Bristol, Nottingham and Liverpool, and the
'new towns' of Wythenshawe and Speke, contain much that was
innovative and can still delight the eye, while the fact that private
sector suburbs were seeking in some ways to imitate them was
testimonial in itself. The Wheatley programme came nowhere near its

intended target, and was closed down altogether within ten
years: nevertheless the estates of 1924-34 represent most people's
image of council housing and most council tenants' ideal.

HOUSING FOR WHOM?

Access to council housing, however, had to be rationed. Demand
exceeded supply not only because it was subsidised and therefore
a bargain, but also because it was good housing and for most
people the only good housing that was conceivably attainable.
Rents actually were high compared with other obtainable, but
inferior, accommodation, so the households competing for council
houses tended to be a select class of well-paid working people in
regular employment. Like byelaw housing before it, council housing was mainly benefiting an already advantaged group. An
awareness was growing that council housing was not reaching
those who were worst housed; it simply was not being built fast
enough to meet increasing demand.

The radical housing movement had put its faith in massive supply rather than in the reformist approach of slum clearance and
replacement. John Wheatley had been emphatic about that in his
evidence to the Scottish Royal Commission.[25] This was not acceptance of a free market approach, for it presumed subsidy of new
rented housing for the working population. Even if rents were
initially affordable only by the better paid, they would vacate
their present housing where rents would be depressed by the new
supply. A filtering process would be set in motion that would
eventually eliminate bad housing because nobody would be prepared, or obliged, to live in it. The failure to achieve any such
thing was now clear.

Our current concern with late nineteenth-century byelaw housing inclines us to forget what the slums of the inter-war period
actually were like. They included great masses of dwellings now
unimaginably bad, many of them still as they were described by
nineteenth-century commissioners, despite the limited affects of
railway and road works and the improvement schemes of a handful
of local authorities.

Generally, the housing shortage after the First World War was
such that slum clearance could not be thought of; any dwelling,
however bad, was better than none. The 1923 Act did contain
specific subsidy provisions for clearance and replacement, but
they were used by only a few authorities, mainly to deal with
areas identified before 1914 where action had been delayed.

The garden-suburb line established by the Tudor Walters Report had, before 1930, almost everywhere been held. Exceptions
were in a few inner London boroughs and in Scotland, where flats
were traditionally accepted, but even there densities were low and
extensive communal gardens were provided. Rehousing was another matter, and flats were still usual for a variety of reasons,
including the need to use inner-city sites, nearness to work,

cheapness and a presumption that flats were appropriate for the
supposedly dangerous classes that were being moved.

The result was a distinctive and special type of housing, resem-
bling tenement estates of the nineteenth century rather than the
garden-suburb model. The LCC, in two large slum clearance estates
of the 1920s, sought to compensate for the depressed environmental
standards by improved domestic equipment and communal facilities. In their major flatted schemes at Tabard Street, Southwark
and at Ossulston Street in St Pancras, electric power circuits,
central boiler houses for heating and hot water supply, and lifts
were proposed. In his first design for Ossulston Street the LCC's
architect, Topham Forrest, proposed a 'mixed development' with
penthouse studio flats, to be let at high rents, on the top floor
(albeit served by a separate entrance and lift) and an under-
ground car park. These excesses were eliminated by the ministry,
but the splendid buildings of Ossulston Street, opened by Neville
Chamberlain in 1929 and visited by the Prince of Wales, show both
in their history and their architectural treatment an awareness of
the dangers that lurked in a two-class housing system.[26]

That was to become the great dilemma for those involved in
housing in the 1930s and some of its problems are still with us. In
1929 bad housing had become a major concern, central to that
year's general election campaign. Arthur Greenwood became Minister of Health in the second Labour government and proceeded to
implement the party's commitment to a two-pronged housing programme: to go on providing general needs housing under the
Wheatley Act and to demolish and replace the slums. Greenwood's
Housing Act, 1930, simplified the slum clearance process and required all authorities with more than 20,000 population to prepare
schemes for dealing with their slums and submit a five-year building programme.

The act provided a new formula for subsidy, a fixed-rate contribution of £2 5s per year for 40 years for each person rehoused.
The extra cost of building on inner-city sites was allowed for by
an additional subsidy. It was also accepted that many of those
rehoused would be unable to afford the comparatively high rents
of existing council houses, and rent rebates were specifically
sanctioned by the act.

Advice issued by the ministry and the Scottish department
showed some awareness of the dangers in the two-pronged
approach. It was not necessary for all those rehoused to be accommodated in houses built with the new subsidy, but it was made
clear that the subsidy was conditional on an equivalent number of
houses actually being provided by the authority. In the event,
however, advice on allocations and differential rents were of little
help in ensuring any great degree of mix in the council housing
stock.

Considering the sharp decline in council building, from more
than 104,000 houses in 1928 to 55,700 in 1929, and the prevailing
economic climate, it really was very doubtful whether local authorities could continue to provide for general needs and pursue an

effective slum clearance policy at the same time. If that had not
been realised in the ministry in 1930 it must have been made clear
very soon by the slow response of the authorities, which provided
under the Greenwood Act only 2,400 houses in 1931 and 6,000 in
1932.

The Committee on Local Expenditure,[27] set up by the National
government after the crisis of 1931, considered that the expanding
private building industry could cater for necessary general addit-
ions to the housing stock, and that state effort should be concentrated entirely on replacement. The Housing (Financial Provisions)
Act, 1933, represented a retreat from the 'general needs' philosophy even more complete than the ending of the Addison subsidies ten years earlier. The 1924 Act subsidies were abolished
(those under the 1923 Act had been ended in 1929) and councils,
unless they were willing to build without exchequer aid (which
very few were), had to apply their efforts solely to slum clearance
and replacement. It was, as Bowley called it, a return to the sanitary policy of the nineteenth century with a vengeance.[28] At the
same time housing standards were under attack; it was made clear
that councils should build smaller houses and should spend less on
them. There could have been no surer recipe for introducing the
principle of less eligibility into council housing.

The 1933 Act called on all authorities to state the number of unfit houses in their areas and to deal with them in a five-year programme. The total returns of houses to be closed or demolished in
January 1934 was 266,851 in England and Wales, and they were to
be replaced by 285,189 new houses. In the event 273,389 had been
built by March 1939, and as houses were still being completed up
to the early part of 1940, the 1934 target must very nearly have
been met. But the standards of unfitness applied were extremely
low and were very variably interpreted between authorities. As
the campaign continued, more slums were discovered and official
totals were revised in 1937 and 1939 to 378,000 and 472,000 respectively.

Building houses takes time; 1924 Act houses were being completed up to the beginning of 1935 and it was natural that some of
them should have been allocated to families rehoused from the first
slum clearance schemes as well as to others in need. This caused
alarm, amounting in some places to moral panic, both among households generally and the by then traditional occupants of council
housing. Attempts to impose rent rebate schemes had similar repercussions; not only were 'respectable' tenants to have slum
dwellers as neighbours but it seemed they were expected to sub-
sidise them into the bargain.[29] Despite the brave example of Leeds,
where under Labour's scheme of 1934 the poorest tenants could
live rent-free paying only rates, very few authorities operated
effective rent rebate systems.[30]

In most places the question of 'mix' became academic as the supply of general needs houses ceased and rehousing from slums was
necessarily into 1930 Act houses. Subsequent identification of 1930
Act schemes as 'ghettoes' is commonplace in housing literature,

and labelling was made easier and more certain because the estates
were usually distinctly and disturbingly different from other
council housing. The traditional connection between slum clearance
and flat building has already been mentioned, and it was continued
in the 1930s.

In fact only a small proportion of housing built for slum clearance rehousing in England and Wales was in flats, though the
walk-up tenement was dominant in Scotland. Well over three-
quarters of the new houses were in cottage estates on the out-
skirts of towns which did not help people in employment, who
tended to be casual or service workers. But despite the retention
of suburban form, the garden-suburb model had usually been de-
graded almost beyond recognition. Houses were smaller and
narrow-fronted, sometimes flatted four in a block or built in
longer rows with tunnels for back access, road verges were narrower and tree-planting was quite absent. The houses were less
well-built, and are now more expensive and troublesome to maintain. In his study of council housing in North Shields Byrne
estimates that even allowing for lower building costs, flatted
houses built in the 1930s show a reduction of 40 per cent from
expenditure in the previous decade, which can only be accounted
for by reduced standards all round. Byrne also demonstrates the
common experience that (until a recent and expensive up-grading)
these houses were held in low esteem by established council residents and accepted reluctantly by prospective tenants.[31]

COUNCIL HOUSES AND COUNCIL FLATS

Numbers of dwellings built under the inter-war housing acts are
given in Tables 1.1 and 1.2. It has not been possible to categor-
ise house types for this period but council housing after 1930 is
dominated by the image of flats and the problems that attend them,
and it is in the discussion of flats that we cross the break in
house-building that marks the Second World War.[32]

Depressing though the 1930s seem now in this long-range view
of council housing, for those engaged in the crusade against the
slums it was an heroic age, particularly in the London boroughs
and the cities of the North where Labour was achieving power in
local government. The replacement of stinking, broken-down
slums by modern flats held a powerful attraction politically. The
image came from Europe, and particularly from socialist Vienna,
where the 'hofs', paid for by 'rental tax' (levied on the owners of
older property) rather than by borrowed capital, attracted a
stream of visiting architects, housing professionals and politicians
from Britain and other countries in Western Europe. The earliest
example of their influence in Britain had been Ossulston Street,
designed while the 'hofs' were still being built, but later imitations
were architecturally inferior, apart from lacking the gardens,
crèches and other communal facilities of the Viennese models. So
between 1933 and 1939 great blocks of walk-up flats, usually with

*Table 1.1:   Dwellings Completed by Local Authorities in England and Wales,
1920-39 (thousands)*

	General Needs			Slum Clearance (1930-38 Acts)	Over-Crowding (1935-38 Acts)	Without Subsidy	Total
	1919 Act	1923 Act	1924 Act				
1920	0.6	–	–	–	–	–	0.6
1921	15.6	–	–	–	–	–	15.6
1922	80.8	–	–	–	–	–	80.8
1923	57.5	–	–	–	–	–	57.5
1924	10.5	3.8	–	–	–	–	14.3
1925	2.9	15.3	2.5	–	–	–	20.7
1926	1.1	16.2	26.9	–	–	–	44.2
1927	0.9	14.1	59.1	–	–	–	74.1
1928	0.2	13.8	90.1	–	–	–	104.1
1929	–	5.1	50.6	–	–	–	55.7
1930	–	5.6	54.6	–	–	1.6	61.8
1931	–	–	52.5	–	–	3.4	55.9
1932	–	–	65.2	2.4	–	2.5	70.1
1933	–	1.4	47.1	6.0	–	1.4	55.9
1934	–	–	44.8	9.0	–	2.2	56.0
1935	–	–	11.1	23.4	–	5.7	40.2
1936	–	–	–	39.1	–	14.4	53.5
1937	–	–	–	54.7	2.0	15.1	71.8
1938	–	–	–	56.8	7.3	13.9	78.0
1939	–	–	–	74.1	14.3	12.5	100.9
Total	170.1	75.3[a]	504.5	265.5	23.6	72.7	1,111.7

Note: a. Includes 15.4 thousand dwellings under slum clearance provisions.
Source: M. Bowley, 'Housing and the State', (Allen & Unwin, 1945), p. 271.

balcony access round echoing courtyards entered by arched gate-
ways, became part of the inner-city scene in Liverpool, Manchester and several of the London boroughs. A special case was
Leeds where, as has been mentioned, efforts had been made by a
short-lived Labour administration to avoid a two-class housing
system. At Quarry Hill, previously a notorious slum, was planned
the most innovative scheme of all with over 900 flats in long, curving blocks, provided with lifts and a water-borne refuse disposal
system. They were intended to include elaborate communal facilities
but owing to the outbreak of war in 1939 these were never completed.[33] Though the style of these great housing schemes was to
an extent modernist, they owed little to the doctrines of le Corbusier and the Congrés Internationaux d'Architecture Moderne

Table 1.2:   Dwellings Completed by Local Authorities in Scotland, 1920-39 (thousands)

	General Needs (1919/23/24 Acts) and Overcrowding (1930-38 Acts)[a]	Slum Clearance (1923/30 Acts)	Without Subsidy	Total
1920	0.8	–	–	0.8
1921	4.3	–	–	4.3
1922	9.4	–	_[b]	9.5
1923	6.2	0.2	–	6.5
1924	2.3	0.6	–	3.0
1925	3.3	1.5	–	4.8
1926	6.4	2.0	–	8.4
1927	13.5	2.0	0.2	15.8
1928	12.5	2.3	–	14.7
1929	12.0	2.3	–	14.3
1930	6.4	1.5	–	7.9
1931	6.1	2.2	–	8.3
1932	6.7	4.9	–	11.6
1933	8.5	7.3	–	15.8
1934	6.1	8.7	0.4	15.2
1935	2.1	15.1	1.5	18.8
1936	2.2	12.2	1.6	16.0
1937	9.1	3.8	0.5	13.3
1938	18.2	0.7	0.3	19.2
1939	31.1[c]	–	–	31.1
Total	167.3	67.6	4.6	239.5

Notes: a. Official Scottish housing statistics were given under these heads and it is not practicable to separate them. Total numbers of dwellings built under the earlier provisions were
as follows: 1919 Act, 25.1 (thousand); 1923 Act (general needs), 4.0; 1923 Act (slum
clearance), 17.1; 1924 Act, 75.3.
b. Less than 50 dwellings.
c. Includes all houses completed from 1 January 1939 to 31 March 1940.
Source: Department of Health for Scotland, 'Annual Reports'.

(CIAM): the ideology was political. A few of these city-centre
blocks are in demand still because of their locations, but generally
the walk-up flats of the 1930s now present serious management
problems to the councils that own them and form a substantial
proportion of what are now called 'difficult-to-let' estates.

When the outbreak of war in 1939 brought house-building virtually to a standstill, it was clear that council housing had come
to stay whatever the arguments about its precise role. Attempts

to restore the private rented sector had failed, and council houses
constituted something like one-tenth of the total housing stock.
For the majority of people, who could not expect to buy a modern
house of their own, council housing was the only real hope. The
provision of council housing on the necessary scale was to become
the essence of post-war policy.

COUNCIL HOUSING FOR ALL

The general election of 1945 returned a Labour government whose
programme included proposals for major reform of the social services
in Britain. Aneurin Bevan as Minister of Health made explicit his
objective that rented housing should be available to anyone who
required it and that the public sector should be its chief provider.
In 1944 the Dudley Committee had reported on housing standards,[34]
not nearly so comprehensively as Tudor Walters, but recognising
the vast changes in working-class life styles and in domestic
equipment since 1918. Gone, for example, was the scullery (and
for that matter the parlour), to be replaced by the dining-kitchen
and the utility room. The importance of providing adequate stor-
age was recognised and recommended space standards were
restored to something near the 1919 level. Flats were not dismissed,
but it was regarded as self-evident that separate houses were to
be preferred, a conclusion that was confirmed by the parallel
Scottish study. In the course of this study the Scottish Housing
Advisory Committee had conducted a consumer survey among
Scottish service men and women and civilian war workers. Even in
Scotland, with its long tradition of flat-dwelling, barely 15 per
cent of respondents expressed a preference for living in 'a block
of modern flats'.[35]
    Inevitably the first products of post-war building were houses
rather than flats, because they could be produced more quickly.
A high proportion were 'prefabs', ranging from completely factory-
made units, such as an aluminium bungalow delivered in three
sections and bolted together on site, to two-storey houses assem-
bled from steel or precast concrete panels. The smaller prefabs,
in compensation for their size, were exceptionally well equipped,
with built-in refrigerator, cooker and electrically heated hot water
system. Space standards of the two-storey prefabs were good, and
examples of both types (though not of the aluminium ones which
had special troubles) are still giving good service and are liked
by their tenants today. One mistake of 1918 was not repeated: a
strict wartime system of building licensing and control of materials
was maintained for over five years, which ensured priority for
public sector building and prevented the runaway escalation of
costs. Soon housing schemes planned before the war began to
emerge through the pipeline, updated to post-war standards;
these included some flats, for example Finsbury's splendid Spa
Green Estate, by Lubetkin and Tecton, designers of the privately
built luxury flats at Highpoint, Hampstead, before the war.

By 1950, with public sector housing production in Britain rising
to the quite unprecedented rate of over 160,000 dwellings a year,
an increasing proportion of them were in blocks of flats. Not all
were as well designed as Spa Green: the LCC and Liverpool Corporation, the two greatest pre-war flat builders, had been building them since the war ended, completing unfinished estates to
the original designs. But during the 1940s there had arisen a new
idealist attitude to flats, particularly among architects and plan-
ners, but transmitted very effectively to other professionals and
politicians concerned with housing. The ideas were disseminated
by numerous publications, reflecting the increasing public interest
in planning and reconstruction from about 1943. The County of
London Plan of that year was presented to the public in an enor-
mously successful Penguin edition which included a version of a
famous diagram produced by Walter Gropius in 1930, showing that
higher flats, at higher densities, actually enhanced standards of
sunlighting and open space.[36] The plan itself, which contained
tempting coloured perspectives showing high buildings in open
parkland, envisaged new housing areas with high proportions of
flats up to ten storeys high which at that time was the maximum
allowed in London.

Despite the Dudley Committee's reservations there was official
acceptance of the need for some housing being built high in the
early post-war years. The housing manuals of 1946 and 1949
encouraged mixed development of houses and flats, and special
subsidies were provided, both for houses included in high-density
schemes and for blocks of flats more than three storeys high
where lifts were required.

The exemplar of this type of housing layout was to be the LCC's
Alton estates at Roehampton. After the war the LCC had acquired
a number of large houses, their gardens comprising in all about
200 acres of parkland adjoining Richmond Park on the boundaries
of West London, and providing the awaited opportunity to test the
model of high flats in a park, derived from le Corbusier. The
resulting development, designed and built in two phases between
1950 and 1957 by groups of architects in Sir Robert Matthew's
newly formed LCC Architect's Department, was of the approved
mixed development pattern, with just over half the dwellings in
high flats. In Alton East, which was developed first, eleven-storey
point blocks were employed, an innovation derived from Scandin-
avian practice, but at Alton West maisonettes were built in slab
blocks, openly derived from le Corbusier's Unité d'habitation at
Marseilles.[37]

Roehampton, like Well Hall Estate on which LCC architects had
worked 40 years before, is still worth revisiting. Well Hall asserted
the garden-suburb ideal, injecting high-design input despite the
wartime urgency and shortages of materials. Roehampton, conceived in the courageous era following the Festival of Britain in
1951, marked the end of post-war restrictions and made a syn-
thesis out of current ideologies. Mixed development is there and
'pups' of l'Unité d'habitation, as well as Swedish-inspired point

blocks, then representing a social-democratic compromise but
later to become the hated 'multis' of succeeding decades.

But at that time political and economic pressures were once more
forcing reductions in housing standards. The Dudley Committee's
space standards began to be eroded in 1951, and were soon to be
abandoned altogether by Harold Macmillan, Minister of Housing and
Local Government in the new Conservative government. His task
was to achieve the target of 300,000 dwellings per year, which was
accomplished in 1953. It was in part attained by relaxing building
licensing in the private sector and also by substantial increase in
the public supply, to over 229,000 completions in that year. A
drastic reduction in dwelling size in Macmillan's 'people's house'
contributed to the achievement: in 1953 the average five-person
council house was over 110 sq ft smaller than in 1951, a reduction
in floor area of 11 per cent.

In 1953 the White Paper, 'Houses: The Next Step', [38] made the
new housing strategy explicit: production would be maintained at
300,000 dwellings per year, but the supply of homes for general
needs would primarily be met by the private sector building
houses for owner occupation. Housing provided by local authorities
and in new towns by the development corporations would make up
the total but, by implication, output from the public sector would
reduce year by year. The privately let stock, most of it built
before 1914, was to be revitalised by encouraging grant-aided
improvements while rent increases tied to improvement and repair
were permitted. Finally slum clearance was to be resumed as the
prime concern of local authorities. Comparisons with the 1930s are
obvious and the parallel was soon to be drawn more completely.
Later in 1953 local authorities were called upon to make returns of
unfit housing in their areas and prepare programmes for dealing
with them. General needs subsidies were reduced and in 1956
abolished, except for housing for the elderly and other special
categories.

The effects on the types of house that were produced were like-
wise similar to those of the 1930s. Dwellings were smaller: the
average three-bedroom house, which had risen in area from 1,026
sq ft in 1946 to 1,055 sq ft in 1949, fell to 947 sq ft in 1952 and to
897 sq ft in 1959, and they had to be built at much higher densities economically to utilise cleared central sites. This meant more
use of flats; the slab and point blocks from Roehampton were
reproduced throughout the central London boroughs, providing
their occupants not with prospects of glorious parklands but with
sometimes even more sensational views of the rapidly changing city.
Those involved in housing production, particularly architects,
became highly committed to their roles, and a great deal of socio-
logical argument, much of it suspect and some of it certainly
specious, was employed to justify new design approaches. Notable
among such developments was the concept of deck access, employed most rigorously in the huge Park Hill and Hyde Park
schemes at Sheffield in the late 1950s. Though deck access was
sadly misapplied in some later building systems it worked very
successfully in medium-rise housing of a decade or so later.

Roehampton to the Sheffield schemes, spanning the 1950s, represent a second period of flat development. The third period was
impelled by the building industry. In support of central government's concern to encourage higher density development, the
ministry had issued a great deal of increasingly detailed technical
advice which in the early 1960s became formalised in parallel series
of Planning and Design Bulletins, and early issues of each were
devoted to high density and high-rise housing development. At
the same time government was encouraging the industry to develop
forms of system building to keep pace with the increasing rate of
slum clearance. The advantages of system building were seen to
be more rapid on-site construction, the addition of new labour and
production resources to the greatly stretched building industry,
and eventual economies of scale. None of these ideas, nor the conditions that called for them, was really new. The heaviest demands
for house building had always been made when the industry was
overloaded and skilled labour and traditional materials in demand
elsewhere: the Treasury's attitude to housing, as an expenditure
flow that could be turned off when times were hard, had made that
more certain. So system building was nothing new either: many
thousands of 'non-traditional' houses had been built under the
1919 Act; this had continued during the 1920s, and after the
1939-45 war came the prefabs. Most of these earlier houses are
still in use, regarded by their tenants simply as good homes. Thus
there was nothing intrinsically wrong with system building, nor
did it necessarily imply high flats. The pressures of the 1960s,
however, calling for rapid production at high densities, made high-
rise solutions inevitable.

Despite the pioneering work of some larger authorities like the
LCC and Sheffield, most local authorities had no experience of
high-density building, and no way of assessing the quality or
suitability of a system that was offered; nor, since selection of a
system eliminates or at least restricts conventional tendering procedures, could they tell how much it ought to cost. The ministry,
now under Sir Keith Joseph, who himself had connections with the
building industry, eased the way by two new facilities. In 1963
the government proposed a National Building Agency which was
established in the following year to provide services both to the
industry and its customers, one of its duties being to appraise
and certificate building systems. Second, the ministry published
guidance on costs of high-density housing, in the form of a set of
tables called the housing cost yardstick, which related an indic-
ative cost per person housed (called a bedspace) to the principal
variables of dwelling size and density.[39] Publishing the yardstick
was a new and radical move: ever since 1919 government departments had refused to disclose their notional cost limits, arguing
that to do so would damage the principle of competitive tendering
and increase the cost of building.

On Labour's return to power in 1964 there was no special incentive to interfere with these devices, which, it was hoped, would
enable the industry to provide system-built housing at an

increasing rate without greatly affecting the production of traditionally constructed houses that were the mainstay of the private
sector supply. In 13 years out of office, Labour's attitude to the
private sector had changed, to the extent of regarding owner
occupation as the tenure to which households would naturally
aspire. Consequently, the new government's housing programme,
which was intended to raise the rate of house building to half a
million dwellings a year in Great Britain by 1970 - and even higher
after that - envisaged an equal division between public and private sectors. Because private production had exceeded that of
the public sector by about one and a half times between 1961 and
1964, an initial increase in local authority building was required.
Completions rose substantially to a peak in 1967 (see Table 1.3).

Table 1.3:   Dwellings Completed by Local Authorities, New Towns and
Scottish Special Housing Association, 1945-80 (thousands)

	England and Wales	Scotland
1945-50 (annual average)	96.3	14.3
1951-55 (annual average)	188.1	30.9
1956-60 (annual average)	124.4	25.9
1961	98.5	20.1
1962	111.7	19.0
1963	102.4	21.6
1964	126.1	29.5
1965	140.9	27.6
1966	142.4	28.2
1967	159.3	34.0
1968	148.0	33.3
1969	139.9	34.3
1970	134.9	34.4
1971	117.2	28.6
1972	93.6	19.6
1973	79.3	17.3
1974	99.4	16.2
1975	122.9	22.8
1976	124.2	21.2
1977	121.2	14.3
1978	96.8	9.9
1979	75.0	7.9
1980	77.1	7.0

Source: Ministry of Housing and Local Government/Department of the Environment,
Scottish Development Department and Welsh Office, 'Housing Statistics' and
'Housing and Construction Statistics'.

Since 1963 more than half of all dwellings provided in the public
sector had been flats and by 1968 most of these were being system-
built. Then in May of that year came the dramatic accident of
Ronan Point, a 22-storey point block in West Ham, when a gas
explosion caused the collapse of a corner of the building through

its whole height, by the progressive shedding of load-bearing wall panels. In the popular view, and doubtless in the minds of many local authority members, that incident heralded the end of the high-rise era. Certainly the repercussions were expensive and dramatic, and opponents of high-rise housing made great mileage out of it. But other pressures were also at work; the proportion of high flats in local authority housing programmes had reached its peak in 1966 and was already beginning to fall, as can be seen from Tables 1.4 and 1.5. Disillusion with multi-storey living might have been among the reasons, but more important was the government's reform, in 1967, of housing standards and finance.

Table 1.4: Proportion of Houses and Flats Built by Local Authorities and New Towns in England and Wales, 1960-80[a]

	Houses	Flats[b] 2-4 storey	5-14 storey	15 storey and over	Total flats
	%	%	%	%	%
1960	52.8	33.0	11.1	3.1	47.2
1961	51.3	32.2	12.7	3.8	48.7
1962	50.1	32.6	12.3	5.0	49.9
1963	46.9	31.2	12.9	9.0	53.1
1964	44.8	31.0	12.2	12.0	55.2
1965	48.3	30.2	10.9	10.6	51.7
1966	47.5	26.8	15.3	10.4	52.5
1967	50.0	27.0	13.3	9.7	50.0
1968	49.3	30.8	14.0	5.9	50.7
1969	50.5	35.9	9.8	3.8	49.4
1970	51.5	38.6	8.2	1.7	48.5
1971	50.0	41.4	6.7	1.9	50.0
1972	48.5	44.1	6.1	1.3	51.5
1973	54.9	41.7	2.9	0.5	45.1
1974	55.9	41.6	2.4	0.1	44.1
1975	60.7	38.1	1.2	–	39.3
1976	57.3	40.9	1.6	0.2	42.7
1977	54.6	44.1	1.3	–	45.4
1978	55.2	42.2	2.6	–	44.8
1979	54.3	44.2	1.5	–	45.7
1980	50.2	49.4	0.5	–	49.8

Notes: a. Tenders approved.
b. Including maisonettes.
Source: As for Table 1.3.

STANDARDS AND THE YARDSTICK: THE 1967 ACT

Almost ten years earlier, discontent with the low housing standards of the 1950s had persuaded the government of the time to set up a committee on housing standards under the chairmanship of Sir

Table 1.5:   Proportion of Houses and Flats Built by Local Authorities and New
Towns in Scotland and Scottish Special Housing Association, 1960-80[a]

	Houses %	Flats[b] 2-4 storey %	5 storey and over %	Maisonettes %	Total flats %
1960	46.7	34.4	12.1	6.8	53.3
1961	52.5	31.4	7.3	8.9	47.5
1962	38.2	30.8	13.2	17.7	61.8
1963	40.9	25.0	22.2	11.9	59.1
1964	38.6	26.5	24.6	10.4	61.4
1965	35.2	21.0	28.7	15.1	64.8
1966	41.9	25.1	25.1	7.9	58.1
1967	46.6	24.8	28.6		53.4
1968	59.1	28.2	12.7		40.9
1969	57.2	25.6	17.2		42.8
1970	52.8	25.4	21.8		47.2
1971	61.9	23.3	14.8		38.1
1972	67.2	24.9	7.9		32.8
1973	81.9	13.4	4.7		18.1
1974	86.6	11.7	1.7		13.4
1975	77.0	17.6	5.4		23.0
1976	84.1	13.7	2.2		15.9
1977	79.0	20.7	0.3		21.0
1978	82.2	16.5	1.3		17.8
1979	75.6	24.4	–		24.4
1980	77.7	22.3	–		22.3

Notes: a. Tenders approved.
b. Including maisonettes which are not shown separately from 1967.
Source: As for Table 1.3.

Parker Morris, a former clerk of Westminster, which reported
in 1961.[40] The guidance was intended to apply to all new houses,
in the private as well as the public sector, and it summed up the
changes required as more space and better heating, to permit
more flexible and efficient use of the whole house. The report was
commended to local authorities when it was published, but introduction of mandatory standards based on Parker Morris had to
wait until 1967.

Besides housing standards, local authorities had been concerned
for some years about rising interest rates. The flat-rate subsidy,
which had been the general mode of exchequer assistance since
1923, made no allowance for these, nor for increased land and
building costs which had been rising steadily since 1959.

The scheme incorporated in the Housing Subsidies Act, 1967,
provided a subsidy on new building which in effect made up the
difference between the rate of interest the local authority would
have to pay on finance for new housing and a rate of 4 per cent.
The details of the subsidy need not be discussed here; the

important change was the return to a basically open-ended subsidy,
something the Treasury had not countenanced for general housing
provision since the abandonment of the Addison subsidy in 1923.
Clearly there had to be limits to the expenditure that could be
subsidised, and those limits were provided by updating the hous-
ing-cost yardstick of 1963; the tables were extended to include all
practical densities and to allow for regional variations in building
costs. Finally, to ensure that a proper commodity was obtained for
the subsidisable expenditure, a slightly modified version of Parker
Morris standards was made mandatory. [41]

On the face of it the 1967 arrangements provided ideal machinery
for an administration committed to the provision and expansion of
social housing. They included a generous and easily applied subsidy which at the same time provided a basis for sensible cost
planning by designers and a high standard of accommodation. In
practice, however, the system ran into trouble from the start.
Interest rates soon rose to levels unthought of when the variable
subsidy was devised and building costs began to rise even more
rapidly. In 1969 housing policy was switched from an increasing
programme of new building to concentration on improvement. And
revision of the cost yardstick, which was originally supposed to
be reviewed annually, failed to keep pace with costs. It has been
uncharitably suggested that inadequate cost levels, requiring
individual relaxations, were used in the early 1970s as means of
curtailing councils' expenditure on new building.

THE ABANDONMENT OF COUNCIL HOUSING?

In June 1970 the Conservatives returned to government with a
determination to make radical changes in housing policy. The
Housing Finance Act, 1972, abolished all subsidies attached to
particular houses and instead related exchequer contributions to
what was called 'reckonable expenditure'. The deficit between
reckonable expenditure and rent income was in future to be met
by the government and local rates in specified proportions. The
yardstick limits remained, and expenditure that exceeded them ·
would be met by the local authority alone. The intention of this
complicated structure was the eventual phasing out of all general
assistance by a progression towards 'fair' rents, to be approved
for all houses by independent rent-scrutiny committees. Tenants
unable to afford these rents would be eligible for rent rebates
while better-off council tenants would be encouraged to become
owner occupiers. (In Scotland 'fair' rents were not to be applied
immediately, though councils were required to raise overall rent
income according to a specified programme.)

The 1972 legislation provoked intense opposition from Labour-
controlled local authorities, which in the case of Clay Cross Urban
District Council was sustained to the point of the council's housing duties being assumed by a commissioner appointed by the
Secretary of State for the Environment. [42] In opposition the Labour

Party promised to repeal key aspects of the new subsidy system
on their return to office.

Owing to rapid increases of both building costs and interest
rates, the proportion of councils' housing expenditure met by
government subsidy actually rose dramatically during the Conservative government's period in office. The promised reform by
Labour, in the Housing Rents and Subsidies Act, 1975, cancelled
the 'fair' rents principle, consolidated the existing subsidies at
the 1974-5 level, and provided a new subsidy on interest charges
resulting from the refinancing of existing loans. This was an in-
terim measure pending a more fundamental reform of housing
finance.

Many aspects of the 1972 Act, including rent rebates, had been
assimilated and the principle of a continuing subsidy for council
housing re-established. The 1975 Act excited surprisingly little
political controversy and it seemed for a time that consensus over
the roles of private and public sectors might actually have been
reached. Agreement extended to the acceptance that the whole
subject needed a re-examination, and early in 1975 Anthony Cros-
land, Secretary of State for the Environment, set up a review of
housing finance. There was an advisory group of more than a
dozen people from outside the civil service, all professionally
involved with housing in academic institutions, local government
or finance.

The resulting publication in June 1977 was the green paper,
'Housing Policy: A Consultative Document', backed up by technical
appendices. [43] Its conclusions and proposals showed an overriding
concern to encourage owner occupation and indeed any other form
of tenure, including some which had previously hardly been
thought of, rather than council housing. Ostensibly council housing was to have a continuing and important role but the specific
proposals did little to sustain it. In particular the recommendations
on housing finance left untouched the overwhelming advantages of
owner occupation. The policy of the Conservative government
elected in 1979 towards the public sector has, of course, been
substantially different from its predecessor. Nevertheless, the
Labour government, in its green paper, failed to put forward the
radical changes which could have made council housing an attractive alternative to owner occupation. As it was, the door was
opened to the Housing Act, 1980, and the right to buy, which are
examined in Chapter 2.

Sixty years of council housing is not a story of unmixed success;
it includes great achievements and some miserable failures, but the
failures should be seen in proportion. The public sector housing
stock has become one of the most valuable and obviously socially
useful assets that we collectively possess, but the residual philosophy has never been so uncompromisingly expressed as it is
today. If pursued, it could throw away the achievements and seriously diminish both quality and variety in the stock and make
council housing an unnatural and stigmatised form of tenure, a far
cry from the courageous innovation of Christopher Addison, the

vision of John Wheatley and the apparently achievable expectations of Aneurin Bevan.

NOTES

1   See for example M. Bowley, 'Housing and the State' (Allen & Unwin, 1945); J. B. Cullingworth, 'Housing and Local Government' (Allen & Unwin, 1966), Ch. 1; and, especially for a recent view, S. Merrett, 'State Housing in Britain' (Routledge & Kegan Paul, 1979). For Scotland see R. D. Cramond, 'Housing Policy in Scotland: A Study in State Assistance' (Oliver and Boyd, 1966).

2   History of the Ministry of Munitions, unpublished official history, 1921, vol. 5, Appendix 1; and Local Government Board for Scotland, 'Annual Report for 1918', Cmd 230 (HMSO, 1919).

3   P. Geddes, 'Cities in Evolution' (E. Benn, 1915 and 1949).

4   S. Damer, State, Class and Housing: Glasgow 1885-1919 and J. Melling, Clydeside Housing and the Evolution of State Rent Control in J. Melling (ed.), 'Housing, Social Policy and the State' (Croom Helm, 1980), pp. 73-112 and 139-67.

5   'Report of the Royal Commission on the Housing of the Industrial Population of Scotland, Rural and Urban', Cd 8731 (HMSO, 1917).

6   Ibid., para. 2237.

7   Ibid. (Minority Report), paras. 214-6.

8   Local Government Boards for England and Wales, and Scotland, 'Report of the Committee appointed...to consider questions of building construction in connection with the provision of dwellings for the working classes..., and report upon methods of securing economy and despatch in the provision of such dwellings' (Tudor Walters Report), Cd 9191 (HMSO, 1918).

9   Ibid., para. 2.

10 Ibid., para. 27.

11 For example P. Wilding, The Housing and Town Planning Act 1919 - A Study in the Making of Social Policy, 'Journal of Social Policy', vol. 2, pt. 4 (1973), pp. 317-34.

12 A. Sayle, 'The Housing of the Workers' (Fisher Unwin, 1924), Chs. 5 and 6.

13 Ibid., p. 135.

14 Merrett, 'State Housing in Britain', p. 36.

15 Bowley, 'Housing and the State', Ch. 2.

16 Ibid., p. 27.

17 Merrett, 'State Housing in Britain', pp. 38-41.

18 For example L. Orbach, 'Homes for Heroes' (Seeley Service, 1977); and M. Swenarton, 'Homes Fit for Heroes' (Heinemann, 1981).

19 Sayle, 'Houses of the Workers'; but cf. H. R. Aldridge, 'The National Housing Manual' (National Housing and Town Planning Council, 1923) who gives for England and Wales: gross need

852,275, net need 796,248, and for Scotland: gross need
131,092, net need 115,565.
20   Bowley, 'Housing and the State', pp. 23-4.
21   Merrett, 'State Housing in Britain', p. 26 and note. The
revised estimate is the author's.
22   Sayle, 'Houses of the Workers', p. 140.
23   Griffith-Boscowen introduced a bill in 1912, a product of the
Unionist Social Reform Committee, which proposed state subsidies for housing: see P. Wilding, Towards Exchequer Subsidies for Housing 1906-1914, 'Social and Economic Administration', vol. 6, no. 1 (1972), p. 9.
24   There has been no adequate biography of John Wheatley, but
see K. Middlemas, 'The Clydesiders' (Collins, 1966), for a
brief portrait and a full account of the politics of his housing
bill.
25   Royal Commission on the Housing of the Industrial Population
of Scotland, 'Minutes of Evidence' (4 vols., HMSO, 1921),
para. 22,528 et seq.
26   See A. Ravetz, From Working Class Tenement to Modern Flat
in A. Sutcliffe (ed.), 'Multi-Storey Living' (Croom Helm, 1974).
27   'Report of the Committee on Local Expenditure (England and
Wales)', Cmd 4200 (HMSO, 1932).
28   Bowley, 'Housing and the State', Ch. 7.
29   The most famous instance of such alarm, resulting in walls
being built to separate private and council estates, is described in P. Collinson, 'The Cutteslowe Walls' (Faber and
Faber, 1963). For political effects of rent-pooling schemes see
(on Leeds) A. Ravetz, 'Model Estate' (Croom Helm, 1974), Ch.
2; and S. Schifferes, Council Tenants and Housing Policy in
the 1930s in M. Edwards et al. (eds.), 'Housing and Class in
Britain' (Conference of Socialist Economists, 1976), pp. 64-71.
30   See G. Wilson, 'Rent Rebates' (Fabian Society, 1938).
31   D. Byrne, The Standard of Council Housing in Inter-War
North Shields in Melling, 'Housing, Social Policy and the
State', pp. 168-93.
32   For a full discussion of flats in Britain, see Sutcliffe, 'Multi-
Storey Living'.
33   For a complete study of Quarry Hill see Ravetz, 'Model Estate'.
34   Ministry of Health, 'Design of Dwellings' (Dudley Report)
(HMSO, 1944).
35   Scottish Housing Advisory Committee, 'Planning Our New
Homes' (HMSO, 1943).
36   E. J. Carter and E. Goldfinger, 'The County of London Plan'
(Penguin Books, 1945).
37   See series of articles, Alton Estate, Roehampton, after 25
Years, 'Housing Review', vol. 29, no. 5 (1980), pp. 167-72.
38   Ministry of Housing and Local Government, 'Houses - The
Next Step', Cmd 8996 (HMSO, 1953).
39   Ministry of Housing and Local Government, 'The Housing Cost
Yardstick for Schemes at Medium and High Densities', Design
Bulletin No. 7 (HMSO, 1963).

40   Central Housing Advisory Committee, 'Homes for Today and
     Tomorrow' (Parker Morris Report) (HMSO, 1961).
41   Ministry of Housing and Local Government, Circular 36/67,
     'Housing Standards: Costs and Subsidies'.
42   D. Skinner and J. Langdon, 'The Story of Clay Cross'
     (Spokesman Books, 1974).
43   'Housing Policy: A Consultative Document', Cmnd 6851 (HMSO,
     1977); and Department of the Environment, 'Housing Policy:
     Technical Volume', parts I, II and III (HMSO, 1977).

2 A New Era for Council Housing?

Alan Murie

Historical accounts of the development of council housing identify periods when rates of growth, levels of subsidy and standards of building varied substantially. Some periods have been marked by high levels of building of high-standard properties. Others have been marked by a concentration on building lower quality dwellings for slum clearance or special needs rather than for general needs (see Chapter 1).

Rather less reference is made in historical accounts to the sale of council houses. Much early legislation was based on a view of the direct provision of housing by local government as temporary and incorporated provision for sale of council properties within a given period. However, in the period of greatest growth of council housing since 1919 legislation has included powers rather than duties to sell dwellings. The Housing Act, 1980 (and the Tenants' Rights, Etc. (Scotland) Act, 1980), involved a major break in this tradition. The legislation extended a right to buy to most council tenants of three years' standing and included the right to a mortgage for these tenants. The significance of this measure for council tenants, potential council tenants and the community as a whole was increased by other measures in these acts, by cuts in planned public expenditure and by the longer term general development in the housing situation in Britain.

The combination of changes suggests that the late 1970s and early 1980s are an important watershed in policy. The developments involved imply more than just a speeding up of existing trends. They also imply more than simply a new period of retrenchment and concentration on special needs. They imply a new era for council housing in which a concentration on special needs is accompanied by a reduction in the actual size of the council stock, a minimal rate of new building, a decline in the quality of new and existing council dwellings and a reduction in subsidy for council housing (but not for owner occupation). This combination of developments has not occurred before and marks a more thorough shift in policy than has occurred in the past. It involves a clearer rejection of ideas of optimal public service provision and a reassertion of the role of the market backed by a minimal poor law service. How far and for how long this attitude to housing provision will develop is uncertain. Even if the trend in existing policy was not extended beyond the present expenditure planning period, and if steps to reverse the trend were taken, time lags would extend the period of minimal provision to some eight years. But it is likely that the period will be longer.

It is not inevitable that policy will revert to some 'sensible' norm and that levels of public investment and subsidy will 'have to be' raised. There is at least a possibility that the future role of council housing will be to provide a minimal residual service in an environment of greater housing inequality – both between and within tenures. The logic of current policy is that housing standards in some areas and for some groups will decline. The extent to which such a deterioration will occur depends on the effectiveness of political demands to oppose it.

Whatever occurs in this respect, the current direction of policy and the stage which has been reached historically mean that much of the worst housing will be council housing. Local authorities have already become major providers of the least adequate and least desirable property. In this context, the historic role of council housing in channelling high-quality, high-cost housing to working-class households and those who wish to rent, at rents which are low relative to cost, is being directly eroded by the ageing of the stock and changing financial arrangements. The new situation for public sector housing is one in which it is critically hampered by the limitations of the housing stock under its control, the relative insignificance of other sources of rented housing, and the contrast in quality of service and advantage associated with different tenures. In this respect the rights for tenants embodied in the Housing Act, 1980, are insignificant in the context of the limited resources available to them. It is in this longer perspective of an ageing stock and changing council housing service, rather than the short-term policies of 1979-80, that it is appropriate to talk of a new era for council housing.

In this context it is reasonable to argue that since the last half of the nineteenth century a fundamental change has occurred in the way in which housing has been consumed. In the nineteenth century the most appropriate mechanism for financing housing production and consumption was private landlordism, but for various reasons this situation has changed. Individual private ownership (owner occupation) has emerged as the most appropriate mechanism in the twentieth century. But the period of transition and transfer, of the decline of rentier landlordism and growth of owner occupation and the institutions surrounding it, involved particular strains and shortages which (through political action) have been offset by state intervention. Thus the development of council housing has at the same time redistributed housing resources in the interests of the working class and has served the interests of capital and 'social order' by minimising the effects of the restructuring of the private market. By the 1980s it is arguable that the period of transition is over. The transitional role of council housing is therefore being abandoned and its permanent role is a more limited one. If this view of the changing role of council housing is broadly accepted, then the view that a new era for council housing has emerged is strengthened. What is occurring is not just another phase in its development. If this is so, there is no reason to expect some natural swing in the pendulum

to return it to a more 'normal' role. The coalition of interests
which sustained the growth of council housing arguably no longer
exists. As a result any attempt to influence or change the future
role of council housing will have to face a different political situation than has existed in the past. It is against this background
that the discussion in this chapter is set. The Housing Act, 1980,
and the public expenditure and policy context within which it has
been developed, are the immediate and most evident mechanisms
for changing the role of council housing. But the significance and
effects of these changes derive from longer term developments.

The discussion in the remainder of this chapter and the statistics referred to will be mainly in terms of the position in England
and Wales. Nevertheless, the situation in Scotland is sufficiently
similar for the broad thrust of the argument to apply there as
well.

THE CURRENT HOUSING SITUATION

When the Conservative government took office in 1979 the state of
housing and housing policy was far from healthy. The picture of
the housing situation in England and Wales presented in the Labour government's review of housing policy demonstrated considerable progress in dealing with housing problems. The great
majority of households enjoyed basic housing conditions which
were good by historical standards. The crude national housing
shortage of 800,000 dwellings in 1951 had become a surplus of
approaching one million. Between 1951 and 1976 the number of
households living in dwellings which were either unfit or lacking
at least one basic amenity had fallen from 7,500,000 to 1,650,000;
overcrowded households had fallen from 664,000 to 150,000; and
multi-person sharing households had fallen from 1,442,000 to
275,000. These and other statistics indicated considerable progress. Indeed the British housing situation could be compared
favourably with that of more affluent countries. In 1977 the green
paper 'Housing Policy' asserted that 'Housing in England and
Wales appears to compare reasonably well in terms of basic amenities and space with countries in both Western Europe and North
America'. [1]

The basis for this progress was considerable public and private
investment in housing throughout the post-war period, coupled
with substantial slum clearance and improvement activity. Since
1945 local authority completions exceeded 150,000 a year both between 1948 and 1957 and between 1965 and 1970. Before 1978 they
only fell below 100,000 once (in 1973). Throughout this period
private sector completions boosted the figures considerably - for
example, to a total of 404,000 in 1967. However, the picture of
progress was already misleading in 1979. The problems of financing the housing programme in a period of rapid inflation and of
public expenditure restraint were evident. The very fact of progress and 'housing surplus' made housing an easy target for

expenditure cuts; housing problems could be and were treated as largely residual in nature. They were seen as specific local problems requiring local responses, which would be resolved in time. A smaller budget, allocated according to need and used in the light of coherent local strategies, could cope. Cash limits and Housing Investment Programmes would lead to more efficiency in spending and would encourage more precise identification of problems and solutions.

While it would be wrong to reject such a set of assumptions out of hand, there were flaws in the argument. The housing problems which had become more apparent throughout the 1970s were not all residual in nature but in some cases were new problems deriving from the pattern of policy itself. Problems with quality, physical condition and management of council housing have become more apparent, as have problems of disrepair and inequality in the owner-occupied sector. Problems of housing poverty have ceased to be concentrated in the privately rented sector. However, certain sections of the population, including the single, the mobile and those with low incomes, have not found the effects of the decline of that tenure on their housing opportunities offset by easier access to council and owner-occupied housing. Conditions in the privately rented sector have remained disadvantageous and have been fuelled by continuing scarcity and the pattern of access to other tenures. As a result housing progress has been accompanied by increasing homelessness and increasing evidence of problems in the major tenures. The structure of the housing market has resulted in housing progress and considerable accumulation of wealth through housing for some, but has also resulted in increasing inequality and continuing housing deprivation for others.

Whatever view is taken of the extent of progress and the nature of remaining problems, the Labour government went a long way to erode the rate of advance. Local authority and new town dwelling starts fell from 131,015 in 1975/6 to 69,068 in 1978/9, and to 53,079 in 1979/80. While expenditure on subsidies had continued on a rising trend from 1974/5, capital investment in land and new dwellings declined substantially after 1976/7. The amount of public expenditure available for housing had fallen steadily as a result of government cutbacks since the mid-1970s. The effects of these cutbacks had fallen disproportionately on new building while expenditure on improvement had not risen substantially.

NEW POLICY INTENTIONS?

The Conservative government came into this situation apparently unimpressed by the details of these trends. The 'Conservative Manifesto 1979'[2] referred to housing under the heading 'Helping the Family' and devoted one and a half pages to housing – more than to social security, education, health and welfare or the elderly and disabled. Housing clearly was a priority but the issues

referred to were principally about ownership and the sale of
council houses. Reference to better use of the existing stock,
including empty houses, was linked only with proposals for shorthold tenancies. No reference at all was made to investment in new
building or improvement, to homelessness or housing need.

The preoccupation of the government with the encouragement of
owner occupation to the exclusion of any other objectives was
apparent in parliamentary debates. As early as the debate on
the Queen's Speech, the Prime Minister outlined a simple political
and housing philosophy:

> Thousands of people in council houses and new towns came
> out to support us for the first time because they wanted a
> chance to buy their own homes. We will give to every council
> tenant the right to purchase his own home at a substantial
> discount on the market price and with 100 per cent mortgages
> for those who need them. This will be a giant stride towards
> making a reality of Anthony Eden's dream of a property-
> owning democracy. It will do something else – it will give to
> more of our people that freedom and mobility and that pros-
> pect of handing something on to their children and grand-
> children which owner-occupation provides.
>
> We will also give council tenants who do not wish to buy
> their own homes, and want to go on renting, additional rights
> and safeguards, and we shall take action to halt the decline
> of the privately-rented sector. Our new concept of shorthold
> tenure will encourage new letting of empty property. We shall
> also take steps to tackle the land shortage for new building.
> We shall speed up and simplify the planning system and we
> shall repeal the Community Land Act. We shall substantially
> increase choice in housing. [3]

The Secretary of State for the Environment, two days later, outlined some of the intentions for housing policy:

> We intend to provide as far as possible the housing policies
> that the British people want... We propose to create a climate
> in which those who are able can prosper, choose their own
> priorities and seek the rewards and satisfactions that relate
> to themselves, their families and their communities. We shall
> concentrate the resources of the community increasingly on
> the members of the community who are not able to help them-
> selves.
>
> In terms of housing policy, our priority of putting people
> first must mean more home ownership, greater freedom of
> choice of home and tenure, greater personal independence,
> whether as a home owner or tenant, and a greater priority
> of public resources for those with obvious and urgent need.
>
> We believe that our economic policies in general will create
> conditions in which it will be possible for more and better
> quality homes to be provided by new building, conversion
> and rehabilitation.

As for specific policies, I have announced the direction of
policies to combat the land shortage. We want to speed up
and simplify the planning system. We shall repeal the Community Land Act. We shall also be talking to the building
society leaders on the subject of mortgage funds for home
purchase. We will be looking at a new subsidy system for
public sector housing which will direct help where it is most
needed. We certainly intend to ensure that local authorities
are able to build homes for those in the greatest need - and
I have in mind especially the elderly in need for sheltered
accommodation and the handicapped. [4]

The introduction of shorthold tenancies would 'provide additional
accommodation for the thousands of young single people who are
seeking it, particularly in our cities'. Simplifying the relationship
between government and local authorities would

release the energies of local authorities - elected members
and officials - to deal more effectively with their housing
problems. I also believe that it will enable my officials at the
Department to concentrate much harder on questions of
improving the quality of the environment and securing better
value for money. [5]

The sale of publicly owned houses at large discounts and new
rights for tenants would redistribute wealth, reduce social divisions and increase mobility and independence.
  Priorities and policies developed in opposition and reflecting a
general view about the role of government in housing have determined legislative and expenditure changes. It is naive to believe
that the government would be influenced by some consensus view
of housing need. Many commentators regard the underlying principles and the actions of governments in the 1970s and 1980s - in
particular the rush to owner occupation - as misguided. However,
it is not helpful to regard this as an ill-informed policy aberration
or to deny that ministers were fully aware of the likely implications
of policies. Anyone who reads ministerial statements, or, for
example, the responses of the Secretary of State to the various
enquiries of the House of Commons Environment Committee, is
likely to be impressed by the consistency of views. The intention
behind the new policies is bound up with views about independence, incentive, the role of the state and economic management.

CUTS IN EXPENDITURE

The government's housing policy in 1979-80 was remarkably de-
void of reference to investment targets or housing need. It might
be charitable to believe that the government felt that the statistics
of housing surplus indicated that the housing problem was solved,
or that all that needed to be done was to adjust mechanisms for

distribution and the expression of choice or tenure preference.
It would seem more likely that the government believed that, whatever problems existed, public intervention or provision was likely
to exacerbate rather than relieve them.

But it is at least partly true that the major decisions about
housing and housing policy had not been based on any evaluation
of the housing situation or housing problems. The Public Expenditure White Paper published in March 1980[6] stated that 'the Government in forming [their] judgement of the amount of public
expenditure which the nation can afford to devote to housing...
have had regard to the present size and condition of the housing
stock, trends in household formation and the capacity of the private sector to meet housing needs'. When the Environment Committee sought to be informed of these details, the Secretary of
State replied 'I... do not consider it useful to publish any such
material'. The figures were based on 'what the country could
afford' rather than on any assessment of housing prospects.[7]

The overwhelming impression is that the process of arriving at
decisions about public expenditure on housing did not include
discussion of the housing situation or any coherent evaluation of
the impact of cuts in housing expenditure compared with cuts in
any other programme. A healthy scepticism about projections and
forecasts appears to have become a justification for abandoning
any consideration of information which could raise difficult questions. It became a justification for only looking at material which
confirmed established predelictions. The Environment Committee
stated:

> The Committee believes that, if a proper judgement is to be
> made as to how much the country can afford, it is important
> that careful consideration be given to the impact on employ-
> ment levels and the social effects of a given level of expend-
> iture and that there should be adequate public debate
> regarding the claims which housing has compared with other
> programme areas.[8]

The cuts in housing capital allocations for local authorities and
housing associations had consequences which would have merited
some prior assessment of their impact. A mid-year reduction of
Housing Investment Programme allocations came in July 1979, soon
after the election. The reduction (by £294 million) did not bite
hard and largely eliminated the then predicted underspend. However, there were authorities which had to halt expenditure on
particular programmes. In 1980/1 the removal of certain constraints
on the use of allocations had little effect in view of the substantial
cuts for that year. The allocations involved reductions of one-
third of the previous year's spending. The amount allocated represented only half of what local authorities had asked for. For the
first time many local authorities made dramatic cuts. While some of
this may have had the effect of 'eliminating waste', it is doubtful
if any analysis could identify such rationality.

Various local authorities reduced, froze, suspended or severely restricted one or more elements in their capital programme - letting of public sector contracts, slum clearance programmes, private sector improvement grants, housing association finance, mortgage lending and improvements to council housing. With changes of this scale it could be expected that the Secretary of State would not have had to make mid-year adjustments. However, in October 1980 a moratorium on new local authority housing capital projects was introduced in England. The reason given for the introduction of the moratorium was an anticipated overspending by local author- ities, but there is no evidence to indicate that overspending was likely (and there were other legal checks on this). It is possible to argue that the decision to introduce a moratorium was designed to gear activity down in preparation for further cuts in 1981/2, or to lead to an underspend on investment to offset an overspend on subsidy arising from higher interest rates. These were higher than had been planned for in arriving at the division of housing cash limits between investment and subsidy.

The announcement of public expenditure plans prepared the ground for further cuts in expenditure. The planned reductions in housing public expenditure from 1980/1 to 1983/4 amounted to 48 per cent. [9] These accounted for 75 per cent of the planned reduction in total public expenditure on programmes plus the con- tingency reserve. In 1974/5 housing accounted for 10 per cent of public expenditure programmes. Its share had fallen to 7.5 per cent by 1979/80 and would fall to only just over 4 per cent by 1983/4. The nature of this cut in expenditure and the way it was arrived at make it very difficult to identify what will be its impact. It has not been arrived at by converting targets for levels of housing investment and subsidy into cash figures. The process has been the other way round - the government's overall financial and monetary targets and the claims of other programmes have determined what can be spent on housing. What this level of expenditure will pay for in terms of housing depends on inflation and interest rates, as well as on factors such as rents and revenue from council house sales. These are real uncertainties and as yet the government has not indicated how it expects them to work out.

The Environment Committee's first report provided a detailed discussion of these issues, and indicated the investment impli- cations of the expenditure plans. It incorporated two different assumptions about the rate of rent increase and the rate of council house sales, and was based on what the committee regarded as optimistic economic assumptions. If real rents increased in the way indicated by ministers (by something over 10 per cent com- pared with 1978/9) and if council house sales were 100,000 per year up to 1983/4, the implications were that planned public ex- penditure would imply - assuming no further shift of investment resources from new building to improvement - a fall in public sector starts from 66,000 in 1979/80 to under 30,000 in 1983/4 (and a fall in public sector completions from 89,000 in 1979/80 to 33,000 in 1983/4).

There were not many ways in which the government could obtain higher investment within the stated expenditure ceilings. Very much higher rents would involve higher rebate costs, and the implications of rent increases for investment were relatively small (5,000 completions more in 1983/4 if rents rose by 50 per cent). Similarly, if council house sales were higher - say 200,000 a year - public sector completions would be some 9,000 more in 1983/4. But there were other factors which would reduce the resources available for investment. In spite of, and perhaps because of, council house sales, housing management and maintenance costs could increase. In addition, local authorities might not wish to postpone improvement to their own stock further.

The figures quoted above assumed that the pool rate of interest for local authorities in 1983/4 would be 11 per cent. It would seem unlikely to be lower. If it is 1 per cent higher that implies some 4,000 new dwellings fewer. If the proportion of private funding (including that from savings) for council house purchase declines under the influence of the right to a council mortgage and the drawing in of more marginal buyers, the effects are again to reduce cash available for investment. At the same time rising unemployment and higher rents may increase the rate of leakage to rent rebates and reduce the income derived from rents. Finally, local authorities may find the claims for resources from other parts of the programme than new building difficult to resist. It would not be unreasonable to predict a rate of new building by 1983/4 nearer to 20,000 than 30,000 dwellings.

The Environment Committee's view was that new public sector housing starts in England were unlikely to exceed 31,000 in 1983/4 and could be well below that figure. In view of the considerations above it would seem probable that figures being used within the Department of the Environment were even lower.

The assumptions being made in these figures involved a very large reduction in general subsidies (that is apart from rent rebates) to local authority tenants - falling in real terms from £1,581 million in 1979/80 to between £200 million and £600 million in 1983/4 (depending on the rate of rent increase). Most tenants will be receiving no general subsidy and an increasing number will be receiving means-tested rent rebates. In contrast mortgage tax relief is likely to remain well above £1,000 million in 1983/4.

The other implications of these expenditure cuts depend on what happens to private sector completions. The Environment Committee's conclusion was that even accounting for this there will be a cumulative shortfall of new construction of approaching half a million dwellings by the mid-1980s.

One of the myths about housing expenditure has at least been exploded. The Secretary of State in justifying cuts pointed to local authority underspending as an indication that authorities wished to cut back. In 1980 the concern shifted to overspending and a moratorium to restrict the present (and future) level of spending. There remains a more important point. Whatever the size of the housing capital programme, the accepted view is that resources should be channelled to areas and groups with the greatest need. But the arrangements for use of capital receipts from council house sales appear to undermine this. Local authorities are entitled to retain 50 per cent of capital receipts from sales. Such receipts are, however, taken into account by the government in arriving at the total sum available for capital expenditure on housing. Thus authorities where sales are low (perhaps because of the level of tenants' incomes or the nature of the housing stock) but problems are considerable will have a smaller claim on allocations for capital investment than their needs would justify. While this is not as great an anomaly as the channelling of resources through tax reliefs, it hardly fits the criteria of making best use of and concentrating resources on those in greatest need.

It is against the background of a lack of a clear housing budget and uncertainty about levels of investment, but the certainty of substantial reductions in investment on top of previous cuts, that the Housing Bill was debated. In the short term it is not the 1980 Act or the right to buy that are the major elements affecting the housing situation, but rather it is the plans for housing public expenditure. These plans imply a continuing low level of investment, high rents and increased dependency on rebates. Council housing will increasingly become self-financing and subsidies will be income-related. In contrast, subsidy for owner occupation will continue to grow and be regressive in its distribution. The Housing Act, 1980, provides some of the mechanisms for this but is also likely to result in an actual decline in the size and quality of the public sector housing stock.

THE HOUSING ACT, 1980

The Housing Act, 1980, contained some elements included in the previous Labour government's Housing Bill of 1979. Most importantly the subsidy system introduced by the act was identical to that outlined in the consultative document 'Housing Policy' in 1977. (In Scotland the Housing (Financial Provisions) (Scotland) Act, 1978, had already introduced a substantially similar subsidy system. The Tenants' Rights, Etc. (Scotland) Act, 1980, contains, with a few differences, the other provisions of the Housing Act, 1980). In other respects, and particularly in the right to buy, the act was distinctively a Conservative Party measure. In spite of the large Conservative majority in parliament, the passage of the bill was not without incident. What is noticeable is how little impact was made by discussion in standing committee. Forty-six sittings of the committee produced only minimal changes. Only one opposition amendment, and that only a matter of drafting, was accepted by the government. The discussion consisted of ritual conflict, of filibuster and taking up pre-arranged positions. [10] Discussions elsewhere had more effect and a number of amendments were made to the bill in the House of Lords. The most

important concession made by the government was the exclusion
from the right to buy of accommodation designed or specially
adapted for the elderly, which it is the practice of the landlord
to let to the elderly. The government had been defeated in the
Lords and it wanted the legislation to be passed before the summer recess. Owing to shortage of time for the Commons to remove
the amendment and secure the agreement of the Lords, the government was virtually obliged to accept its substance. A dispute
over business in the last few days before the recess was resolved
through an agreement between the Secretary of State and his
shadow, Roy Hattersley, over the wording of a substitute amendment. (For procedural reasons it was not possible to amend the
Scottish bill and a second bill, which became the Tenants' Rights,
Etc. (Scotland) Amendment Act, 1980, was introduced in the
autumn.)

Other changes to the legislation were achieved[11] but for present purposes three issues are outstanding. First, the essential
elements of the right to buy with the limited exception referred
to above were not altered. Second, the tenants' charter as enacted
does not resolve the inequities faced by council tenants. Third,
the subsidy system, although it aroused very little comment or
conflict, may prove to be more significant than the Housing Finance Act, 1972, would have been had it remained in operation for
a longer period.

The Right to Buy
The most obvious obstacle to previous Conservative governments'
desire to sell council houses was the reluctance of many local
authorities (not only Labour-controlled ones) to use their powers
to sell. For this reason the Housing Act, 1980, was specifically
designed to remove local discretion over the sale of council houses.
The right-to-buy provisions were backed by powers for the Secretary of State to intervene, carry out and charge for sales in
any local authority. (In Scotland powers of enforcement are on a
different basis.) The provision of a right for tenants to buy
involved explicit reductions in local autonomy.

As early as 18 May 1979 the Secretary of State issued a revised
general consent removing restrictions imposed by his Labour predecessor and providing a more generous discount for council
house sales than ever before.[12] (A similar general consent was
issued in Scotland where none had existed since 1974.) The general consent enabled local authorities to offer the levels of discount
promised in the Conservative manifesto. However, previous legislation did not empower the Secretary of State to make council
house sales mandatory. Both the housing and public expenditure
claims of the government required substantial sales of council
houses but without new legislation it was not clear that these
would be achieved. The right-to-buy provisions of the Housing
Act, 1980, were principally directed at recalcitrant Labour councils. But they affected all local authorities, including Conservative
and independent councils, which refused to sell council houses,

and all those which did sell but used their discretion to exclude certain properties (usually flats and smaller dwellings).

While the sale of council houses is an obvious means of extending the role of the private market in housing, it also in the short term is a mechanism to reduce public expenditure. The bulk of funding for council house sales has come from local authorities themselves, but where they own the asset they can offer a mortgage and do not have to borrow again to cover this. Consequently there is no increase in public sector borrowing to facilitate sales. This is a simple and workable arrangement and allows sales to proceed and to be processed relatively quickly within one agency. But it does not have the financial advantages that would arise if the sale was financed by the private sector. If, say, building societies financed sales, the debt associated with dwellings would become part of the private sector housing debt; the local authority would receive substantial capital payments which it could use to write off its debt. In practice less than one-third of sales have been financed through private sector loans, deposits and outright purchase. The government attempted to encourage the building societies to play a fuller role but without success.

The building societies, while they favoured council house sales, were not willing to set aside quotas or give preferential treatment to sitting-tenant purchasers.[13] The short-term financial advantages of sales were consequently reduced but the political and ideological advantages were unaffected. Moreover, the Department of the Environment's appraisal of the financial effects of the sale of council houses (which is discussed in Chapter 3) indicated that the government was determined to believe that it was financially prudent to sell.

The major elements in the right to buy were as follows:
(1) The right of secure tenants of three years' standing to buy the freehold or long lease of their dwelling.
(2) The right to a mortgage, the amount of which is calculated according to regulations issued by the Secretary of State.
(3) A limited range of excluded properties - largely housing designed or adapted for the elderly and disabled.
(4) Clear procedures to be followed including intervention by the Secretary of State and the courts.
(5) Absence of pre-emption or similar conditions except where approved by the Secretary of State (rural areas).
(6) Continuation of discretionary sales outside the right to buy.
(7) Clear procedures for valuation and calculation of price including arrangements for discount and for appeal to the district valuer.
(8) Tenants not qualifying for a 100 per cent mortgage are entitled to defer completion of purchase for two years; this involves freezing the appropriate price (and discount).
(9) Repayment of part of discount if the property is disposed of within five years.

The effect of both the legislation and the regulations issued subsequently is to do everything possible to enable purchase and

to remove potential obstacles. Furthermore, the burden of decisions about, for example, whether the costs of purchase or maintenance can be afforded or whether family circumstances are
likely to change is placed on the tenant rather than on the local
authority. The likely consequences of these provisions in terms
of the numbers and types of dwellings sold is discussed in Chapter 4. The general conclusions which must be drawn are that the
sale of council houses will exacerbate the problems of tenants who
do not buy and of potential tenants. The number and variety of
dwellings available to these households will decline and the choice
of dwelling and quality of service available will also be adversely
affected.

The Tenants' Charter
Although continuing tenants and potential tenants are unlikely
to benefit from the right to buy and indeed may be disadvantaged, they are not unaffected by other parts of the Housing
Act, 1980. During the 1970s it had become the conventional wis-
dom that problems over the quality of service in the public sector
and inequalities of rights in different tenures could be at least
partly remedied by reform of the rights and conditions of tenancies in the public sector. The measures included in the 1980 Act,
however, are not as strong as those in the previous Labour government's bill. The principal elements in the tenants' charter are
as follows:
(1) Security of tenure and grounds for possession are defined.
(2) The right of succession of a widow, widower or resident mem-
    ber of the family is laid down.
(3) The right to take lodgers or to sub-let is established.
(4) A right to carry out improvements (subject to a landlord's
    permission) and apply for improvement grants is laid down.
(5) Rights to information and consultation are defined. (The
    absence of a right to consultation is a significant difference
    in the Scottish legislation.)
(6) In addition to these rights for tenants, the public at large is
    entitled to information on the rules and procedures governing
    allocations and transfers, and information on arrangements
    for consulting secure tenants; they also have the right to
    check certain details of their own application for housing.
   The terms of the legislation in these areas is not as radical as
the phrase 'tenants' charter' implies. It is important that for the
first time certain rights are backed by the law. However, in most
cases the tenants' charter does not require substantial changes in
existing practice. For example, many local authorities go beyond
what is required under the right of succession, while practice in
relation to lodgers or sub-letting is often already in tune with the
act; the requirement in respect of information and consultation is
minimal. This is not to deny the importance of providing a legal
basis to even minimal rights. It does mean, however, that the
tenants' charter in the Housing Act, 1980, does not represent a
revolutionary change. Most tenants in most local authorities will

not appreciate any difference. Rather they will be aware of rising
rents, reduced transfer opportunities, and possibly worsening
repair and maintenance services resulting from other (and more
substantial) aspects of government policy. In many ways the key-
note of the tenants' charter is the right to buy rather than the
rights associated with continuing tenancy. Those tenants who are
unable or do not wish to take advantage of the right to buy will
not find that the tenants' charter changes their position or significantly erodes the inequalities between housing tenures. In
this sense, while legal rights are strictly less unequal, this
advance is likely to be overwhelmed and rendered insignificant
by the effects of the right to buy, cuts in expenditure and rising
rents.

The New Subsidy System

As has been outlined, the government's expenditure plans assumed
a substantial decrease in subsidy for council tenants. Even if new
investment declined to a minimal level, the subsidy bill would have
to be cut if expenditure targets were to be realised.

The basic mechanism for this is provided in the new housing
subsidy system in the Housing Act, 1980. The act provides for a
deficit financing system and has some similarities with the system
introduced in the Housing Finance Act, 1972. It enables the Secretary of State to base his subsidy on a notional calculation in
which he assumes certain levels of local contribution. While this
can (unlike the 1972 Act) be raised through any combination of
rent and rates, the powers under the Local Government, Planning
and Land Act, 1980, enable the Secretary of State to check any
tendency to shift costs to the ratepayer. In effect his ability to
prescribe a local contribution for the purposes of subsidy calculation is an ability to lay down rent increases.

Especially for authorities whose Housing Revenue Account is in
deficit, there is only limited discretion to act differently. Thus
the most important additional mechanism to implement housing
expenditure cuts, and through that the broader strategy of the
government, is a cash limit system coupled with controls over new
investment (Housing Investment Programmes) and controls over
the size of the subsidy bill. The exact size of this latter bill will
still be dependent on rates of interest and other factors, but is
nevertheless more 'controllable' under the new arrangements with
their implications for rents. The Secretary of State announced in
1980 that calculation of subsidy would be based on an assumption
that rents would rise by £2.95 per week per dwelling; but for most
authorities an even greater actual rise in rents was implied. All
the indications are that neither the opposition nor local authorities
had appreciated the potential of the new subsidy to realise such
substantial changes.

Three points are important to note in this context. First, the
subsidy system in the Housing Act, 1980, could be used differently
to have a different or slower impact. It is simply a mechanism for
implementing policies and does not presuppose certain policies.

Second, the reduction in housing public expenditure is partly offset by an increase in social security expenditure associated with supplementary benefit payment for rents. Third, both the cuts in investment and the new subsidy system substantially erode local autonomy in housing.

IMPLICATIONS AND CONCLUSIONS

The package of policies associated with the Housing Act, 1980, has other aspects not discussed here. For example, the government explicitly encouraged local authorities, by the offer of the ability to keep capital receipts, to embark upon certain policies. In particular these involved sales of land for starter homes, partnership building of starter homes, shared ownership, improving homes for sale, selling unimproved homes and mortgage guarantees. The Local Government, Planning and Land Act, 1980, included measures to restrict the activities of direct Labour departments and to repeal the Community Land Act, 1975. At the same time changes in planning legislation and procedures were designed to remove constraints on the private sector. Registers of unused and underused land in public ownership, powers for the Secretary of State to direct release of registered land, and detailed measures to streamline development control and appeals procedures were all designed to create the climate for private development. Sales of land by new town development corporations, the Property Services Agency and the Housing Corporation, and reduction in the rate of Development Land Tax were directed towards the same end. Proposals were also advanced to replace the cost-yardstick procedure in project approval and subsidy arrangements with a market-related value for money formula, and to abandon insistence on Parker Morris standards in public housing developments.
    These changes taken together represent a determined break with previous policy. If the direction indicated by the plans outlined in 1979/80 is maintained for, say, ten years there can be no doubt that the housing market will be substantially different as a result. The first year of Conservative government in the housing field has been marked by a single-minded pursuit of linked objectives: the expansion of owner occupation and reduction in direct public expenditure on housing. The government has been willing to breach major areas of local autonomy and to ignore the conventional planning and forecasting assumptions rather than to compromise its primary goals. The greatest embarrassments for the government in achieving its aims involve the impact of high interest rates on housing-related public expenditure, the unwillingness of building societies to earmark funds for council house sales, and the effects of high interest rates and unemployment on owner occupiers.
    Just as these 'problems' originate beyond the housing field as such, so has the government's perspective on housing moved

beyond a bricks and mortar approach. The emphasis on the redistribution of wealth and on encouraging labour mobility has
been greater than the emphasis on homelessness, overcrowding
or problems of house condition. In this sense the most interesting
feature of their policy has been a redefinition of the terms of the debate about housing. While it would no doubt be wrong to argue
that this redefinition involves a disregard for problems of housing stress, it does involve some strong competing concerns.
Indeed, it would seem that the concern to make council housing a
self-financing residual service, and to encourage (through maintenance of tax relief and other privileges) private individual
investment, involves both an explicit intent to foster certain inequalities and reward 'merit', and a general abandonment of social
service objectives. In essence the government regards housing as
a commodity best provided through the market, with little justification for state intervention. The thoroughness with which this
shift in policy is being pursued, the legal and financial measures
developed to implement it, and the housing situation in which the
changes are being introduced mark it as at least as important as
previous periods of reaction. Arguably it involves a new era for
council housing. Owner occupation provides the most likely mechanism for ensuring that the consumption of housing is governed
by market processes. In this sense increased owner occupation is
not simply an end in itself but is a means of achieving other goals
concerned with public expenditure, market processes, incentives,
choices and self-help.

The counterpart of such a policy of privatisation is one of residualisation of the public sector and clearer definition of the role of
the state in housing provision. Policies directed towards new
investment, as well as the sale of council, new town and housing
association dwellings, offer a limited continuing role for publicly
provided housing. This role is largely concerned with meeting the
needs of a residual population who cannot fend for themselves in
the owner-occupied market and cannot obtain adequate housing
in the privately rented sector. The tendency to see public housing as only necessary for the elderly, the poor and certain groups
with special needs is apparent. It is fully consistent with a view
that public resources should be channelled towards those in 'real
need'. What is anomalous in such a proposition is the relationship
with policies which, in order to encourage private ownership,
channel resources towards those with higher incomes, more wealth
and better housing. In this sense the residualist approach to public housing can only be regarded as a product of ideas about
private ownership and the role of the state as such, rather than
about the best use of resources and channelling them to those in
greatest need. This view is sustained by assessments, for example,
of the financial effects of the sales (see Chapter 3).

The right to buy extends considerable privileges to particular
tenants. It involves a redistribution in favour of these individuals
and as a result will in most cases extend their housing opportunities and ability to accumulate wealth. What is surprising in the

policy is the consistent assertion by the government that all tenants will benefit, or that no one will 'lose' as a result of the benefits accruing to some. The most ludicrous assertion has been that
there will be no loss of re-lets and therefore no loss of housing
supply to households who must rent. The government has been
unwilling to accept that there are substantial costs involved in
the right to buy or that sales will be concentrated in the better
parts of the public sector stock. It has been unwilling to acknow-
ledge the possibility that sales will exacerbate problems in a public sector which in certain areas is already becoming a second
best, a welfare housing service. The longer the combination of
low public investment and council house sales continues, the more
unequal the housing experience of different families will be. The
public sector will deteriorate and become increasingly a poor law
service. Even the principle that such a service should pay for
itself will begin to be realised.

Those who remain public sector tenants will be even more disadvantaged compared with owner occupiers. The disparity in
financial support between tenants and owners (who also accumulate wealth through housing) will be increasingly marked.
Unemployment, growing economic inequality, the problems
created by the continuing decline of the private rented sector,
and the effects of sustained high levels of council house sales
alongside low investment in public and private improvement and
new building are likely to reinforce one another. While there are
other important dimensions to housing inequalities, including those
between different groups of owner occupiers, the changing role
of council housing is an important element in increasing housing
inequalities.

NOTES

1   'Housing Policy: A Consultative Document', Cmnd 6851 (HMSO,
    1977), para. 2.01.
2   Conservative Party, 'Conservative Manifesto 1979' (Conser-
    vative Central Office, 1979).
3   'House of Commons: Official Report', vol. 967, cols. 79-80
    (15 May 1979).
4   Ibid., col. 407.
5   Ibid., col. 408.
6   'The Government's Expenditure Plans 1980-81 to 1983-84',
    Cmnd 7841 (HMSO, 1980).
7   House of Commons, 'First Report from the Environment Com-
    mittee', HC 714/1979-80 (HMSO, 1980).
8. Ibid.
9   'The Government's Expenditure Plans'.
10 M. Ferman, The Tragicomedy of the Housing Bill, 'New States-
    man', 21 November 1980.

11 D. McCulloch, How the AMA Fought – and Improved – the
    Housing Bill, 'Municipal Journal' (October 1980).
12 Department of the Environment, Circular Letter, 18 May 1979.
13 House of Commons, Environment Committee, 'Council House
    Sales: Minutes of Evidence', HC 535 – vi/1979–80 (HMSO,
    1980).

3 The Financial and Economic Implications of Council House Sales

Bernard Kilroy

The financial let alone economic implications of the sale of council houses are not widely understood since, surprisingly, they have not been fully explored until recently.[1] Instant and one-sided verdicts still abound. In this chapter, therefore, three main interests are considered in turn: the purchaser's, the local community's and the national interest. For each a time perspective is required since long-term effects can reverse the short term. Further, the financial implications in money must be distinguished from the wider economic implications for resources.

Before the late 1970s sales were debated primarily in social terms even when decisions with major financial implications were taken by government; for instance when from 1968 Labour restricted sales to a proportion of a council's stock, or when from 1972 the Conservatives permitted discounts larger than 20 per cent in some circumstances.[2] Even in the 1980s political commitments for or against sales are not likely to be changed by a wider appreciation of the financial arguments.

The financial and economic implications have come to the fore along with the debate about housing finance as a whole, which was the main impetus behind Labour's 'fundamental' housing policy review that eventually reported in 1977.[3] The effects of sales naturally reflect the misunderstandings and political compromises of the whole housing finance system, when analysed according to all the very different interests involved. Indeed sales are but one aspect of a more general argument about the balance between tenures, with an implied reduction in council housing and increase in owner occupation. So sales cannot be debated in isolation. Yet the two main parties are unwilling to tackle the real issues in housing finance.

The issue of sales is now so politicised that critical standards have been abandoned by both political camps; hence the confusion. First, advocates of sales have been allowed to argue the magic that everyone gains financially from sales: not only tenants who buy but taxpayers and ratepayers too, and even other tenants indirectly. No one could dispute the individual bargain of buying one's council house when the price is discounted by between one third and a half under the provisions of the Housing Act, 1980. Yet such generosity is an exception to the Conservative government's otherwise austere tone about the stark choice between immediate and lasting benefits, for instance that one man's pay rise is another man's job. Discounted sales of council houses would, the government claimed, also save the rest of the community millions of pounds.

52

The Labour government, however, had not contradicted claims that everyone could benefit from sales;[4] it did not publish studies which it had commissioned from civil servants that proved otherwise. The reason was embarrassment. Conservatives could and did put Labour on the spot by accusing them of denying to tenants access to personal tax-free gains in wealth.[5] Detailed figures would have again highlighted the contrast in financial advantages between owning and renting, which Labour had not felt able to alter after its housing policy review.

Second, the widespread speculation whether the public purse will 'gain or lose' has been an abdication of responsibility. Since 1976 a series of sale appraisals have been carried out akin to investment appraisals of commercial projects.[6] They have looked at income and expenditure over future years. Alas, attention has generally focused on them as predicting what is going to happen, that is whether sales will prove to be profitable. Instead attention should surely have focused, as with any investment appraisal, on the sensitivity of the outcome to changes in the assumptions and therefore what should happen – what decisions are called for about rents, subsidies and discounts. Commercial investment appraisals are not for 'crystal-ball gazing' about whether a product will be profitable; they are to clarify what the rates of production and selling price should be. Both the two appraisals by the Department of the Environment (DOE) are also predictive. The first of these, the 'old' appraisal prepared under the Labour government in 1978, was not published but was leaked late in 1979. The 'new' appraisal under the Conservative government was hurriedly published (the scissors and pasting actually show) two days before the second reading debate of the Housing Bill in January 1980.[7]

The faults are not obvious in these or similar appraisals. By selecting some historical data on past trends in rents and extrapolating into the future, a 'factual' impression is given. Yet rents cannot be isolated from other financial trends in the past like take-home pay and interest rates. Had any attempt been made to test whether sales in the past would have been profitable under the actual circumstances of the time on terms comparable to those offered now, the results would have been very different. Unfortunately, whatever the purport of the appraisals, it has been an open secret among both parties that policy about sales is made on other than financial criteria.

Third, an artificial association has been created between the all too evident institutional weaknesses of council housing, its consumer insensitivity for example, and its alleged financial weaknesses. The link has been created not only on the moderate right by Mr Peter Walker, Environment Secretary in the Heath government,[8] but from the left by Mr Frank Field, now a Labour MP, when director of the Child Poverty Action Group.[9] The link is based on a misunderstanding about why housing expenditure and particularly housing subsidies seemed 'out of control' from 1973 onwards. Housing has been uniquely vulnerable to inadequacies in the inflation accounting of debt interest in the annual white papers on the government's expenditure plans.[10] During the 1970s there was an explosive increase in mortgage tax relief to owner occupiers for the same reasons which was criticised much less. In future the cost of tax relief cannot but grow unless interest rates drop, while public housing subsidies are planned to fall in any case.[11] However, tax uncollected is not counted in the United Kingdom as a 'cost' to public spending. Further, the Labour Party was ambivalent. On the one hand, it had been slow to commit itself about the extent to which rents should reflect costs when the latter were increasing faster than inflation. On the other hand, for the sake of the marginal voter, it was anxious not to appear opposed to owner occupation. So Labour was in no position to do other than patch the existing system.

Fourth, because the sales debate has taken place within the claustrophobic world of housing finance, the financial implications have been wrongly equated with the economic ones. One speech by the Minister for Housing epitomised this. In approving the vast shift of wealth into home ownership since 1914, he quoted a recent editorial in the financial press which had commented that the postwar rise in home ownership and in house prices had done more to redistribute wealth than any tax devised or proposed by his opponents. But he overlooked the main claim in the editorial that the trend had depended directly on distortions in the financial markets and the tax system which were now threatening the economy on a scale that the government could not afford to ignore.[12]

The process explains why the sales issue has become prominent. As the Building Societies Association (BSA) has pointed out, the privately rented sector has now so shrunk that, if much more than the present 55 per cent of households are to become owner occupiers, the growth must now come at the expense of the public sector.[13] Of the three tenures, private renting has for the last half century been steadily penalised financially as the other two tenures have been encouraged. But public housing cannot now compete with the privileges accorded to owner occupation.

More rational discussion will be achieved only in a wider context and if several factors are connected in the public mind. Not only will housing have to cede the political stage to employment, but tax neutrality will have to be seen as essential for our economic health. Not only will the housing 'system' have to be seen as failing, as in 1972/3, but reform will have to be appreciated as providing benefits, not sacrifices. Indeed, much of the so-called financial assistance to housing will have to be understood as causing, not alleviating, housing problems like shortages, immobility, high prices and deterioration of the stock.

THE PURCHASER'S INTEREST

Actual Outgoings
The only thoroughly documented evidence remains that from

Birmingham by Alan Murie in the early 1970s before the leap in house prices and when discounts averaged 15 per cent.[14] The mortgage repayments of tenants who bought were then most often one and a half times their rent. By 1975, however, even 50/50 equity sharers in a Greater London Council (GLC) scheme for new houses in Hertfordshire were paying (without discounts) 22 per cent of regional average earnings or as much as twice the 11 per cent for conventional renting.[15] In 1980, the all-party House of Commons Select Committee on the Environment was able to obtain only a range of estimates. For instance, the BSA suggested that initial outgoings of tenants who bought could be, net of tax relief and at the then 15 per cent mortgage rate, some 80 per cent more than an assumed national average weekly rent then of £8 for council dwellings of all types.[16] The BSA was using notional 1980 amounts from the DOE 'new' appraisal, where tenants are assumed to buy houses valued at £14,000, discounted by 40 per cent to £8,400, with an 80 per cent mortgage of £6,700. Were the mortgage rate to fall to 11 per cent, the BSA said, net weekly cost could fall to less than £11.50.

However, Leeds and Birmingham City Councils both suggested that to rent might soon cost a sitting tenant as much as to buy.[17] This is likely to have become more common since successive increases will have brought national average weekly council rents to £11.50 by mid-1981 while the mortgage rate and the increase in house prices have fallen back.

Comparisons of outgoings usually omit maintenance. The Family Expenditure Survey showed that in 1979 council tenants spent an average of £0.65 per week on repairs, maintenance and decoration whereas mortgagors spent a wider range whose average was £3.43. This could be even more significant in the 50/50 shared ownership schemes which the government is promoting for marginal purchasers because shared owners become responsible for all, and not half, the maintenance costs. For flats purchased, service charges cannot be disguised. Wandsworth Council thought they might be so high as to deter tenants from buying unless they were capitalised into increased discounts or lower valuations.[18] . More recently, Southwark Council has claimed that the legislation is unclear as to how liability for structural repairs is to be shared.

How Outgoings are Viewed
Consumer surveys confirm that most people think it right for buying to cost significantly more than renting.[19] The Birmingham council tenants who purchased in Murie's survey invariably saw their increased outgoings as a bargain.[20] They contrasted their fixed mortgage commitments with ever-rising rents which they saw as 'dead money'; their outgoings were now accumulating a capital asset (for trading-up, retirement or bequest) which was a more worthwhile investment than putting savings elsewhere. Two Conservative Environment Secretaries have emphasised the attraction: that by 1978, after paying out similar amounts for the last 25 years, a council tenant had nothing while an owner occupier had an asset which had appreciated in value from £2,000 to £16,000.[21]

Family circumstances and employment prospects are still an obstacle to home ownership for many. However, growth in post-war incomes has changed perceptions. Studies suggest not only that the demand for housing rises strongly as real income levels in general rise but also that it increases as people move up from one income level to another. More significantly, the purposes which housing serves change, through a spectrum from a basic necessity to a luxury to an investment asset. [22] Elsewhere, in Sweden, Switzerland and West Germany, prosperity and low rates of owner occupation are compatible. In this country, the tax regime is such that a rise in the standard of living must inevitably imply a shift towards owner occupation.

In consequence, even the Labour Party has had to change its philosophy. In contrast to its Bevanite traditions, the housing policy review of 1977 saw public housing as merely filling a basic gap not otherwise catered for. The shift may explain why Labour did not even test the accuracy of the Conservative comparisons quoted above. The increase from £2,000 to £16,000 in house values is in fact an exaggeration: it ignores the effect of changes in the value of money. The buyer's real gain is the extent to which the eight-fold rise in house prices has been faster than the five-fold rise in other prices after deducting the repair, insurance and transaction costs of owning. The true cost to the tenant has been the rent paid in real terms net of maintenance, say £4 per week at 1978 prices over 25 years, that is £5,000, plus the extent to which rents (and maintenance) have risen faster than prices generally. Overall, the owner occupier might have become £7,500 better off than the tenant; that is just over half the Conservative claim.

Labour would have been swimming against the tide had it drawn the conclusion that, if buyers usually benefited from ownership, the gain ought not be compounded through mortgage tax relief and exemption from capital gains tax. Even though council tenants were a potential Labour constituency of a third of all households, the party was slow to face their inevitable losses from the system. Compensations could have been sought through better housing services plus savings bonds, available only to tenants, as well-proofed against inflation as home ownership.

The underlying logic of the situation explains why Labour failed to challenge its opponent's argument that both councils and purchasers could gain from sales. If the public purse gains from not selling, then individual tenants would presumably lose by continuing to rent – which was precisely what Conservatives argued. Thorough analysis would have forced Labour to admit that the financial scales were tipped in favour of ownership, something which was too politically sensitive to broach. So, apart from the minor measures in its 'new deal for council housing' announced not long before the 1979 election, Labour sat on the fence. Without radical changes in housing finance, however, Labour's opposition to sales was, and still is, an impossible task.

Maintenance
Owners are known to be more conscious of the investment value
of home ownership than tenants. But less prominence has been
given to the value tenants attach to maintenance. As maintenance
costs are likely to go on rising in real terms, it is important to
know whether they can be passed on to tenants. If not, it might
be more attractive for councils to sell. Consumer surveys suggest
that among council tenants the highest popularity score of renting is that 'the council sees to repairs'. This is mentioned more
often than their highest unpopularity score of 'lack of independence and choice'. Conversely, among owners as well as tenants,
the highest scoring disadvantage of owning is the responsibility
for repairs. This is mentioned more often by owners than their
highest scoring advantage, the investment value. [23]
    There is more practical evidence which confirms the opinion
surveys. The Family Expenditure Survey figures already quoted
and the do-it-yourself boom at first suggest that home owners'
spending on upkeep is not negligible. But there is a growing
awareness that this tends to be mainly by able-bodied households
and much of the work is cosmetic. The growth of disrepair shown
by government surveys of house condition suggests that neglect
is more widespread than had been believed. [24] On the other hand,
the National Consumer Council's survey concluded that council
tenants would pay more for better maintenance. [25] Yet sale
appraisals by the DOE (and others), which assume that higher
maintenance costs cannot be passed on in higher rents, favour
the case for selling.

Discounts and Encouragements to Ownership
Meanwhile, to help home ownership, both major political parties
have concentrated on helping would-be buyers to surmount the
'threshold' costs. But house prices and, more so, mortgage repayments have continued to rise faster than prices in general and
during the last decade faster than earnings. Hence, both parties
have favoured savings/bonus schemes for first-time buyers
(introduced by Labour in 1978) and have also promoted low start
mortgages.
    Mounting threshold costs have been the stimulus for discounts
on sales to become more generous than the 20 per cent permitted
since 1967. Any higher discount is even harder to justify on valuation grounds. For discount was not, as often supposed, by
virtue of the sitting tenancy. With nothing to prevent council
rent increases as inflation continues, this does not lower the
'investment value' as it does in the private rented sector. Before
1980, discount was in return for the obligation on the purchaser
to give the authority first refusal at the original price if he sold
within five years. In 1972 the government encouraged local authorities to increase the maximum discount to 30 per cent in special
cases with a correspondingly longer pre-emption period of eight
years.
    However, in imitation of Birmingham Corporation (the pioneer

large-scale seller), councils had commonly varied the discount
according to length of residence, though within the maximum 20
or 30 per cent range. There was no logic in this approach. Nevertheless, it was never challenged by Labour in office, though
within the party a 'no discount, no strings' policy was adopted in
1979. Now the illogicality is enshrined in the Housing Act, 1980,
which increases the discount from a basic 33 per cent after a minimum three years' residence by one percentage point for every
extra year to a maximum of 50 per cent. This is repayable on a
sliding scale if the purchaser sells within five years. Only in the
House of Lords was the logic itself criticised.[26] It turns upside
down a familiar argument of the political right, that council tenants do not pay an economic rent: why then should they be
treated more generously the longer they have rented? Alternatively,
if discounts are in some sense a compensation, why should only
those tenants fortunate enough to buy be rewarded? One has to
conclude that the basis of discounts is purely political.

Other generous incentives, besides discounts, have been added
to the right to buy in the 1980 Act. Shared ownership schemes for
the sale of existing housing to sitting tenants, including proportions other than 50/50, are facilitated. Apart from management
complictions, these must increase the risk of foreclosure among
marginal buyers.[27] The same risk applies to the new right to a
joint mortgage. There is also a new two-year option to buy at today's price on payment of a £100 deposit. This would increase a
50 per cent discount to 62 per cent if house prices lose by 15
per cent each year.

Lifetime Comparisons
The sales debate has lacked lifetime comparisons of housing outgoings, even 'guesstimates', between tenants who buy and tenants
who continue to rent. Their respective finances can be simulated
as in Table 3.1, based on the DOE 'new' appraisal's average middle
aged purchaser or his surviving spouse, who are assumed to live for
35 years more in the house. Rents, mortgage interest rates and
maintenance are assumed constant in real terms.

THE LOCAL INTEREST

The local authority's financial interests should represent the ratepayer. Its economic interests are those of the local community in
the local housing service and housing market. Unfortunately the
debate about whether the public purse will gain or lose from sales
is confused. There is a widespread feeling that 'the figures can be
made to prove whatever one wants'. For instance, the widest difference between the range of possibilities in the DOE's old and new
appraisals for each house sold is, over the long term, a possible
gain of £9,218 and a possible loss of £8,535, that is a gap of
£17,753 (over twice the assumed discounted sale price of £8,400).
A gain of £9,218 from selling would mean houses could be given
away with a bonus of £818 before the public purse lost.

Table 3.1: Tenants' Lifetime Outgoings From Age 45 in 1980

Housing costs over 35 years at constant value	Tenant who buys £14,000 market value	Tenant who rents Rent @ £8.64 p.w.	(Rent @ £8 p.w.)
	£	£	£
Purchase price	8,400	–	–
Mortgage relief	– 2,268	–	–
Rent	–	15,725	(14,560)
less Rebates	–	– 2,022	(–1,872)
Rates	same	same	same
Maintenance paid	7,076	1,425	(1,425)
House insurance	417	–	–
Gross Outgoings	13,625	15,128	(14,113)
less Value of estate	– 14,000	–	–
add Renovation liability	3,500	–	–
Net Outgoings	3,125	15,128	(14,113)

Sources: Broadly derived from Department of the Environment, 'Appraisal of the Financial Effects of Council House Sales' (DOE, 1980), the DOE 'new' appraisal. An alternative average rent of a three-bedroom, post-war house assumed at £8.64 per week has been added in order better to represent the rent of houses sold than the all-dwelling average of £8 used by DOE. Constant values give simple multiple totals, for example £8 x 52 weeks x 35 years gives £14,560. Purchase price is after 40 per cent discount on market values with tax relief at 30 per cent on a 90 per cent mortgage; nil rent rebates for the first 20 years, then 30 per cent of rent for 15 years (half of the 60 per cent of tenants eligible); repair, maintenance and decoration costs from 'Family Expenditure Survey 1978' giving an average of £2.88 per week for owners and £0.58 per week for council tenants, updated by the retail price index; renovation costs from DOE 'new' appraisal.

The politicisation of the debate has encouraged authoritative voices to take refuge in the 'unpredictability' of the results. The Chartered Institute of Public Finance and Accountancy (CIPFA) is not immune from this fault. It is begging the question to sug- gest that 'results depend on the range of assumptions fed in'. By paying so much attention to what might happen, this attitude con- tradicts the purpose of investment appraisal as a business tool for indicating what decisions should be made about the factors one can control, rents in particular. Such an attitude also forgets that the different factors of rents, earnings and interest rates tend to vary in combination, not independently. They are not set on some predetermined course; as the financial environment has changed in the past, so decisions about them have tended to fol- low suit.

Changes in the law as well as inflation have also obscured the clear financial responsibility for the outcome of sales. In 1952 the principle that houses, like other public assets, should be sold at the best price was removed. [28] This paved the way for discounts for which there is no valuation basis. Inflation in values, moreover,

helped to hide real losses. By contrast, the corresponding principle that houses should be let at a fair balance between tenant,
ratepayer and taxpayer remained.[29] In this case the lack of
inflation accounting helped create the impression of rental losses
when councils' borrowing costs were rising faster than rents. In
the confusion, both advocates and opponents of selling have been
able to argue plausibly.

Two-dimensional Comparisons: the Flaws
The main financial advantage of sales used to be thought of erron-
eously as the immediate capital gain to the local authority. It is
true that if a house is sold at the current market value (less discount) this is invariably more than the outstanding debt incurred
at historic prices in the past, particularly as sales have been
prohibited at less than historic costs. Thus, before the 1979
election it was claimed that since 1976 Nottingham City Council
had sold £40 million worth of council houses and made a 'profit' of
£18 million over the cost of building them, which was nonsense.

This kind of comparison has persisted because opponents of
sales did not challenge its logic. They accepted it by implication
by arguing how much it cost to replace houses sold. As Birmingham Corporation had shown as far back as 1971 this was not valid;
the majority of houses would have continued to be occupied by the
same households whether sold or not. Only a proportion, probably
less than the national average turnover rate of some 4 per cent a
year, would need replacing. So for every 100 houses sold, re-
placements could be spread over a period of 25 years. Some areas
without housing shortages might never need to replace houses.

On the surface, the immediate gain from sales undermines the
principle at the core of local housing finance and confidence in it.
Apparently in revenue terms, too, the older houses seem most
profitable to sell: the ones with 15 years or more of life behind
them, capable of producing an income surplus to set against the
losses on newer building. The debt on a 1930s house built for
£500 costs only £1 a week to service. That on a 1950s house built
for £1,500 costs only £3. Yet the mortgage income which a council
receives after sale is determined by 1980s values.

It is irrelevant, however, to count either the apparent capital
gain or to think in terms of the outstanding debt charges (which
must be paid anyway). These give a two-dimensional view which
omits the future. What matters is the opportunity gain or loss
between all future revenues and all future costs on the house.
Otherwise ordinary commercial standards of investment appraisal
are ignored.

Counting the capital 'gain' is also technically incorrect; any
cash received from selling cannot be counted as part of an authority's income. It is only the authority's borrowing requirements
which are reduced by the extent of the debt cancelled. Whether
the gain is received in mortgage instalments or debt charges not
incurred is immaterial. So in income terms it makes no difference
if sales are financed externally by, say, a building society. The

distinction has been academic since in practice less than 30 per cent of sales proceeds have been received in cash, out of tenants' savings as well as mortgages.[30] The proportion is likely to drop because of the right to a mortgage guaranteed under the 1980 Act and if sales to poorer tenants increase. Nine out of ten sales have always been financed, on what amounts to a hire purchase agreement, by authorities themselves. They make a book transfer and mortgage repayments take the place of rents.

Some alternative representations, which have shown the income effect on the housing revenue account, have also been 'two dimensional' by showing only the first year after sales. Both the Royal Institution of Chartered Surveyors (RICS) and the GLC have made this error.[31] Invariably, mortgage repayments and interest are more than the rent at first. So the council appears to make an immediate surplus on all types of houses; Table 3.4 (page 87) shows past examples. In addition, the management and maintenance costs are now carried by the purchaser, though this is not always obvious except through service charges in the case of flats sold.

Figure 3.1: Relationship Between a Council's Income from Sold Houses

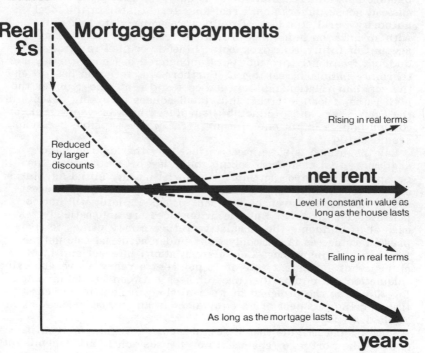

Instead, the value of the initial surplus must be qualified 'three dimensionally' according to projections of income and expenditure in succeeding years, which the RICS and GLC omitted to do. Projections would then show that the fixed income from mortgage repayments on sold houses would probably have been overtaken by rising income from rents after between five and fifteen years. Put another way, income from mortgage repayments will fall in real terms as time goes by whereas rents should keep their value constant if they keep pace with inflation, as in Figure 3.1. This principle is no longer contested. The point at issue, such as in the DOE new appraisal, is just when the cross-over occurs; whether the gains from sales in the years before the cross-over exceed the losses in the years after the cross-over. [32]

Three-dimensional Appreciation: the Obstacles

Inflationary Distortions. Unfortunately, 'three-dimensional' appreciation of sales is clouded by inflation. This should not be surprising. Even in the commercial world, inflation accounting has been slow to develop. For instance, asset stripping during the stock market boom of the early 1970s was encouraged by undervaluations of companies' assets, particularly their property, on balance sheets. Presentations of endowment mortgages commonly mislead house buyers about real long-term costs. In the local authority world, the lack of political commitment to link rents with an inflation index has prevented treasurers from taking account of future rent prospects. Indeed, council revenue budgets frequently project rents unchanged in money terms, and therefore falling in real terms. Furthermore, inflation has upset the constant relationship between cost and rent since, under the high rates of loan interest, individual houses incur big deficits in the early years and produce big surpluses in later years. Sale of council houses is but one of many areas where sensible decisions are obscured.

Lay discussion is sometimes confused by the 'bird in hand' argument, that cash from selling today is worth more than the prospect of cash from letting tomorrow; that any initial surpluses on current account can be invested and the cumulative interest reinvested so that even higher rent prospects later will not compensate. This is true. But the differences are automatically taken care of by reducing the cumulative future money values to their present value, as is commonly done under actuarial calculations for, say, life insurance. Consider inflation, interest and incomes all rising at a constant rate of 10 per cent a year. A present value calculation can equate the three choices between £1,000 invested for 10 years, the prospect of its capital equivalent in 10 years time and the prospect of its equivalent in an annual income, as in Table 3.5 (page 88).

Some people imagine that if rental income foregone is eventually to overtake mortgage repayments on houses sold, this depends on high inflation continuing and rents therefore rising faster in nominal terms. This is not so; if inflation eases, mortgage interest

will drop too. Besides, sales could make losses if inflation were
nil. Then the full value of a house sold would equal its site and
construction cost less depreciation; any discount must represent
a deficit. If such a sale were by mortgage, to the instalments
repaid would be added simply a charge for the use of money borrowed, say 2 per cent. Under inflation any gain from selling at a
price nominally higher than original cost is illusory, except to the
extent that house prices have risen faster than general prices.
Similarly the high initial mortgage payments ('front-end loading')
of inflated interest rates simply compensate the lender for the
anticipated decline in the real value of repayments later; there is
no real difference overall.

Now consider rents under nil inflation. Rents would consist of
(a) running costs or service charges, (b) wear and tear (technically capital consumption) and (c) the cost of the use of money.
The rent net of upkeep paid by the tenant is, by definition, the
rent of the money borrowed to use the asset at the real rate of
interest (that is the nominal rate minus the rate of inflation).
Alternatively, net rent could be paid as a capital sum or lease for,
say, 99 years of nominal life. In both cases the unexpired value
of the asset would be excluded since this returns to the landlord.

Under inflationary conditions, however, a gap automatically
opens between rents and costs, even when the real rate of interest is negative, as during the 1970s. For borrowing is front-
loaded and not indexed as are rents. Alas, the connection between
rents and the use charge for money is broken; periodic decisions
to increase rents are required, which are easily politicised. And
tenants see a never-ending and rising commitment to paying 'dead
money'.

Treasury Cash Distortions. Three-dimensional appreciation of
sales is even more frustrated by Treasury cash conventions,
which contradict normal (including local government) accounting
practice and tip the medium-term balance in favour of selling. For
the Treasury counts as income whatever, and only whatever, is
received in cash. This practice is bound to undervalue any long-
term investment, such as rented housing, where future income is
realisable only over a period of years. It has been well caricatured
as favouring the 'quick buck' by selling the 'seed corn', terms
actually used about the profitable presentation of the government
sale of British Petroleum shares in 1979. The reason is that the
public expenditure accounts do not distinguish between capital
and current accounts. All government spending is counted in cash
terms against tax revenue; any excess becomes the government's
borrowing requirement; any reduction is treated as a cash gain.[33]
This is why, in Treasury but not in local government accounting,
there is an artificial capital 'gain' when sales are financed externally by, say, a building society.[34]

The DOE's 'new' appraisal of sales during a 20-year period is
therefore bound to favour the case for selling. For cash proceeds
from sale are almost bound to exceed 20 years of net rental value;

non profit-making houses are generally expected to pay for themselves only after a longer lifetime, notionally of up to 60 years.
To require sale values to be balanced by 20 years, rent income
could be undervaluing the rental asset by two-thirds and ignoring
40 years of potential earning. Other appraisals have suggested no
more than: (a) that sales would make profits during the first ten
years (say the 1980s) and gradually turn to losses for the second
ten (say the 1990s); and (b) that the present value of losses
would start to exceed gains after that (say the year 2000).

Estimates in the DOE 'new' appraisal for houses sold in 1970
(which are not highlighted) show that, after eight years, surpluses to councils had died away and the combined government
surplus had never existed except by including as income the 30
per cent of sale price received in cash in the first year.[35] Alas,
neither the DOE nor any of the other published appraisals have
been able to draw upon the actual records of authorities, such as
the GLC or Birmingham, which have sold houses on a large scale
since 1970. So, what could be factually settled remains open to
speculation.

The DOE 'cash versus value' deception is compounded because
its new appraisal is inconsistent. Whereas rents receivable after
year 20 are ignored, sale proceeds are included as if received in
full before year 21 and the costs of renovation in year 15 as if
paid in full. In fact, only the loan charges actually saved or
incurred on current account are cash savings. Between 75 and 85
per cent only of sale proceeds of £8,400 would be received before
year 21 (reducing them by between £2,100 and £1,300) and only
five years' interest charges on renovation would be paid (reducing the £3,208 cost by around £1,200). Such corrections alone
could reverse the DOE's 20-year 'gain' from selling.

Three-dimensional Comparisons: Theory and Practice
A true 'three-dimensional' assessment therefore calculates the
streams of income and expenditure over the expected life of the
dwelling. In theory this principle has been observed by the DOE
long-term 50-year appraisal, by CIPFA, Leeds City and various
other local authorities although practice varies. The money distortions of income and expenditure received at different times are
removed mathematically by deflating them to 'present value'. Similarly, 'present value' calculations can add in the value of the
unexpired life of a house or its site and subtract any liability for
renovation which might take place beyond the period over which
the appraisal is carried out. In other words, a break-even sale
price, equal to the rental value of a house when let, can be calculated according to standard principles of valuation.

The DOE long-term appraisal preserves these principles in so
far as the sale proceeds of £8,400 from the house are the same,
whether received in a single cash sum or in annual mortgage
instalments, when deflated to a capitalised sum (the instalments
are fixed in nominal money terms and therefore decline in real
terms as the years go by). Conversely, so long as rents keep

their value in spite of inflation, the net annual income from rent would remain at the DOE's 1980 sum of £256 a year in <u>real</u> terms (without rates, £8 per week gross is £416 per year less £160 for management and maintenance) returning annually some 3 per cent of the selling price. Apart from other factors, and assuming management and maintenance costs remain the same in real terms, break-even point should therefore be reached after 33 years' rental value (£8,400 divided by £256). <u>A shorter life expectancy would produce a deficit from continuing to let rather than to sell, a longer one a surplus.</u>

Understanding the relationship between the factors is crucial before attempting to measure them. The higher the price discount, the lower the value of mortgage repayments and thus the sooner they are overtaken by rents (see Figure 3.1). So a shorter rental period is needed to break even, and vice versa. Similarly, if net rents were to rise faster than an annual index-linked value, real rental income would tilt upwards, thus shortening the rental period required, and vice versa. Unfortunately the pros and cons of sales may not be understood in such simple terms since rental value calculations are unfamiliar now; the housing market is dominated by sales for owner occupation, not by letting. Houses are therefore no longer thought of as assets producing a stream of income in kind and in which owner occupiers invest their savings as an alternative to other investments. The final abolition of Schedule A taxation in 1963 helped to sever the link. A 'rate of return' from housing has therefore become more and more a merely theoretical concept. Also, the politicisation of rents has cast them in terms of equitable proportions of income rather than a method of recouping costs.

What do actual sales show? During 1977/8 council houses were being sold at prices equivalent to rental values of around 36 years after discounts of around 15 per cent, less than now (see Table 3.6 on page 89). Had no discounts been given, the prices would have been equivalent to around 43 years' rental value. The net rents in these statistics could be expressed in terms of an annual rate of return of some 2.8 and 2.4 per cent respectively of selling price. The pattern seems constant. Such rates straddle the average of 2.5 per cent which an independent study calculated as the 'profitability' of local authority housing in the 1970s by expressing net rent income from all council dwellings as a proportion of their aggregate value.[36] Therefore, so long as these rental values do accord with remaining life expectancy, to increase discounts must risk selling at a loss.

Indeed, had discounts averaged 40 per cent in 1977/8, as assumed by DOE for 1980, selling prices would have been equivalent to about only 26 years of rental income. This is shorter than in the DOE appraisal, where selling prices are equivalent to 33 years. But that is because the DOE used the prices of houses actually sold (updated) but the lower average rent of all council dwellings. Once this bias is corrected, all the indications are that, provided rents do retain their value and provided houses sold do have a remaining life of longer than 25 to 30 years (the usual terms of mortgages), selling must represent a loss on present terms.

Rent Prospects. How then can sales be shown as profitable on present terms? The reason is that the DOE, among others, has argued that rents are likely to lose their value as time goes on. Rents are the kingpin in any sales appraisal (though other components, considered later, may tip the balance) and misleading evidence has been convincingly presented. Also, quite small changes in the assumptions are magnified when projected far into the future; hence the implausibly wide range of possibilities between the two DOE appraisals. Keynes's dictum, 'better roughly right than precisely wrong', is apposite. Past trends can be checked in Figure 3.2 (or Table 3.7 in the Appendix).

One must first appreciate that whether rents 'keep their value' depends on the extent to which they keep pace with interest rates and the level of earnings, as the DOE recognised. Lay opinion tends, wrongly, to think of rents being 'constant' in real terms if they keep pace with inflation (usually the retail price index). However, unless rents keep broadly in line with interest rates, that is the rent of money, it would be financially worthwhile for an authority to sell houses and invest the proceeds on the money market rather than to let them. So the DOE correctly used money market interest rates to equate or 'discount' expected rent income to real present value, as should any business appraisal. On this test, post-war council rents paid better than the money market. For instance, between 1949 and 1979 rents rose at an annual average of 9.0 per cent while interest rates averaged 7.3 and inflation 6.6 per cent.

Alternatively, the rate of earnings growth can be compared with rents. For if rents do not keep pace with earnings, a rented house is a wasting investment since it will become steadily more expensive to replace and to manage; its rents are not paying for the real capital consumption which the users of the house are exploiting. Also, as house prices have inflated with earnings trends, councils would find it more profitable to sell out whenever a house falls vacant than to re-let it. On this test, average post-war (1949-79) council rents rose annually on a par with gross earnings and faster than wage rates, at 9.0 and 9.1 and 8.3 per cent respectively.

Interest and earnings rates ought to be broadly interchangeable because, taking one year with another, they indicate the underlying growth of the real economy. When they diverge substantially, as happened in the 1930s, during both world wars or after the post-oil crisis of the 1970s, it is a reflection of some serious temporary economic disequilibrium. So comparisons (like the DOE's) of rent trends with interest or earnings rates separately during such periods are unreliable.

According to such value guidelines, future rent prospects can be gauged by comparing policy commitments against past experience. Some appraisals have lacked realism on this score. For instance, in 1976 when Leeds City Council announced its intention of selling 5,000 houses, gains of 'millions of pounds' were talked about.[37] Leeds assumed, however, that rents would rise at only 5 per cent a year or half as fast as inflation, which it assumed at 10 per cent, ignoring the national average post-war trend for rents to rise at one and a half times the rate of inflation. In fact in the following year Leeds increased its rents by some 25 per cent, also about one and a half times the current rate of inflation.

In 1978, the DOE 'old' appraisal assumed that rents would keep their value by keeping in line with earnings, the explicit policy since 1977 of the then Labour government and also the post-war record.[38] However, the DOE 'new' appraisal took a different stance by assuming that rents could be continuously held down as they had been sometimes during the past. For this uncertainty, a token hesitation by the opposition was to blame. For Labour had long delayed an explicit commitment to the indexation of rents, even in broad principle, in spite of its insistence upon indexation of pensions and other social security benefits. Labour's philosophy had been preoccupied with housing as a social service. Although chronic shortages had been overcome and poor tenants were now protected by rent rebates, it had taken time to grasp that public housing must pay its way. Otherwise only welfare housing could be justified. However, Labour did put its new commitment into practice in the only two mechanisms where central government could influence rent decisions before 1980, the rate support grant and housing subsidies to high-cost areas. The Conservative government has demonstrated no less a commitment by using its 1980 housing and rate support grant legislation, which effectively centralises rent decisions, to restore rents to their proportion of earnings before 1974.[39]

It might be argued that past circumstances are no guarantee of future behaviour. Previously rent decisions were within the discretion of housing authorities, and throughout the post-war period rents of existing houses were undoubtedly pushed up through rent pooling as the costs of massive construction programmes were passed on. In any case the 'average' rent trends are for all dwellings, new and old, and probably overstate rent increases because of the new, perhaps higher quality, houses and flats added each year. On the other hand, before 1972, when rebates became universal, many councils restrained rent increases to ease the burden on families and pensioners. And before the introduction of rent pooling in 1935 there was no really 'average' rent; rents of existing houses remained unchanged while prices generally were falling and rents of new houses with them.

So the crucial question is: did past rent decisions by policy-makers respond to changes in the economic environment, that is trends in prices, interest rates and earnings? The overwhelming statistical evidence is that they did. Now there is a tendency in housing policy to measure rents as some ratio of earnings. But previously the trends confirm that, consciously or by chance,

Figure 3.2(a): Nominal Trends in Rents, Interest Rates, Earnings and Prices, 1929–82 (post-war shown darker)

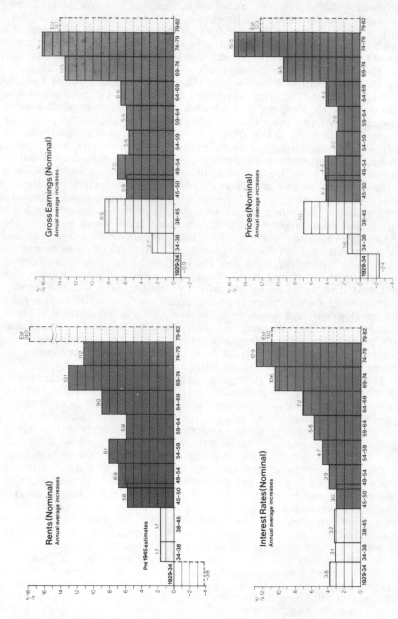

Sources: See Table 3.7.

Figure 3.2(b): Real Trends in Rents, Interest Rates, Earnings, Wage Rates and Disposable Incomes, 1929–82 (post-war shown darker)

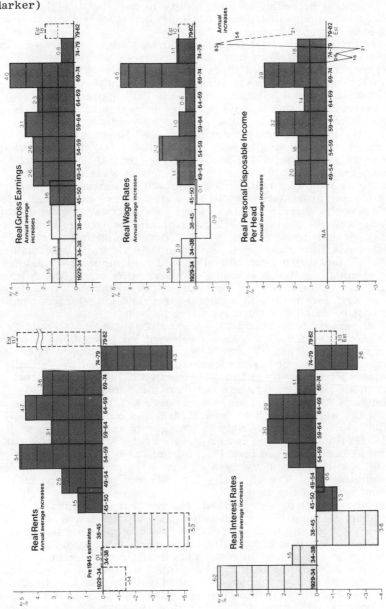

Sources: See Table 3.7.

housing authorities generally matched cost changes with a 'feel' about what could be fairly shared between tenant and taxpayer or ratepayer according to their ability to pay. So there is every reason to suppose that policy decisions in future will respond to the economic environment.

Yet the DOE appraisal (and some others) suggest otherwise on the basis of selective evidence: that rents would grow at most as fast as earnings and that there is an equal possibility they would grow by considerably less, even by as little as three-quarters the rate of general inflation. First, the DOE appraisal creates a deceptive impression that its coverage is representative by using alternatively the last 5-, 10-, 20- and 50-year averages. During only two peacetime periods during the last 50 years did rents fall in real terms, the stagflation years of 1974-9 and the depression years 1929-34. The 1974-9 decline is so strong that it seriously biases the 10- and 20-year averages. The 50-year average is biased by including both periods, as well as wartime.

A clearer presentation would show that during the period 1929-79 it was the norm for rents to keep pace with earnings and that, throughout the post-war period, rents always exceeded interest rates, except in the period 1974-9. Therefore letting council houses was financially more profitable than selling them. During 1974-9 interest rates did indeed exceed rent increases, though not earnings. But this is using new borrowing rates, which were exceptionally inflated, not local authorities' pooled interest rates,[40] which arguably represent a more appropriate long-term opportunity cost to match long-term rent trends.

The periods 1929-34 and 1974-9 should not be singled out. Pre-war circumstances seem scarcely relevant for projections into the twenty-first century. The 1974-9 trend in rents can be explained not only in terms of the unsuccessful experiment of the 'social contract', but also by the fact that between 1974 and 1977 real take-home pay (strictly, real net disposable income per head after tax) did not increase, as had never before been the case since the war.[41] Also data from 1979-82 (as indeed from 1972-3) could be used as misleadingly to exaggerate rent increases as data from 1974-9 can be used to exaggerate rent decline. Even if Labour had been returned in 1979, rent increases (albeit smaller) would also certainly have followed the sharp upward trend in disposable incomes. Therefore the pre-1979 and post-1979 periods should be taken together.

Besides, as already mentioned, the real rate of return on local authority housing during the 1970s probably ranged around 2.5 per cent. Not only is this a perfectly respectable rate for social investment but it is in line with post-war average growth in real earnings and in excess of real yields in the money market. Yet, over the decade, the DOE 'new' appraisal presents the real value of rents as negative because overall they then rose less than inflation and earnings. The contradiction arises because the 2.5 per cent return represented (even underestimated) real income since borrowing costs were negative over the decade. In other words, had local authorities invested in the money market (including their sale proceeds) instead of letting houses, they would have lost money.

Second, the DOE's projections are not based on its own statistical evidence. It did not combine actual rent records over the four periods analysed (the last 5, 10, 20 and 50 years) with what actually happened over the same periods to interest rates and earnings, but with how they 'ought to' have behaved. Thus the DOE assumed that, whatever the rate of future inflation: (a) earnings would always be equal to or less than interest rates, never more; and (b) rent increases would always be equal to or less than earnings growth, never more. In fact, apart from the depression years between 1929 and 1937, during the entire half century analysed by the DOE this combination never occurred.

The DOE's imagined relationship also sways the balance for the public purse in another way. For the interest rate is the basis for discounting future money sums to their present value. Even if rents keep pace with earnings, a mere 1 per cent edge in interest rates over earnings (as the DOE assumes) writes down the aggregate value of rent income over 20 years by 14 per cent and over 50 years by 23 per cent, and also correspondingly reduces the capitalised cost of mortgage tax relief on houses sold.

Third, the financial environment of past and future is least accurately reflected where the DOE appraisal seems most sophisticated.[42] The DOE has projected two pairs of economic 'scenarios' of low/high inflation and low/high growth. But whatever the scenario, the same six (and biased downwards) rent assumptions are always projected, making 24 equally possible alternatives. Yet had the DOE taken the periods in the past 50 years which most closely matched its four 'scenarios', it would have revealed that rents were almost always increased in excess of its assumptions. To illustrate: during the two classic decades of economic growth of the 1950s and 1960s, overall real rent increases averaged one and a half times real earnings growth and more than twice the rate of inflation. Yet the DOE's projection assumes that rent increases under the same future circumstances could range from (at most) being in line with earnings down to three-quarters the rate of inflation (astonishingly only one-third of the historical parallel) because of what happened under quite different circumstances.

An unreal world is thus postulated by the DOE new appraisal. In the future it implied that earnings could rise between one and a half and two and a half times in real terms over 50 years (not far from the post-war trend) but that rents could fall to as low as between one-third and two-thirds their 1979 level (reversing the post-war trend). Rents might then become only between 2.5 and 1 per cent of average earnings as against 7 per cent in 1979.[43]

For the past, the DOE implies that in 1929 it would have been financially more sensible for a council not to let a house it had just built for £346; it could have sold it for £208 (40 per cent less) and gained by investing the proceeds on the money market until 1979 (£3,486 cumulative value). But since rents have kept pace

overall with interest rates, a council following the DOE's investment guidance would have lost £2,313 (1979 cumulative value of
1929 discount) and the faster appreciation of the house and site
value - as many councils selling or letting 1929 houses can testify.

In sum, the DOE's proof that council house sales can be financially profitable, on the grounds that rents are unlikely to keep
their value according to interest rates and earnings, is based on
an imaginary world which came nearest to materialising during the
wartime and some of the depression years.

In spite of all their polemic, neither opponents nor advocates of
sales have tackled the key policy decision for the future of council housing: what is a reasonable rent? On the one hand, if rents
and earnings are linked, is not higher productivity and overtime
indirectly penalised? Again, should rents rise even if costs fall?
On the other hand, if a public landlord's rental income were
reduced would not selling become attractive so long as house
values, geared with tax relief, go on rising with gross earnings?
Perhaps continued expenditure on housing investment might maintain councils' costs as in the past, so making such questions
academic. Nevertheless, a choice remains. Tenants can be enabled
to anticipate future capital appreciation through low rents. Alternatively, since tenants lack any medium of savings which is as
inflation proof as home ownership, the solution might be for them
to become shareholders in their own property. If rents were
indexed to earnings they would reap a dividend income or a capital rebate if houses were sold. Then the investment equation
between sale prices and rental value would remain, as it must.

Management and Maintenance Costs. The two DOE appraisals do,
however, differ in their conclusions even according to the one set
of options where the new appraisal is nearest the old, with rents
rising in line with earnings (see Table 3.8 on page 91). The
difference is attributable to other factors, the most important of
which are now considered.

If net rents are to keep their value, management and maintenance costs must not rise in real terms, unless they are passed on.
Is that realistic? In a small but well publicised minority of authorities, such costs have even overtaken rents for a while. But in
practice the financial environment ensures that costs and charges
vary over a period broadly in unison, not independently. It is
scarcely conceivable, as the DOE 'new' appraisal postulates, that
rents would be allowed to fall in real terms on a national scale
from £8 a week to £2.62 in 50 years time, and average management
and maintenance costs to rise from £2.34 now to £5.25. It is also
scarcely conceivable, as one-third of CIPFA's examples suggest,
that the capitalised cost of management and maintenance over the
remaining life of houses could be four times their selling prices.[44]
Not surprisingly, in such examples sales appear profitable. These
considerations are far more significant than the widespread
recognition (shared by the DOE) that, because organisational

costs are relatively fixed, savings on running costs cannot be in proportion to houses sold.

The challenge of rising costs must be met, however, even if the final solution of selling is rejected. Management and maintenance costs persuade many people to favour sales when they are convinced against sales on grounds of investment value and rental income alone. So there is a strong case for separate presentation of service charges, necessary in any case for sales of flats. Separating service costs would also increase consumer consciousness. Then innovations to increase cost effectiveness, productivity increases, self-help or extra charges might be feasible. Separation would encourage records to be more accurate and ensure that only true housing costs are charged and not social and planning costs too, as commonly happens. Also the advantages of financing renovation costs from borrowing rather than from current income would be clearer.

Renovation Costs. These explain most of the difference between the DOE 'new' and 'old' appraisals where rent assumptions are closest. The DOE 'old' appraisal used a common assumption that renovation costs would be broadly offset by the value of the unexpired house or the site. This is plausible since extra life and rental are generated by improvement. Indeed, in practice, the unexpired values of unimproved pre-war council houses sold invariably exceed their renovation costs. Conversely some allowance might also be made for the exchequer's liability eventually to give improvement or repair grants on houses sold or pay supplementary benefit towards the repair costs of elderly owner occupiers.

How realistic are the renovation costs sometimes assumed? The DOE allowed between £2,500 and £5,500. CIPFA allowed between £3,500 and £8,000. [45] But both count these costs as incurred during the life assumed for the house. This is bound to tip the appraisal scales since they are between some 42 per cent and 65 per cent or 42 per cent and 95 per cent respectively of the sale proceeds of £8,400. Surely the costs of renovation which literally give the house a new life should not be charged against its first life.

The life expectancy of a house is crucial in calculating its rental value. The DOE itself put the renovation of the 'representative' house between 40 and 50 years from now (not from date of construction), but had to use an average cost which included the higher renovation costs of acquired stock since there were no separate statistics for purpose-built stock. CIPFA allowed for the possibility that as many as 55 years might elapse between the date of construction and renovation, and that the house would expire only after a further 25 years life. In practical terms, a sale price of £8,400 for a house rented at £256 net is equivalent to an assumed remaining life expectancy of 33 years. If its life expectancy is nearer 40 years, its price ought to be £10,240 and if 55 years, £14,080. To sell for less is to sell at a loss.

However, both the DOE and CIPFA cogently argue that as housing standards rise renovation will be done sooner and cost more.
CIPFA include a possible first life as short as 30 years from original construction as well as 45 and 55 years. The DOE assumes
that the representative period before renovation of houses now
standing will shorten to 30 or even 15 years. These assumptions
become less plausible when it is realised to what a massive extent
even existing rates of renovation, for which spending allocations
are being reduced, would have to be increased. Assuming that
the life elapsed on existing dwellings averages 25 to 30 years and
in CIPFA's assumption that renovation occurs once in an 80-year
life, one might still deduce an overall remaining life expectancy
for houses sold of not less than 40 years value.

As before, decisions should matter more than predictions. A
life expectancy of 40 years means that to sell a house at 33 years
rental value is automatically to sell at a loss. Conversely, however,
a rent of £276 is too cheap to justify selling without discounts at
£14,000 since that would require 51 years rental value. So traditional accounting for a notional life of 60 years - too long for the
first life, too short for overall life - needs to be reconsidered.

Subsidies. Subsidies prevent the equation between investment and
rental value from being a simple one, though obviously they must
reduce the life expectancy required for a house to break even.
There is an additional complication. Until the 1980 Act, each
authority's total subsidy was in broad proportion to its total
housing debt. Therefore the subsidy lost on each house sold
could be computed broadly according to the debt outstanding on
the individual house. With the introduction of a deficit subsidy
system in 1980, each authority's subsidy will vary according to
the reckonable deficit (if any) which it happened to carry on its
current account in 1980. The DOE 'new' appraisal assumes that
councils will lose from each house sold an average of just over
£2,000 in subsidy over 20 years, which might be equivalent to
almost eight years rental income. Then the rental value required
for houses sold to break even is shortened to only some 21 to 25
years after 40 per cent discounts and to some 43 to 47 years if
sold without discounts (depending on whether assumed weekly
rent is £8.64 or £8). In fact, some authorities will be entitled to
subsidies higher or for longer than the average, others vice versa.
Therefore the new subsidy system has a built-in bias for or
against sales according to the chance variations in council finances.

Under the new subsidy system, it is proposed that councils also
forfeit the revenue equivalent of half the nominal (and illusory)
capital gain from sales. Under the old system they stood to forego
an average of £260 in subsidies in the first year after each house
was sold. Now they will forego £518.[46] Indeed, it seems that central
government could reduce its total subsidy bill to nil by selling
only a proportion of the stock. The new forfeit will advance the
cross-over date at which councils' rent losses on houses sold start
to exceed gains from sales. It will penalise those authorities whose

housing revenue accounts are now approaching surplus. The
effect was not widely appreciated because in the DOE 'new' appraisal capital receipts are counted as cash in the first year. Had
receipts been counted only as reducing borrowing liability (which,
as was pointed out above, they should have been) an authority's
first-year revenue gains from each house might be as low as £126.
Only two or three years could elapse before such benefits dis-
appeared. The DOE has been considering replacing the proposed
forfeit by more severe claw-backs of councils' nominal gains
through both the new subsidy system and the rate support grant.

Local Economic Implications. The effect of sales on the local housing services and market can be anticipated even if the range of
dwellings sold turns out to be wider and purchasers younger than
hitherto. The stock is so composed that it is statistically likely for
the concentration of sales on 'middle vintage' houses to continue.
Half of all local authority dwellings in England and Wales have
three bedrooms; of these 90 per cent are houses. Most of these
houses (81 per cent) were built before 1964 and thus will carry a
low historic debt. Of these, a slightly higher proportion are post-
war and in all likelihood (available statistics cannot prove this)
are cheaper to maintain and need less renovation.
  If sales tend to be earlier post-war three-bedroom houses, the
financial effect on each authority's portfolio will be disproportionately significant because their market value so far exceeds their
outstanding debt. Were central government to observe correct
accountancy procedures this illusory capital gain would be irrelevant. However, as proposed, the new subsidy forfeit counts it.
If confirmed, this would have the effect of increasing the average
outstanding debt on the dwellings remaining available for rent and
the costs of their management and maintenance are all likely to
rise. As a result the average deficit to be met by tenants, ratepayers and taxpayers would grow.
  In these circumstances, the local authority housing service cannot but become more dependent on central government and so
encourage a more selective welfare housing; wider responsibilities
would be seen as incurring an extra burden on subsidies and
rates. Then some households might be excluded from reasonable
accommodation to rent as well as being unable to buy in the open
market because of modest incomes or family commitments.

Traditional Clientele. Any likelihood of housing expectations rising
in future could coincide with a falling ability of authorities to satisfy their traditional clientele. Notwithstanding the temporary
pause in economic growth, real incomes may well continue to rise
not much more slowly than the average of two and a half per cent
a year by which they have risen since the war. On the evidence,
housing demand will increase by at least two-thirds as much, possibly more. [47] Thus a 30 per cent increase in real incomes over a
decade would cause housing demand to increase by at least 20 per
cent.

If this increased demand were expressed in space only, a house-hold would expect one extra room in five. However, it is likely to be expressed not so much in traditional terms of space and basic amenities but more, to judge from the new phenomenon of 'difficult-to-let' council housing, in wider terms like estate envir-onment, gardens and neighbourhood facilities - factors which post-war high density housing drives were often forced to over-look.

Rising demand is unlikely to be dampened even if average real incomes of local authority tenants fall behind, through a greater incidence of unemployment than the population in general because of their distribution of ages and skills. For expectations of coun-cil tenants in general are probably influenced by comparisons with better-off owner occupiers, who form the majority tenure, and with those tenants whose incomes continue to rise in parallel with the rate of national economic growth.

New Clientele. Authorities may be frustrated from catering for new needs unless they have well-balanced portfolios. In the past, local authorities concentrated on family housing. But now younger households need the ready access which private letting used to offer. And older households, including the now ageing post-war 'bulge' of owner occupiers, are living longer and need manage-ment support - preferably in their own homes.

Renewal policies are at risk too. Moreover, government surveys of house condition have been showing that two-fifths of house-holds in properties needing renovation could not, or would not, improve their houses even if grants or publicity were increased substantially. Not more than half of these households were elderly.[48] The more serious the state of disrepair, the more likely it was for occupants to underestimate its severity. Yet the back-log must be dealt with eventually, even when so many said they were satisfied with their conditions. Besides, they may feel con-demning their housing reflects on them personally. So people blame the 'area' instead,[49] and migrate away from towns if they have the means.

It is sometimes argued that the net effect of sales on the local market will be nil: that fewer council tenants moving into the private market to buy will be counterbalanced by more would-be tenants buying privately, once they know there is less chance of a council vacancy. This presupposes either that both are potential purchasers of the same kind of house or that a 'filtering-down' process quickly adjusts houses to households.[50] The more likely effect would be a temporary easing of demand for houses com-parable to council houses, that is above the lowest price ranges. However, the House-Builders Federation thought sales would cause a significant loss of custom only in some exceptional areas like new towns; in any case demand would increase later every-where as tenant purchasers traded-up.[51]

If sales of council houses cut the supply of houses for the 'in-between' households on the borders of renting and buying, the shortage may drive up house prices at the lower end of the market, making it difficult for skilled workers with families to move from one area to another. House prices have already risen considerably faster than other prices since the war, generally in line with incomes. In future they could well rise faster than incomes, as the now unique tax concessions on home ownership bid up prices. Hitherto excess demand for housing could draw upon a reservoir of cheap housing transferred from private letting: 37 per cent of owner-occupied homes standing in 1975 had originally been rented. [52] That source is now dwindling; an argument, incidentally, for selling the poorest council houses and flats, not the best. So any dampening effect on house prices must be less.

A comparatively smaller number of council houses sold may also dampen demand and prices at first, but also temporarily. For once purchasers (or their heirs) sell their houses, they will scarcely ask less than the going rate. So the discount which enabled them to purchase cheaply will have enhanced their purchasing power when they buy again and so help to bid up house prices.

THE NATIONAL INTEREST

Subsidies and Tax Relief
Debates on housing subsidies have often been misled by comparisons on new houses. Familiar examples quote the subsidy on a new council house at four times the cost of mortgage relief on a new owner-occupied house. When council houses are sold, however, new houses are a tiny minority. The DOE estimated that before the 1980 Act the subsidy saved on each council house sold and the cost of mortgage relief after sale both averaged about £260 in the year after sale. Each sale is now expected to reduce exchequer subsidy by £518 because of the proposal for councils to surrender half the annual revenue equivalent of their nominal (and artificial) capital gain. So average mortgage relief will now cost £258 less.

Nevertheless, the DOE acknowledged that on rented council housing the exchequer subsidy liability would die away after an average of 20 years. By contrast tax relief on sold houses would give the exchequer a new perpetual liability; more tax relief has to be reinjected each time the house is resold and remortgaged as prices rise, as Figure 3.3 illustrates diagrammatically.

Some writers, including the present author, have exaggerated the frequency of reinjection by basing it on the length of an average mortgage (seven years) rather than the as yet unknown movement of tenant purchasers. Some of these, particularly the middle-aged, may not move for the rest of their lives - perhaps 35 years. Accordingly, the DOE allows for two alternative frequencies of moving to accommodate these as well as the more frequent moves of younger households. Depending also on inflation, relief would then cost the exchequer between some £1,000 and some

Figure 3.3: Relationship Between Exchequer Subsidy on Sold and Rented Houses

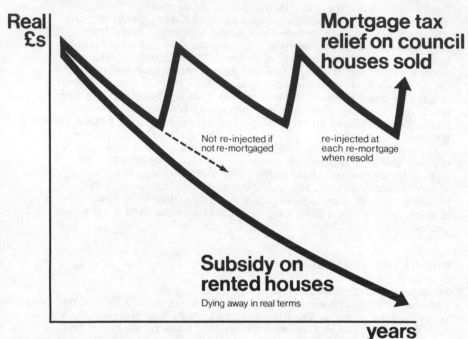

Real £s

Mortgage tax relief on council houses sold

Not re-injected if not re-mortgaged

re-injected at each re-mortgage when resold

Subsidy on rented houses

Dying away in real terms

years

£3,000 over 20 years, and between some £2,000 and almost £5,000 over 50 years. By contrast, had the house remained let, a subsidy of some £2,000 in all would have been paid by the exchequer, provided rents retained their value. The cost of tax relief is more likely to tend towards the higher than the lower amounts, since the sales campaign must surely increase the growing awareness of the investment potential of home ownership among younger tenants. Indeed, it is hardly the government's intention to confine the 'social revolution', which sales are designed to achieve, to middle-aged tenants. To date, the only available sample suggests that as many as 45 per cent of 1972/3 tenant purchasers had moved in only seven years, mostly after the five-year pre-emption period. [53] But all this sample bought their council houses with a building society mortgage and so cannot be representative.

The familiar contrasts between rental subsidy and tax relief should not, however, be imported directly into the arithmetic of sale appraisals showing the effects on the combined public purse (central and local). Appraisals are best based on respective net income figures. In the case of public income from let houses, the subsidy is counted automatically by using rental income, which is already net of subsidy. In calculating the income from houses sold,

the rental subsidy can be ignored; the subsidy which an authority loses on each house sold is the exchequer's gain - they offset
each other. It is the sale proceeds which are relevant, netted by
the cost of mortgage tax relief.

Rent Rebates
It has been suggested that however high the cost of mortgage
relief if tenants buy, this can be no more than the cost of rent
rebates had they continued to rent. In the DOE's 'new' appraisal,
if the typical tenant purchaser were aged 45 and stayed put for
35 more years, rebates would become significant in the years
between retirement and the death of his widow. Over the DOE's
50-year comparison, mortgage relief and rent rebates are shown
as almost identical in cost if inflation is high and if rents keep
pace with earnings.

Such assumptions about the loss of rent income were exaggerated. Each rebated rent would indeed be a loss of about the half
the rent. But the DOE assumed that all purchasers would have
had their rents rebated had they remained tenants once they
reached retirement age, not just the 60 per cent of them it suggested by implication. [54] Also, retirement age was assumed to be
60 years old. As a result, the DOE counted the rental value over
the tenant's remaining 35 years as if it was equivalent to 25 years
(that is 15 years before retirement plus 20 years after retirement
when half the rent would be rebated). Instead, the rental value
should surely have been nearer 30.5 years (that is 20 years
before retirement plus 15 years after retirement when half the
rent of 60 per cent of tenants would be rebated and the remaining
40 per cent would continue to pay full rent).

Second, the introduction of new state earnings-related pensions
as well as the spread of savings and occupational pensions will
substantially reduce rebates to pensioners, perhaps to a third of
their present level. Third, the crucial assumption is that the
average purchaser would be aged 45 and would never have moved.
Yet younger sitting tenants are expected to buy instead of moving privately. Moreover, the DOE has since agreed that it underestimated the re-letting rate; at the end of 35 years 66.5 per cent
of purchasing tenants would have moved anyway. [55] Had the
houses sold remained in letting, rental income foregone in rebate
would therefore have been closer to the average for all dwellings
(one-tenth). If so, the potential rent income on sold houses during the next 35 years would only have been reduced to 31.5 years,
rather than 25 years as the DOE assumed.

More fundamentally, is it appropriate to compare mortgage
relief with rent rebates? For the tax relief is automatic, is for
housing, and increases the higher the income and mortgage. Rebates are means-tested, are for income support, and increase the
lower the income. Indeed, since the DOE 'new' appraisal does not
include payments under supplementary benefit for housing, not
all the total government subvention of tenants (or owner occupiers
for that matter) is counted. Also, if tenants had bought at a full

average price of £14,000 without discount, they would have needed more state assistance, first in increased mortgage relief and then possibly in supplementary benefit as pensioners. How can the public purse save on its liabilities if it gives away its assets?

The lifetime comparisons point up the flaw in this argument. Table 3.1 shows that during the remaining 35 years of the 'representative' tenant's life, so long as rents retain constant value, his outgoings are not dissimilar (around £14,000) whether he buys or continues to rent, and the mortgage relief or rent rebate he would receive is comparable (around £2,000). Only in the latter part of this period and afterwards does the let house give the public purse a net surplus, as Table 3.2 suggests. However, the propsect of this surplus is rendered uncertain by the DOE's assumption that rents could equally well have fallen substantially in value by this time. This has the effect of concentrating attention on the apparently certain and comparable costs of assistance instead of the investment potential which the public purse retains. Had the house been sold, this value (£14,000) would have been handed over in the new owner's equity.

Table 3.2:   Public Purse Receipts Over 35 Years

Receipts: equivalents from Table 3.1	From tenant who buys	From tenant who rents @ £8.64 p.w.	(@ £8 p.w.)
	£	£	£
Sale price (net)	8,400	–	–
less Mortgage relief	– 2,268	–	–
Rent income	–	15,725	(14,560)
less Loan Charges	same	same	same
less Rent rebates[a]	–	– 2,022	(– 1,872)
less Repairs & Management	–	– 5,600	(– 5,600)
Gross Receipts	6,132	8,103	7,088
add Value of house	–	14,000	14,000
less Renovation costs	–	– 3,500	– 3,500
Net Receipts[b]	6,132	18,603	17,588

Notes: a. Income lost in rebate is from a 'representative' tenant only; rebates to average tenants would be one-tenth of rent income throughout to take account of re-letting rates (see p. 79) but void losses should then be added.
b. Net receipts before deduction of the present value of the development cost of the house (say £14,000) or the loan charges equivalent.
Source: Broadly derived from Department of the Environment, 'Appraisal of the Financial Effects of Council Houses Sales', with assumptions as in Table 3.1.

The comparison between rebate costs and mortgage relief ignores the fact that the benefits of home ownership are no longer taxed, either annually in Schedule A or finally in the taxation of the capital gains. Therefore, the cost of the tax foregone by the exchequer is forgotten. But the owner lives in the house rent-free. Some of the surplus between what the public purse receives when letting the house over what it receives by selling it is, put another way, what it foregoes by not taxing the owner's benefit of ownership.

The Borrowing Requirement

Council house sales are supposed to reduce the public sector borrowing requirement (PSBR) provided outside agencies like building societies fund sales. However, receipts in cash now average less than 30 per cent of value after discount and are likely to fall, as argued earlier. Indeed, in 1979, when the year's gross value of total sales increased by £139 million (to £543 million), associated lending by councils increased by £131 million, making the net increase in receipts a mere £8 million. [56]

Even if building societies do fund sales, under present policies the PSBR will not be reduced because local authorities as a whole can increase their capital spending by an equivalent amount (half by the authority selling, the rest through national housing investment allocations). But this trade-off is not the good news for the construction industry or employment which it seems. For public capital investment then has to wait upon the variable fortunes of the building societies and their willingness to fund sales. Meanwhile the private building industry fears that its housing investment will suffer from a mortgage famine if societies do fund sales on any significant scale. [57] Either way, sales thus tend to jeopardise rather than promote housing investment.

Building societies have intimated that they will not reserve funds for council house sales; with tenant purchasers they will also exercise their normal lending criteria and give preference to existing depositors. No doubt pleas to societies and other lending institutions will persist. However, if all the government's target of 250,000 sales per year was funded by building societies, they would have to increase their net receipts by around one-quarter, or more than three months' inflow (that is by £1,680 million against their net annual increase in funds of some £6 billion in 1980). [58] This assumes an average mortgage on council houses sold of £6,720, after 20 per cent of the net market price of £8,400 is paid for by cash deposits totalling £420 million from tenants' savings. But a substantial proportion of such savings will have been held in building society accounts; [59] their withdrawal will reduce societies' balances. Sales of, say, 100,000 a year would require funds in proportion.

For societies to maintain funds for traditional lending (perhaps reduced if fewer council tenants buy in the open market) they would have to increase the competitive edge which their deposit rates offer over other institutions. This is already 1.3 to 2 percentage points. [60] Mortgage rates would have to follow suit.

Over the last two decades, the net annual increase in all loans for house purchase has quadrupled as a proportion of gross domestic product (GDP). This could not have been accommodated without an unexpected tripling of savings flows as a proportion of GDP,[61] which appears to be a reaction to inflation and which may well not be permanent. It is commonly believed that, since house purchase funds are recycled, a net increase in funds is required only to finance a net increase in the number of owner occupiers. However, the steady real increase in house values has ensured that, as houses are continuously and more frequently remortgaged, there is a net increase in the private 'housing sector borrowing requirement' (HSBR).

By 1978 the private HSBR was two-thirds as big as the entire PSBR. The DOE's housing policy review estimated that, during the decade 1976-86, with only a modest increase in house prices and not counting fresh increases in demand, the annual volume of finance for building societies' house purchase transactions would have to increase by some 50 per cent in real terms. Societies' own later estimates made in 1979 suggest an increase of some 75 per cent.[62]

The private HSBR for all agencies totalled some £6.75 billion in 1980. After adding the net funds for rented housing by housing authorities and associations of some £1.5 billion and £0.5 billion respectively, the total HSBR was some £8.75 billion at 1980 prices. However, in its borrowing requirement, public rented housing is less demanding because debt increases only when real investment takes place. Over the last decade the number of public tenancies increased by some 20 per cent as did the number of owner occupiers. Whereas the outstanding debt on all local authority housing tripled, that on owner-occupied housing quadrupled. Other projections indicate that, as councils' building programmes are being reduced, their housing debts will actually decline in real terms. However, as council houses change tenure they will create a new borrowing liability.

The volume of available funds to finance the HSBR is comparatively finite and can increase only temporarily with a high savings ratio or, more permanently, with the growth of the productive economy, which itself requires investment funds. The average mortgage now needs five savers (smaller and poorer than before) to finance it as against 1.8 in 1960. The building society movement already doubts that the housing market in the 1980s can be financed on existing terms,[63] even though they have rejected this author's criticism and claimed that the system is self-financing.[64] Elsewhere, another financial intermediary has been mooted to attract wholesale funds on more favourable terms - but inevitably from other uses.[65]

The effect on the economy of discounted sales is more significant than is the case with the sale of other public assets, such as British Petroleum shares. First, the PSBR is reduced initially by only 60 per cent of the value of the house. The cost of the average discount of 40 per cent represents a loss of potential income which still has to be raised in later years; the liability does not evaporate. Second, the tenant purchaser enjoys the benefit of a fixed mortgage tied to the lower discounted price instead of the

eventually higher outgoings he would have paid in rent; a proportion of this will undoubtedly be used by him for consumption.
This 'leakage' of borrowed funds will be additional to that which
already occurs in the housing market when owners move house or
they or their heirs sell for the last time. A substantial proportion
of their proceeds is spent rather than saved or reinvested.[66]

If, instead of staying put, the original tenant purchaser sells
his house after, say, five years the flow is capitalised into a
single year. Additional funds of up to £5,600 per house will be
needed since the succeeding purchaser will now need to fund the
full market value of the house of £14,000. If the original purchaser
were to save (with a building society) the value in full of the discount he receives when he sells his house, nil additional funds
would be needed. However, the normal leakage is likely.

Investment Effect
It is sometimes claimed that the net resource effect of sales is nil
because only the tenure of the house changes. However, an
investment effect does arise because in time council houses sold
will tend towards the lower average occupancy rates of owner-
occupied houses. Even those rented council houses which are
underoccupied would eventually tend towards the (higher) average occupation rate of local authority housing. This is between
25 and 40 per cent denser than the average for owner occupiers,
depending on household age, as Table 3.3 shows.

Table 3.3: Average Persons Per Room by Tenure (England and Wales)

Age of head of household	(1) Owner occupiers	(2) Local authority and new town tenants	Ratio (Col. 2 ÷ Col. 1)
Under 25	0.52	0.73	1.40
25-34	0.65	0.88	1.35
35-44	0.71	0.92	1.30
45-54	0.59	0.74	1.25
55-64	0.44	0.57	1.30
65 and over	0.36	0.48	1.33

Sources: Department of the Environment, 'Housing Policy: Technical Volume', part I, (HMSO,
1977), Table II. 18.

The eventual effect of sales would therefore be to increase the
real demand which the housing sector makes on the economy. This
is already excessive. The fact that capital formation in housing
takes proportionately less in Britain than in most other major
economies is not relevant; the crude proportion of GDP tells us
little. It is its composition which matters. There should be less
need for Britain to devote so much to fresh housing investment.
Its urbanisation took place earlier than that of its Western counter-
parts, whose faster growing economies allow more scope for

housing investment; only the North Americans are as well-housed as ourselves. Given the age and condition of housing in Britain, the share of investment absorbed by net increases to the stock in order to accommodate new households and rising standards should not compete with the priority of renewing the existing stock, whether by maintenance, improvement or replacement. [67]

In fact underinvestment in renewal helps disguise overinvestment in higher standards. Both features get overlooked because the overall proportion of GDP devoted to housing is low by international comparisons. Also the organisation and skills of the construction industry have always favoured new development while the structure of housing finance in both public and private housing stimulates excessive demand for housing quality and space. So investment in higher standards naturally exercises prior claim over renewal; both could not be accommodated within the existing capacity of the construction industry or without increasing the distortions in the UK economy. The problem can only get worse, for as many as one in three of all existing dwellings were built before 1919, the majority in the Victorian building boom between 1875 and 1900. Council house sales on any large scale will add further to the problem by increasing the quantity of underused housing. This will then have to be made good by further investment though resources are already stretched.

CONCLUSIONS

The financial implications of sales of council houses must distinguish three different interests and the long term from the short term. The individual sitting tenant who buys at a discount almost certainly obtains a bargain although age, family circumstances, employment prospects and maintenance costs may be deterrents to purchase. The local authority seems to make short-term gains even from selling at below real cost. But these are illusory because of the lack of inflation accounting. They are turned into real long-term losses because average selling prices are the equivalent of no more than 30 (or perhaps fewer) years of rental income, even net of upkeep costs. There would be no financial objection to sales without discounts. Then selling prices and rental income could represent approximately the same investment value.

Sales at discounts could become more profitable to the public purse than letting only if the rental income relationship did not hold. Not only would costs have to increase because, for instance, council houses were renovated much more frequently and at higher costs than now, or because maintenance costs increased in real terms without being passed on in the service element paid by tenants, but, more significantly, political decisions would have to be taken repeatedly to ignore such changes in costs as well as to allow rents to fail to keep pace with earnings and interest rates. This is a quite implausible prospect in the light of the post-war record. In presenting statistics in a way which apparently proves otherwise, the DOE's financial appraisal cannot be excepted from the charge of political bias and of distorting the historical evidence. On the other hand, opponents of sales, by withholding an explicit political commitment to a balance between costs and rent, cannot be excepted from the charge of lacking responsibility.

Central government is virtually certain to lose from sales because of the additional cost of mortgage tax relief and other tax exemptions on owner occupation. These can be falsely represented as no more than the cost of rent rebates were houses to continue in letting, partly through unrealistic assumptions such as are made in the DOE appraisal and partly because other tax exemptions are ignored.

The economic implications of sales must be distinguished from the financial. Local concern is bound to focus upon the risk of distortions such as shortages causing house prices to rise, in spite of the temporary benefits of filtering cheaper homes into the local housing market. Sales may also hinder local housing services from becoming more responsive to the changing requirements of different age-groups and an increasingly obsolescent housing fabric.

In the national context, the sale of council houses on any large scale is likely to be increasingly understood as prejudicial to our real housing requirements. The borrowing requirement of the housing sector is likely to increase, not diminish, while construction programmes and employment may suffer an extra element of instability. Meanwhile the discounts available may encourage the further leakage of productive capital into consumption. Sales will also tend to increase underoccupation in the housing stock. So housing investment will be diverted into making good the loss in supply. Already too much housing investment is attracted into raising housing standards and away from the basic priorities of renewing the existing obsolescent stock.

If the financial and economic implications could be so big, why have they not been aired more widely? The explanation must lie in anomalies in housing finance and widespread misunderstandings about them. These need remedying first, particularly in relation to housing subsidies. Since the cost of mortgage tax relief has been very similar to the cost of council housing subsidies, a neat political stalemate has been created. Too much attention has been paid to what subsidies cost, not enough to what they do.

In the owner-occupied sector other tax exemptions, on housing capital gains and the abolition of Schedule A as well as an effective exemption from capital transfer tax, have all been overlooked. Meanwhile mortgage tax relief has been defended on the grounds that neither house builders nor house buyers could survive without it, thus ignoring the way it bids up house prices and how the potential encouragement to production is transferred to the price of land and to existing owners. Alternatively, relief has been justified as the best offset against a tax structure which is too progressive. [68]

More effort should have been made to compare the benefits

enjoyed by tenants and owners in return for what they pay, not between the amounts paid to them by the exchequer. Unfortunately the nearest set of official (and annual) comparisons which are designed to show the redistributive effects of subsidies have been marred by the way they are presented. So the case for reform is less obvious. In the case of local authority tenants, subsidies have been shown explicitly. They have been calculated according to the difference between what a tenant actually pays and an imputed value rent. In the case of owner occupiers, however, the value of tax exemptions has not appeared explicitly. An imputed income 'in kind' from their housing has also been calculated. But in this case it cannot be picked up from the tables because it has been hidden in their 'original income'. It is this already adjusted income which has been used as the basic income for showing the effect on all households of taxes deducted and cash benefits added. And those deductions have only been shown net, that is including mortgage relief. Therefore the real benefits and their redistributive effects have been disguised in the case of owner occupiers whereas subsidies to tenants appear as inevitably concentrated on the lower income bands.[69]

The housing finance debate will only be settled outside the closed world of housing on grounds of tax neutrality within the general economy. This would emerge if the cost of 'tax expenditures' were better known since those attributable to housing are the largest of all (not counting the personal income tax allowances). The distortions are evidenced by the real increase of house prices over most other commodities and the major transfer of wealth out of stocks and shares into land and dwellings.[70]

In spite of the prospect of a steady increase in the value of tax foregone by the exchequer to support home ownership, public housing has a bad name. This is serious because public authorities must surely be the main agents for the massive reinvestment in housing which we need, whoever ends up owning or managing that investment. The serious institutional shortcomings of council housing are not to be confused with its financial strengths. For subsidy and borrowing requirements only increase in real terms when fresh investment takes place. In home ownership they increase just because houses are exchanged and are remortgaged, without any productive impact.

There has recently been a backlash against the artificial 'explosion' in public expenditure on housing which took place during the 1970s. This was because Treasury conventions run counter to normal accounting practice: real capital investment, which declined, is added to current expenditure on subsidies, which are transfer payments. Subsidies ballooned when interest charges rose at double the rate of inflation.[71]

The distortions could be remedied. First, indexed loans would be required. At present any development is frustrated by the Treasury convention which would even count interest deferred as public expenditure the same as if it was subsidised borrowing. At least current expenditure which is properly financed from trading revenue or taxable capacity should be distinguished from capital investment (including capitalised interest) which is legitimately financed from borrowing. Second, the principle of cross-subsidisation would need to be extended across the boundaries of each local authority so that the fluctuating needs and resources of different localities were balanced out in national or regional investment pooling. Then public housing could be set on the path of self-sufficiency and away from the sterile politicisation of its finances.

The grave financial and economic implications of selling council houses on a large scale cannot be separated from all these wider considerations. Otherwise, the opportunity will be lost of re-cycling the national asset value of council housing built up over the last 60 years, which is comparable in value to North Sea oil. It is needed to assist the renewal of the existing housing stock, both rented and owned, especially when there is so much pressure on our financial and economic resources.

ADDITIONAL TABLES

Table 3.4: First-year Revenue Gains from Sales (1976)

	Pre-war (1931) house £	Post-war (1955) house £	Modern (1972) house £
Market price less 20% discount	3,100	5,000	5,280
Income gained			
Mortgage (@ 10.5%) receipts	343	553	584
Management and maintenance saved	85	85	85
Total gained	428	638	669
Income lost			
Rent foregone	201	246	291
Subsidy foregone	10	52	166
Total foregone	211	298	457
Net gain	217	340	212

Source: Leeds City Council 1976 papers quoted in B. Kilroy, No Jackpot from Council House Sales, 'Roof' (May 1977).

Table 3.5   Equivalent Investment Alternatives

£1,000 invested @ 10% with inflation at 10% p.a. giving value at end of each year

End of year	1	2	3	4	5	6	7	8	9	10
£s nominal	1100	1210	1331	1464	1611	1772	1949	2144	2358	2594
PV factor[a]	0.91	0.83	0.75	0.68	0.62	0.57	0.51	0.47	0.42	0.39
£s real	1000	1000	1000	1000	1000	1000	1000	1000	1000	1000

Capital equivalent in 10 years' time of £1000 now

End of year	..	..	..	..	..	..	..	..	..	10
£s nominal	..	..	..	..	..	..	..	..	..	2594
PV factor	..	..	..	..	..	..	..	..	..0.3855
£s real	..	..	..	..	..	..	..	..	..	1000

Annual income for 10 years which is equivalent to £1000 in the hand now[b]

End of year	1	2	3	4	5	6	7	8	9	10
£s nominal	163	163	163	163	163	163	163	163	163	163
PV factor	0.91	0.83	0.75	0.68	0.62	0.57	0.51	0.47	0.42	0.39
£s present value[c]	148	135	122	111	101	93	83	77	68	63

Notes: a. Present value from formula $\dfrac{1}{(1 + \frac{r}{100})^n}$ rounded to two places or valuation tables of 'present value of £1'.
 b. £1000 divided by factor from tables of 'present value of £1 per annum (the sinking fund being invested at the same rate of interest)'.
 c. Sums to £1000.

Table 3.6   Actual Rental Values Compared with DOE Assumptions

	Discounts from selling price	Rate of return (actual rents as % of selling price)		Rental value equivalent
		gross	net	
Council houses actually sold in 1977/8	%	%	%	years
at actual discounted price	15	4.4	(2.8)	(36)
if nil discount had been given	nil	3.7	(2.4)	(43)
if discounts had been given as now	40	6.3	(3.9)	(26)
At DOE new appraisal assumed average sale price of £8,400 after discount of 40% in 1980	Gross rent per annum			
at DOE assumed average rent for all dwellings @ £8 p.w.	£ 416	5.0	3.0	(33)
if DOE had assumed same actual rent return of 6.3% as in 1977/8	(529)	6.3	(4.4)	(23)
if DOE had assumed average rent of post-war 3-bedroom houses @ £8.64 p.w.	449	(5.3)	(3.4)	(29)

Sources: D. Webster, Financial Consequences of Council House Sales: Why Do Assessments Vary?, 'CES Review No. 9' (Centre for Environmental Studies, 1980), p. 44 for 1977/8 gross returns; Department of the Environment, 'Appraisal of the Financial Effects of Council House Sales' (DOE, 1980), the 'new' appraisal, for 1980 rent and price assumptions. Net re- · turns and rental values are the author's derived approximations. For 1977/8 these are based on the same relationship between general management and maintenance deductions from rents in the all-dwelling average returns by the Chartered Institute of Public Finance and Accountancy for non-metropolitan districts (as being the least distorted), that is £110 out of £296 per year. Net returns for the DOE appraisal in 1980 assume a constant £160 deduction from each gross rent. How much the DOE all-dwelling average rent of £416 should be corrected to reflect rents of houses sold is debatable. To reflect the same return as in 1977/8 is undoubtedly an overcompensation since the resultant rent of £529 seems too high for 1980. If the rent of post-war three-bedroom houses is assumed (as the DOE 'old' appraisal), break-even is after 30 years.

Table 3.7   Inflation, Rent Increases, Interest Rates and Earnings Growth:
Annual Averages, 1929-82

Period	Years[a]	Inflation	Rent[b] increases		Profitability and growth					
					Interest Rates		Earnings (gross)		Wages rates	
			nom-inal	real	nom-inal	real	nom-inal	real	nom-inal	real
		%	%	%	%	%	%	%	%	%
Five year bands[a]										
1929-34	5	−2.4	−3.8[c]	−1.4[c]	3.8	6.2	−0.9	1.5	−0.9	1.5
1934-38	4	1.6	1.7[c]	0.1[c]	3.1	1.5	2.7	1.1	2.5	0.9
1936-45	9	6.0	1.7	−4.3	3.2	−2.8	7.4	1.4	5.5	−0.5
1938-45	7	7.0	1.7	−5.3	3.2	−3.8	8.5	1.5	6.1	−0.9
1945-50	5	4.3	5.8	1.5	3.0	−1.3	5.9	1.6	4.2	−0.1
1949-54	5	4.4	6.9	2.5	3.9	−0.5	7.0	2.6	5.5	1.1
1954-59	5	3.0	8.1	5.1	4.7	1.7	5.6	2.6	5.2	2.2
1959-64	5	2.8	5.9	3.1	5.8	3.0	5.9	3.1	3.8	1.0
1964-69	5	4.3	9.0	4.7	7.2	2.9	6.6	2.3	4.9	0.6
1969-74	5	9.5	13.1	3.6	10.6	1.1	13.5	4.0	14.0	4.5
1974-79	5	15.5	11.2	−4.3	12.9	−2.6	16.3[d]	0.8	16.6	1.1
1979-82 (est.)	3	12.3	24.0	11.7	11.0	−1.3	14.1	1.8	13.3	1.0
Averages used by DOE as 'representative'										
1929-79	50	5.0	5.8	0.8	5.8	0.8	7.2[d]	2.2	6.2	1.2
1959-79	20	7.9	9.8	1.9	9.1	1.2	10.5[d]	2.6	9.7	1.8
1969-79	10	12.5	12.2	−0.3	11.8	−0.7	14.9[d]	2.4	15.3	2.8
1974-79	5	15.5	11.2	−4.3	12.9	−2.6	16.3[d]	0.8	16.6	1.1
Other post-war averages										
1945-74	29	4.6	7.8	3.2	6.0	2.4	7.4	2.8	6.3	1.7
1949-69	20	3.6	7.7	4.1	5.4	1.8	6.2	2.6	4.8	1.2
1949-79	30	6.3	9.0	2.7	7.5	1.2	9.1	2.8	8.2	1.9
1945-82 (est.)	37	6.6	9.5	2.9	7.3	0.7	9.2	2.6	8.2	1.6

Notes:
a. Gaps in data prevent a 5-year banding before 1945.
b. Local authority rents only.
c. Approximations only.
d. Using a slightly different series, the DOE appraisal calculated average earnings at 6.9% for
1929-79, 10.2% for 1959-79, 15.0% for 1969-79 and 16.4% (est.) for 1974-9.
Sources: Statistics are extracted from the same sources used by the DOE 'new' appraisal. For
inflation, the consumers' expenditure deflator (more reliable than the retail price index

before 1956) is from C.H. Feinstein, 'National Income, Expenditure and Output in the United Kingdom 1855-1965' (Cambridge University Press, 1972), Table 61; and from National Income and Expenditure', 1981 Edition (HMSO, 1981), Table 2.6. Local authority rents (England and Wales) are from Department of the Environment, 'Housing and Construction Statistics'; S. Merrett, 'State Housing in Britain' (Routledge & Kegan Paul, 1979), p. 181 (reproducing some Institute of Municipal Treasurers and Accountants statistics); and 'House of Commons: Official Report', vol. 922, cols. 305-6 (9 December 1976). Pre-war estimates are from Ministry of Health, 'Annual Reports'; 'Rents of Houses and Flats Owned by Local Authorites', Cmnd 5527 (HMSO), 1937), Table 1 (for the 1936 survey benchmark); and M. Bowley, 'Housing and the State' (Allen & Unwin, 1945). Interest rates are from B.R. Mitchell and P. Deane, 'Abstract of British Historical Statistics' (Cambridge University Press, 1962), p. 455 (for 1929-55); and Central Statistical Office, 'Economic Trends: Annual Supplement 1981' (HMSO, 1981) (from 1956). The representative money market is assumed to be the 2.5 per cent consols rate throughout. Earnings (gross and wage rates) from Feinstein 'National Income, Expenditure and Output in the United Kingdom, 1855-1965', Table 65 (for 1929-65, both series for manual workers); Central Statistics Office, 'Economic Trends: 1981 Annual Supplement', Table 110 (for 1965 onwards, 'whole economy' series for gross earnings and wage rates for manual workers); also Department of Employment, 'British Labour Statistics, Historical Abstract' (HMSO, 1972), Table 38; Central Statistical Office, 'Monthly Digest of Statistics'; and 'Department of Employment Gazette' (New Earnings Survey data).

Table 3.8   The Old and New DOE Appraisals: Closest Assumptions Yet Differing Outcomes

Long term average annual rates	'Old' appraisal (1978)		'New' appraisal (1980)	
	nominal	real	nominal	real
Inflation	(7%)[a]		(9%)	
Interest rates[b]	(10%)	3%	(12%)	3%
Earnings growth	(9%)	2%	(11%)	2%
Rent increases	in line with earnings		in line with earnings	
Range of outcomes per house sold				
+ = GAIN			+ £2,185	
			to	
− = LOSS	£5,530 to − £4,500		− £3,635	
	(always losses from		(sometimes gains	
	selling)		from selling)	

Notes: a. By implication from para. 26.
b. Also used for discounting rates to present values.
Sources: The unpublished 'old' appraisal is quoted in B. Kilroy, From Roughly Right to Precisely Wrong, 'Roof' (January 1980); the 'new' appraisal is Department of the Environment, 'Appraisal of the Financial Effects of Council House Sales', para. 30, fourth combination (higher inflation, higher earnings growth). The original of this table was supplied by D. Griffiths.

NOTES

1   Material published on the financial and economic implications
    of council house sales (* works of particular relevance).
    * A. Murie, 'The Sale of Council Houses', Occasional Paper
    no. 35 (Centre for Urban and Regional Studies, University of
    Birmingham, 1975) is the standard authority but explored the
    financial implications from a limited angle, mostly only the
    purchasers. F. Griffin, 'Selling More Council Houses' (Con-
    servative Political Centre, 1971) is an old-style pamphlet by
    the Leader of Birmingham Council unanswered for five years.
    T. J. Gough, A Consensus on Council House Sales?, 'Housing
    and Planning Review' (July/September 1976) was once useful
    but is now superseded. * B. Kilroy, No Jackpot from Council
    House Sales, 'Roof' (May 1977) was the first published (but
    brief) case study about Leeds City Council's sales drive.
    * S. Weir and B. Kilroy, Equity Sharing in Cheshunt, 'Roof'
    (November 1976) on the Greater London Council's experiments
    is a complementary study. 'Housing Policy: A Consultative
    Document', Cmnd 6851 (HMSO, 1977), the Labour govern-
    ment's green paper, was reticent and non-commital. J.P.
    Wilson, 'Accounting for the Sale of Council Houses'
    (Institute of Cost and Management Accountants, 1977);
    Nottingham Alternative Publications, 'Where Have All the
    Assets Gone?' (NAP, 1979); *Chartered Institute of Public
    Finance and Accountancy, 'Institute Statement: The Sale
    of Council Dwellings' (CIPFA, 1979); and * Shelter, 'Facts
    on Council House Sales' (Shelter, 1979): these four studies
    all attempt assessments which remove inflationary distor-
    tions but Wilson is not always correct. * Department of the
    Environment, 'Appraisal of the Financial Effects of Council
    House Sales' (DOE, 1980) is the 'new' appraisal, hurriedly
    published for the second reading of the Conservative Housing
    Bill. The DOE's 'old' appraisal prepared under Labour in 1978,
    never published, had been leaked not long before. * B. Kilroy,
    From Roughly Right to Precisely Wrong, 'Roof' (January 1980)
    is a brief comparison of both appraisals. * D. Webster, Fin-
    ancial Consequences of Council House Sales: Why Do Assess-
    ments Vary?, 'CES Review No. 9' (Centre for Enfironmental
    Studies, 1980) is the most systematic analysis of the DOE
    'new' appraisal (but omits the 'old' appraisal). It also boils
    down (somewhat aridly and without 'in the round' conclusions)
    the bones of six classic studies (DOE new, Kilroy, NAP,
    CIPFA, Wilson, Shelter) but sometimes suffers from poor ed-
    iting (Kilroy is misdated and mistitled). Webster's more sub-
    stantial work has been as one of the advisers to the House of
    Commons Environment Committee inquiry into the social and
    financial implications of council house sales which supersedes
    much earlier analysis. Written evidence is only published sep-
    arately where oral evidence was also taken and is referenced
    as follows:

House of Commons, Environment Committee, 'Council House Sales: Minutes of Evidence' [Session 1979-80]: * 'London Borough of Southwark', HC 535-i; * 'London Borough of Wandsworth', HC 535-ii; South Lakeland District Council' and 'Allerdale District Council', HC 535-iii; * Leeds City Council', HC 535-iv; * 'B. Kilroy' and * 'Chartered Institute of Public Finance and Accountancy', HC 535-v; * 'Building Societies Association', HC 535-vi; 'Catholic Housing Aid Society' and * 'House-Builders Federation', HC 535-vii; (HC 535-viii was procedural note only); 'Thamesdown Borough Council' and 'Crawley Borough Council', HC 535-ix; * 'Greater London Council' and * 'City of Birmingham', HC 535-x; and * 'Department of the Environment', HC 535-xi. See also memoranda submitted to the committee which are listed in the Appendix on page 197. * B. Kilroy, Council House Sales: Was the Government Misled by the DOE's Evidence? 'Housing and Planning Review' (Summer 1981) adds more details. Some high-quality analysis has also been carried out by D. Griffiths for the Labour Party and is the basis of its booklets on the implications of sales.

2 Murie, 'Sale of Council Houses', p. 48.
3 'Housing Policy: A Consultative Document'.
4 Ibid., p. 106.
5 Secretary of State for the Environment (Mr Michael Heseltine), speech to the Institute of Housing, 1979, 'Housing', vol. 15, no. 9 (1979), pp. 26-31.
6 Summarised by Webster, Why do Assessments Vary?
7 Department of the Environment, 'Financial Effects'.
8 P. Walker, The Real Tenants' Charter, 'Guardian', 15 November 1978 and letters, 17 November 1978.
9 F. Field, 'Do We Need Council Houses?' (Catholic Housing Aid Society, 1975); and 'Roof' (May and July 1976).
10 B. Kilroy, Housing in A. Walker (ed.), 'Public Expenditure and Social Priorities' (forthcoming Heinemann, 1981).
11 House of Commons, Environment Committee, 'First Report, Session 1979-80', HC 714/1979-80, pp. 28-35.
12 Minister for Housing and Construction (Mr John Stanley), speech in 'Home Ownership in the 1980s' (Shelter Housing Aid Centre, 1980), quoting from 'Financial Times', 12 November 1979.
13 House of Commons, Environment Committee, 'Council House Sales', HC 535-vi.
14 Murie, 'Sale of Council Houses', Ch. 6.
15 Weir and Kilroy, Equity Sharing in Cheshunt.
16 House of Commons, Environment Committee, 'Council House Sales', HC 535-vi.
17 Ibid., HC 535-iv, p. 125; and HC 535-x, p. 304.
18 Ibid., HC 535-ii.
19 National Economic Development Office, 'Housing for All' (NEDO, 1977), Ch. 4.
20 Murie, 'Sale of Council Houses', pp. 119-24.

21   Walker, Real Tenants' Charter; and Heseltine, speech to the
     Institute of Housing.
22   M. Ball and R. Kirwan, 'The Economics of an Urban Housing
     Market, Bristol Area Study' (Centre for Environmental
     Studies, 1975).
23   British Market Research Bureau, 'Housing Consumer Survey'
     (National Economic Development Office, 1977), Tables 4.1 and
     4.2.
24   Department of the Environment, 'English House Condition
     Survey 1976, Part I: Physical Condition' (HMSO, 1978); and
     'Part II: Social Survey' (HMSO, 1979).
25   National Consumer Council, 'Soonest Mended', (NCC, 1979).
26   'House of Lords: Official Report', vol. 411, col. 10 (30 June
     1980).
27   V. Karn, Pity the Poor Home Owners, 'Roof' (January 1979).
28   S. W. Magnus and F. E. Price, 'Knight's Annotated Housing
     Act 1957' (Charles Knight, 1958), p. 221.
29   Ibid., p. 232.
30   Department of the Environment, 'Housing and Construction
     Statistics' (June quarter 1980, part 2), Table 2.13.
31   Royal Institution of Chartered Surveyors, 'Housing - The
     Chartered Surveyor's Report' (RICS, 1976), Ch. X; and
     Greater London Council Housing Committee reports.
32   Kilroy, No Jackpot; and Nottingham Alternative Publications,
     'Where Have All the Assets Gone?'
33   Kilroy, Housing in Walker, 'Public Expenditure and Social
     Priorities'.
34   Chartered Institute of Public Finance and Accountancy,
     'Institute Statement', p. 6; and House of Commons, En-
     vironment Committee, 'Council House Sales', HC 535-v,
     p. 155.
35   Department of the Envrionment, 'Financial Effects', para.
     55.
36   A. B. Atkinson and M. A. King, Housing Policy, Taxation
     and Reform, 'Midland Bank Review' (Spring 1980), p. 9.
37   Kilroy, No Jackpot; and House of Commons, Environment
     Committee, 'Council House Sales', HC 535-iv.
38   'Housing Policy: A Consultative Document', para. 9.37; and
     Housing Bill (March 1979), Clause 45 (7).
39   House of Commons, Environment Committee [First Report,
     Session 1979-80], 'Minutes of Evidence', HC 578-i/1979/80,
     p. 17 (evidence by Secretary of State for the Environ-
     ment).
40   Department of the Environment, 'Housing Policy: Technical
     Volume', part III (HMSO 1977), Table VIII.18.
41   Central Statistical Office, 'Economic Trends: Annual Supple-
     ment 1981' (HMSO, 1981), Table 45; and 'Social Trends 1980'
     (HMSO, 1980), Chart 6.17.
42   Kilroy, Was the Government Misled?
43   'House of Commons: Official Report', vol. 997, col. 200 (20
     January 1980) gives post-war trends of rents as a percentage

of earnings.

44 Chartered Institute of Public Finance and Accountancy, 'Institute Statement', Table IV.

45 Ibid., Table IV.

46 Department of the Environment, 'Financial Effects', para. 49.

47 Department of the Environment, 'Housing Policy: Technical Volume', part II, Ch. 6, para. 44 gives references.

48 Department of the Environment, 'English House Condition Survey, Part II', Ch. 2 and Table D2.1.

49 Department of the Environment, 'National Dwelling and Housing Survey' (HMSO 1978), Tables 43, 44, 82, 83, 122, 123.

50 A. Murie, P. Niner and C. Watson, 'Housing Policy and the Housing System' (Allen & Unwin, 1976) analyses the limitations of filtering.

51 House of Commons Environment Committee, 'Council House Sales', HC 535-vii, pp. 229 and 233.

52 Department of the Environment, 'Housing Policy: Technical Volume', part I, Tables 1.23, 1.24.

53 Anglia Building Society, 'Occasional News', no. 2 (July 1980).

54 Webster, Why Do Assessments Vary?, p. 44.

55 Department of the Environment, unpublished letter to House of Commons Environment Committee.

56 'The Government's Expenditure Plans 1980-81 to 1983-4', Cmnd 7841 (HMSO, 1980), Table 2.7.

57 House of Commons, Environment Committee, 'Council House Sales', HC 535-vii.

58 Ibid., HC 535-vi.

59 Building Societies Association, 'Mortgage Finance in the 1980s' (Stow Report) (BSA, 1979), Table 13.7.

60 Committee to Review the Functioning of Financial Institutions (Wilson Committee), 'Second Stage Evidence, Vol. 3, Building Societies Association' (HMSO, 1979), Ch. VI.

61 B. Kilroy, Housing Finance - Why So Privileged?, 'Lloyds Bank Review', no. 133 (1979), p. 38.

62 Building Societies Association, 'Mortgage Finance', Appendix I, Annex 3.

63 Ibid., Summary and Conclusions.

64 Building Societies Association, 'Bulletin', no. 21 (BSA, 1980), p. 14.

65 'Housing Policy: A Consultative Document', para. 7.62.

66 Department of the Environment, 'Housing Policy: Technical Volume', part II, p. 116.

67 Kilroy, Housing Finance - Why So Privileged?, pp. 44 and 49.

68 'Housing Policy: A Consultative Document', para. 5.37.

69 Central Statistical Office, The Effects of Taxes and Benefits on Household Income, 1979, 'Economic Trends', no. 327 (HMSO, 1981), p. 115; and 'Social Trends 1980', (HMSO, 1980), Chart 6.24.

70   Kilroy, Housing Finance – Why So Privileged?, p. 43.
71   B. Kilroy, Why is Housing Investment Being Cut So Much?,
     'Housing Review', vol. 30, no. 2 (1981), pp. 46-8.

4 The Social Implications of Council House Sales

Ray Forrest

The nature of housing and housing provision occupies a central position in society. The rhythms of social and economic change can bring about fundamental transformations in the housing sphere. Over this century the dramatic decline of private landlordism provides an obvious example. More generally, the early development of capitalism and the growth of cities completely changed the living conditions of the working classes. It is worth emphasising the inevitability of change at an early stage in this chapter. Too often discussions of council house sales contain an unquestioning defence of the current pattern of public sector provision or, alternatively, implicitly accept the 'normality' of home ownership. There is nothing immutable about housing tenure. Whilst this chapter focuses on the social consequences of the sale of council houses, it should be recognised that the pressure for sales is itself a consequence of broader social and economic processes. A combination of factors has pushed the issue to the forefront of domestic politics.

The present political conjuncture, with the election of a highly market-oriented Tory government is clearly important. But perhaps of greater importance is the fact that there is little scope for the further expansion of home ownership through the dissolution of private landlordism. Private renting is now characterised by a residue of elderly tenants on the one hand and a group of young, highly mobile people on the other. Neither of these groups is at a position in the family life cycle where owner occupation is particularly attractive or appropriate. Moreover, many properties which remain in the privately rented sector are in considerable disrepair or structurally unsuited for owner occupation. Increasingly, therefore, owner occupation and public renting are in direct confrontation. For those whose interests are closely tied to higher levels of home ownership the existence of a large public sector is of understandable concern. Basically, if home ownership is to expand, public renting must contract.

The social consequences of the sale of council houses have a number of different dimensions and can be discussed at different levels. The consequences for those who remain as public sector tenants have been the main topic of research and debate. There are also consequences for those tenants who buy. The policy may affect existing owner occupiers and those currently seeking to buy in the private sector. Indeed, council house sales cannot be divorced from more general concerns about the social consequences of the expansion of owner occupation and, particularly, the

position of low-income households. Council house sales also im-
pinge on questions of labour mobility, unemployment and broader
patterns of wealth and inequality.

Some of these questions can only remain matters of speculation
at present. Even the more direct policy questions, such as the
types of dwellings being sold and the characteristics of purchasers,
have only been researched in a very fragmented way. There is
now, however, growing evidence from the aggregate of local
studies that certain trends are under way. The overall impact of
these trends will depend on the level of sales and thus will vary
according to local circumstances. Nevertheless, if sales reach the
levels some advocates of the policy desire, the consequences are
likely to be increasingly clear cut, more profound and to alter
significantly the structure and pattern of opportunities within the
housing market. Many of the trends referred to below will become
more marked. In that sense (to borrow an appropriate aphorism)
what is important is not so much where we are but in what direction we are moving.

THE DESIRE FOR HOME OWNERSHIP

Advocates of council house sales would have us believe that we
are moving inexorably towards increased owner occupation. The
sales policy is presented as just one part of a natural progression,
the fulfilment of the innate desire to own a home. Of course, this
is nonsense. While there may be a universal desire to improve one's
housing conditions and standards, owner occupation need not
necessarily be the only route. The fact that over 50 per cent of
British households are now owner occupiers is no more a natural
phenomenon than was the situation at the turn of the century
when almost all households rented from private landlords.

No one seriously suggests that natural desires are being inhib-
ited in other Western capitalist societies with very different tenure patterns. In West Germany and the Netherlands, for example,
only 40 per cent of households are currently owner occupiers.
Patterns of public and private renting also vary markedly among
Western European countries. The privately rented sector is considerably smaller in Britain than elsewhere. It is clear therefore
that tenure patterns are the result of specific social and economic
circumstances and have little to do with innate desires. It is also
the case, however, that general trends in the development of
modern capitalist economies have created the conditions and pressures which make mortgaged owner occupation the favoured tenure.
Indeed, without the massive extension of consumer credit it would
not be possible as a mass tenure.[1] National governments have
influenced tenure patterns by pursuing policies which favour one
tenure rather than another; what Kemeny has referred to as 'political tenure strategies'.[2] In Britain the tax benefits which accrue
to owner occupiers and the public investment in council houses
can be contrasted with the position of private renting.

The supporters of council house sales argue that a large number of council tenants want to be owner occupiers and, surely, that that is adequate justification for providing such an opportunity. The fact that a large public sector in housing exists precisely because owner occupation was not available to many households through normal market processes is consequently ignored. More to the point, however, there is a fine but important distinction between what council tenants <u>want</u> to be and what council tenants <u>ought</u> to be. It is hardly surprising that many council tenants express the wish to buy a council house when the incentives to do so are progressively enhanced. With the Housing Act, 1980, the 'right to buy' for many tenants is an offer they cannot refuse. Behind all the rhetoric about council house serfdom and the wishes of public tenants is a simple belief held prominently, but not exclusively, by the present Conservative government that council housing should be downgraded as an alternative tenure. This was most clearly expressed by Julian Amery, a former Conservative Minister for Housing, in a 1978 parliamentary debate: 'What I care about is that we should aim to make house purchase not merely attractive, but irresistibly attractive to the council house tenant'.[3]

Statistical claims to show a high level of demand for home ownership often ignore the context in which the relevant questions were set and the different housing situations of the respondents. The extent and nature of the demand for owner occupation revealed in various surveys is discussed in Chapter 5. Without discussing these research findings at this stage, it is apparent that the desires and opportunities for purchase will vary across the council stock. What is presented as an equitable policy to meet the demands of council tenants is thus nothing of the sort. The benefits will be selective and individual, and the overall effects grossly inequitable. As Murie comments:

> it seems fair to assume that one of the main reasons for the general popularity of owner occupation is that owner occupiers have better, or more desirable homes. Most building for owner occupation is surburban semi-detached houses with gardens, and 68 per cent of mortgaged accommodation is a detached or semi-detached house, according to the General Household Survey (GHS).
>
> If, however, it is the image of a pleasantly situated house which attracts would-be home owners, then the scope for council house sales is strictly limited; for the GHS also shows that nearly two-thirds of local authority accommodation is flats or terraced houses.[4]

The nature of the council stock also varies between cities and this will affect the pattern of opportunity available to different groups of tenants. In London, for example, two-thirds of the stock are flats, in Leeds 35 per cent and in Manchester 30 per cent. While this may mean that in some areas only a small number of dwellings

are sold, it is the nature and pattern of sales which is important
rather than the overall numbers. If we reinterpret the desire for
home ownership among council tenants as a desire for a house
with a garden in a pleasant location, then the implication of the
sales policy becomes very different. For those tenants living in
high-rise flats and seeking transfer to just such a dwelling the
advantages of the right to buy become rather less obvious.

WHO BENEFITS? WHO LOSES?

On the broadest level the benefits of council house sales accrue
to all those tenants in a position to exercise their right to buy,
who occupy a desirable dwelling and who have sufficient income.
The benefits also accrue to those agencies and institutions whose
political or economic interests are closely tied to the extension of
home ownership; for example, the building societies, estate
agents and other exchange professionals. In terms of who loses,
all those sections of the community who are not offered an equivalent opportunity to benefit can be regarded as excluded. They
can in particular be regarded as losing out because as ratepayers
and taxpayers they have a share in the public assets which are
being sold at prices below their value.

More specifically we can examine the potential effects of sales
on four different groups within the housing market: (a) the
buyers of council houses; (b) those who remain as public sector
tenants; (c) those seeking to enter owner occupation or public
renting; and (d) existing owner occupiers.

The Buyers of Council Houses
For the majority who purchase the advantages are clear. They are
enabled to buy at substantially less than market value an asset
which will almost certainly appreciate. In most cases the dwelling
will be well constructed and well maintained. They will have more
freedom in relation to improvements and opportunities to 'person-
alise' their dwelling than council tenants. The combination of the
discounted purchase price (for sitting tenant purchasers) and the
general effects of house-price inflation will promise a substantial
gain on resale, although some portion of the discount will be repayable to the local authority if resale occurs within five years.
Generally, a large deposit will be available to enable purchase
elsewhere in the private sector. Purchasers will also possess an
asset which they can pass on to their children.

Past research has, however, shown that purchasers are a highly
selected group of tenants. In Birmingham, Murie found that the
typical purchaser was 'a long established tenant, in middle age,
with a fairly large family growing up, earning above average
wages, in a skilled manual occupation and often with more than
one earner in the household'.[5] Niner found a similar pattern in
five other West Midlands authorities.[6] With the statutory right to
buy and high discounts contained in the Housing Act, 1980, these

characteristics may change. Nevertheless, it seems unlikely that the dominant relationship between relatively high incomes and desirable dwellings will change markedly. In this context it is of some interest that even in the public sector there is a correlation between level of household income and value of dwelling occupied. [7] In other words it is highly likely that those tenants with the highest incomes will be occupying the most valuable dwellings. This is the inevitable outcome of the subtlety of allocation criteria, with the tendency for various minority groups such as black people, single-parent families and those regarded as problem tenants to end up in low-status dwellings and estates. [8]

Does the policy extend the opportunity to enter owner occupation to those not already in a position to do so? The evidence available suggests that the majority of those who buy could, on income criteria, have bought elsewhere in the private sector. [9] On age criteria, however, many council house purchasers could have experienced difficulties obtaining a building society mortgage. Moreover, many tenants are choosing to buy a home they have occupied for a number of years rather than choosing to enter owner occupation as such. There is thus some truth in the argument that those who buy would not have moved out of the public sector and created vacancies for other existing tenants. But the act of becoming an owner occupier considerably increases the likelihood that sometime in the near future those who buy will choose to realise a capital gain and move elsewhere in the private sector. [10] Besides, in the longer term, and given the age of the typical purchasers, there is little doubt that dwellings would outlast tenants.

More importantly, though, those who buy are able to purchase a high-amenity dwelling at considerably lower cost than a similar dwelling elsewhere in the private sector. In this way council house sales will act to reduce the normal level of movement from public renting to owner occupation. Why choose to purchase an older, terraced dwelling in need of repair and improvement when a modern, semi-detached house can be purchased for less? As discounts become more generous this factor will become more important. It has been suggested that the demand for council housing will increase because of the opportunities on offer for low-cost entry to owner occupation. [11]

The increased discounts and the two-year option to purchase in the Housing Act, 1980, may well bring council house purchase within reach of many lower-income households. Unfortunately, the act of house purchase does not necessarily present a solution to housing problems. Whilst mortgage payments may not appear financially onerous, repairs and maintenance and associated outgoings make the real costs much higher. Karn's work in Birmingham has shown the hardship which can arise with arrears and repossessions for low-income households with local authority mortgages. Of households who had taken out mortgages between 1964 and 1971, 16 per cent had failed to maintain payments. [12] Specifically, in relation to council house sales, the casualties of owner occupation may increase if more tenants are encouraged to buy at a time of high unemployment and record interest rates. There is evidence that such a trend is already under way. According to a recent article in a national daily, Birmingham City Council had bought back 250 homes and fresh appeals were being handled at the rate of ten a week. Whilst this hardly constitutes hard evidence, it is worth noting Friend's comments: 'Nationally, mortgage default is already as significant a cause of homelessness as rent arrears - each accounting for 6 per cent of those accepted by local authorities during the first half of 1978'.[13]

In this context it is necessary for housing market analyses to begin to differentiate more precisely between mortgaged owners and outright owners, since it cannot be assumed that the former all necessarily become the latter. A more sensitive appreciation of the relationship between the 'real' costs of home ownership and household incomes is needed. While house-price inflation represents a potential capital gain, it is generally not realisable in a liquid form. The increasing value of a dwelling is therefore of no real benefit when inflation is having a parallel effect on rates and on fuel, maintenance and repair costs. In relation to council house sales, while purchasers are mostly better-off tenants buying the best dwellings, few households may experience financial difficulties. As discounts are increased and less desirable and less well-maintained dwellings are sold, those least able to afford the day-to-day costs of home ownership may be tempted to buy.

This brings us to the question of resale. Evidence on this issue is scant, which is unfortunate since it is at the point of resale that market criteria take over from notions of need and previously publicly owned dwellings are absorbed by the private sector. What evidence there is suggests that the rate of turnover of bought council houses outside any pre-emption period is roughly equivalent to turnover in the public sector generally (around 4 per cent).[14] The collective impact of the process will be discussed later. At this stage it is the individual experiences of purchasers which is of concern. The perceived advantages of home ownership revolve around the ownership of an asset, an investment which can be realised and reinvested in a more desirable dwelling or passed on to the next generation. If an owner-occupied dwelling proves to be a liability rather than an asset then all the other supposed attractions of house purchase pale into insignificance. Indeed, it is this aspect of the policy of council house sales which has been most strongly emphasised by the present government. Margaret Thatcher in the debate on the Queen's Speech in May 1979 remarked that the right to buy 'will give more of our people that freedom and mobility and that prospect of handing something on to their children and grandchildren'.[15] In the housing debate two days later Michael Heseltine stated: 'I believe that, in a way and on a scale that was quite unpredictable, ownership of property has brought financial gain of immense value to millions of our citizens.'[16]

It is this promise of financial gain which constitutes the 'hard

sell' in the sales programme, and relates to broader debates concerning the effects of council house sales on the distribution of
wealth.[17] But some council houses are liabilities rather than
assets. What this means (apart from the fact that some tenants
are occupying dwellings unsuitable for purchase) is that for some
buyers the promise of a financial gain will not be fulfilled. They
may be trapped on predominantly council-owned estates, facing
high repairs and maintenance costs, and unable to sell on the
open market. More generally, the private market response to
high-rise flats or houses in the middle of large council estates
has yet to be determined. This may not prove to be a problem on
popular, high-sales estates and there is evidence to indicate that
former council houses can be highly desirable commodities.[18] It
may be a different story on less popular estates, where individual
flats have been sold or where the overall number of sales are low.

Those Who Remain as Public Sector Tenants
The effect of sales on those who remain in the public sector has
been the subject of most research and critical comment. No one
has seriously suggested that all tenants are in a position to purchase or that the sales policy can offer any advantages for those
who are unable or unwilling to buy. It is difficult to see how such
a claim could be justified. As with almost any social or economic
policy, it is impossible to confer a benefit on one group without
at the same time creating an absolute or relative disadvantage for
another group. Public housing offers collective benefits in terms
of housing standards and mobility, and the impact of the sales
policy must be evaluated on that basis. Thus the advocates and
critics of sales occupy opposing ideological positions which are
fundamentally irreconcilable. While the protaganists of the sales
programme argue for the benefits which accrue to individual tenant purchasers, at root the critics are saying 'A should not buy
because of the effect on B'. In a society where the cult of posses-
sive individualism dominates, and in terms of electoral appeal, the
former position is clearly easier to defend and propound than the
latter.

No one would deny, therefore, that a large number of individual
tenants will derive substantial material advantages from buying
their council house. But will this process affect the structure and
pattern of housing opportunities for those who remain as public
sector tenants? The Housing Act, 1980, contains a number of provisions for allowing greater freedom for those who do remain. In
themselves these represent welcome moves towards a less paternalistic public housing service. Unfortunately, in the light of
other trends and particularly council house sales, they must be
seen in the context of a general process of residualisation of both
public sector tenants and dwellings.

It was suggested earlier that overall numbers were of less importance than the pattern of sales and that the impact will vary
according to the nature of particular local authority housing
stocks. Many of the criticisms of the sales programme hinge on

the argument that the selective nature of sales will adversely
affect the transfer and exchange opportunities of those who remain. For example, families living in high-rise flats may have to
wait longer for a transfer to a dwelling more appropriate to their
needs. More generally, the overall quality and range of choice in
the public sector will be reduced. There is now a growing body
of evidence from different areas which indicates that this is precisely what is happening. Since the research undertaken in Birmingham in 1975 concluded that 'council houses which have been
sold are concentrated according to location and type of "popular"
housing',[19] various other studies and reports have begun to confirm these findings. Friend found a similar process under way in
Leeds and Bromley.[20] A study of sales in South Oxfordshire
found that:

> While the variations in quality of housing are less than in
> urban areas and present sales policy limits sales to the best
> stock, where we can discern differences in quality due to
> age, situation and style, it is the best council housing which
> is being sold.[21]

In Oxford itself, research by Brough reached similar conclusions,[22]
as did research by the National Council of Social Service on rural
housing in East Hampshire.[23] The selective pattern of sales is
hardly surprising. Only those tenants with sufficient incomes are
in a position to exercise their right to buy, and in general only
those occupying desirable properties will choose to do so. Of
course, house purchase involves a complex set of decisions and
Popplestone has recently indicated the specific influences which
may affect the pattern of sales on council estates. In relation to
financial influences he comments:

> People's chances of future career advancement depend on
> what jobs they have. The income disparity between various
> occupations increases as people get older. There is a sharp
> contrast in the pattern of income over any life cycle between
> manual workers on the one hand, and managers, executives
> and professionals on the other.
>
> Most earn the same early in their working life, whatever
> their jobs (in 1970, earnings for 21-24 year olds were bet-
> ween £20 and £25 per week, whatever the job). But after
> 25, earnings diverge sharply. Managers and professionals
> are likely to double their salaries in real terms by the time
> they reach their forties.
>
> By contrast, manual workers reach their peak earnings
> by their thirties. That peak is only 15 per cent more than
> what they earned in their mid-twenties.

One of Popplestone's conclusions from this is that:

Inequalities in income between different occupational groups and the low prospects of work advancement for many council tenants make it unlikely that young married couples will buy council housing. Instead, it is likely that only those tenants who can squeeze in the necessary mortgage payments between the end of their family rearing and the beginning of retirement will be able to buy, when the inducement of a discount for length of residence is also highest. [24]

These are important considerations both for those who are seeking to increase the level of sales and for those seeking to investigate the uneven pattern of sales. Nevertheless, while there is clearly no simple relationship between tenants' incomes and the costs of purchasing, factors such as the position in the family cycle are unlikely to modify substantially the dominant trend in sales of the 'best dwellings on the most popular estates'. We can draw one important conclusion at this stage. The selling of council houses has been presented as a policy which will increase social mix in the public sector and diminish the differences between owners and tenants. In reality, the evidence suggests that it will have precisely the opposite effect. While it may increase the overall number of owner occupiers, the distinctions between this tenure group and those who remain as public sector tenants will become more marked. The belief that the sale of council houses could reduce social segregation in supposedly one-class council estates derives in any case from the false assumption that council tenants are all drawn from particular occupational groups. (This contention sounds strange when expressed by those concerned with the number of wealthy council tenants who should not be in receipt of subsidy.) Alternatively, it is assumed that the sale of houses will make inroads into those estates which have become distinct because of local authority grading, unpopularity and policies towards problem families. These are the very estates which will be affected by council house sales only indirectly because of the reduction in the availability of alternative housing, in choice and in mobility in the public sector. It is these estates which will become more reminiscent of residual welfare housing in the American mould.

Moreover, some allocation policies may be sensitive to complaints from new owner occupiers about problem families being moved in. If so, this could exacerbate further the tendencies towards the ghettoisation of particular estates and the adverse consequences of the selective nature of council house sales. Indeed, a policy document from the Conservative Central Office makes this consideration quite explicit in relation to the sale of flats. 'In particular, purchasers will want undertakings that problem families are not housed nearby in homes unsold since this would adversely affect the value of the property.' [25] To return therefore to the question of the effect of sales on the opportunities for transfer and exchange within the public sector, the policy will adversely affect tenants in a number of ways.

First, the asset stripping effect of sales combined with low level of replacement building will reduce the overall quality of the council stock. Second, allocation policies may be seriously distorted by some estates being perceived as suitable for purchasers and others for long-term tenants. Third, fewer vacancies for transfer will arise, particularly in the most sought-after parts of the stock. Whilst there may have been some justification in the past and in the short term for the claim that those tenants who bought would not have moved anyway, this argument is quite misleading in a number of ways. The argument that those who bought would not have moved out of the public sector derives from the evidence which indicated that it was mainly stable, long-established, elderly tenant households who were purchasing.[26] As suggested earlier, however, it is also the case that, with this group of households, dwellings would almost certainly outlast households. In the longer term these dwellings would have been vacated. If the higher discounts now available dramatically change the characteristics of tenant purchasers (for example, by drawing in more younger households) then the argument is eroded in a different way. It is more likely in these cases that some of the tenants would have bought elsewhere in the private sector. Furthermore, and to reiterate an earlier point, sales will inevitably reduce normal movement from public renting to home ownership. These are all ways in which the housing opportunities for those who remain as tenants will be reduced.

Moreover, the above discussion only takes account of the effect of sales to sitting tenants. The effects are more direct and more damaging when vacant dwellings are put up for sale rather than re-let, and when a sales policy generally begins to dominate the traditional functions of local authority housing. This has happened in a number of authorities. In Nottingham, the Conservative council only returned vacant dwellings to the lettings pool if they remained unsold after three weeks. A family in London were told by the Greater London Council (GLC) that one of the reasons for the shortage of larger properties was that 'some of the vacant houses are being reserved for sale'. This was despite the family being a high-priority case in terms of overcrowding and medical disability. In Bristol a single parent with two young children living in a high-rise block was told that applications to buy were 'being given priority over lettings to the waiting lists, clearance rehousing and all other categories of rehousing, including transfers'.[27] Epping Forest Council offers commission to their staff for council house sales. The GLC appointed a 'Sales Director'.

Of course, this kind of evidence is anecdotal and impressionistic and no firm conclusions about the overall effects of sales can be drawn from it. But there is sufficient basis for concern that, even with a relatively low level of sales, the social function of public housing is already being seriously undermined. While individual cases of hardship and housing deprivation may be dismissed as unrepresentative, it is worth reminding ourselves that behind the cold statistics and broad policy conclusions people are already being materially affected.

Those Seeking to Enter the Public Sector or Home Ownership
For households and individuals who are neither public sector tenants nor owner occupiers, the effects of council house sales will
vary according to individual preferences and circumstances. For
those wishing and able to buy, as former council houses are resold on the open market, greater choice and value for money may
be available. Evidence which is available on this issue indicates
that, while former council houses are valued slightly lower than
similar dwellings elsewhere in the private sector, they are unlikely to be the cheapest properties available. [28] In other words,
former council houses do not add an extra rung at the bottom of
a notional housing ladder and thus do not create opportunities for
purchase for those households who would not have been in such
a position anyway. In Birmingham, 25 per cent of purchasers of
former council houses were already existing owner occupiers.
Compared with the original sitting-tenant purchasers, the new
purchasers were younger, at an earlier stage in the family cycle
and a considerably higher proportion were in middle-class employment.
    Predictably, as public sector dwellings become subject to allo-
cation through market processes, they become part of a general
pool of houses available for purchase. They no longer have any
specific function in the housing market. Claims, therefore, that
'when a house is subsequently resold after the pre-emption period a cheap house for sale is provided which may well go to a
family on the waiting list' reveal a considerable misunderstanding
of housing market processes. [29] While the above suggestion may
have some limited validity where local authorities operate open
waiting lists on which anyone can register, it is extremely unlikely
that the resale process represents an alternative route for households in categories of need. The benefits accrue to a group of
households more directly comparable to first-time buyers generally than new council tenants. [30] Many would not have been allocated dwellings, and certainly not the particular ones they had
purchased, on grounds of need.
    For those households in the privately rented sector, concealed
and sharing households, and the homeless there is likely to be
less opportunity to enter the public sector and less choice available. There are of course suggestions that measures to revitalise
private renting through legislative changes, increased involvement of building societies in the rental market and the growth of
housing associations could create an adequate substitute for public renting. Whether such measures can ever generate adequate
accommodation in sufficient quantity and at sufficiently low rents
is, however, unlikely. If there is one element of consistency in
the history of British housing it is the failure of the private
sector to provide working-class dwellings. Those who advocate a
freer market in housing must accept the consequences of their
ideology. They must accept either the need for state intervention
in relation to those groups unable to pay the going rate or a high
degree of deprivation and homelessness.

This takes us on to the feasibility of universal ownership. If such a situation were foreseeable, then it could be argued that the temporary inequalities would ultimately disappear. But certain sections of the population – the poor, those in insecure employment, the unemployed and those dependent on welfare benefits – will never gain access to credit for purchase on the open market. Households in the privately rented sector (particularly those renting from resident landlords), those living with parents and all those denied access to owner occupation for various reasons could not benefit from a once-and-for-all transfer of public housing into private ownership.

Existing Owner Occupiers
Some brief comments are also appropriate in relation to the position of existing owner occupiers. The misconception by some owners that public sector tenants benefit from a higher level of subsidy seemingly does not extend to the more valid conclusion that a number of public tenants are indeed benefiting from highly subsidised purchase. The fragmenting and isolating nature of owner occupation perhaps militates against the realisation and expression of collective concern that the sales policy is highly inequitable in this respect. For example, first-time buyers on the open market will pay substantially more than sitting-tenant purchasers for a dwelling which is likely to be of considerably lower quality. Moreover, a purchasing council tenant is likely to make a significantly larger capital gain on resale. Thus, a first-time buyer on the open market will have substantially less to reinvest in the next house. The housing market effects of this process will clearly depend upon the number of resales involved, but potentially there could be a large group of second-time purchasers with unusually large deposits to reinvest.

RESIDUALISING THE PUBLIC SECTOR?

This chapter has focused mainly on the housing market effects of the sale of public rental dwellings. It was, however, argued in the introduction that council house sales must be seen in a much broader context for the social consequences to be correctly understood and assessed. For example, it is impossible to make an assessment without considering what might be termed conjunctural conditions. The sale of public dwellings is not inevitably damaging to the function of public renting. What this chapter has tried to argue is that the policy in its present form and in present conditions is contributing towards greater inequalities in housing, is stigmatising and segregating in its effects, and will generally reduce the opportunities available for those who are or wish to become public tenants. If we interpret the intentions of the Housing Act, 1980, benevolently and assume that the purpose is indeed to create greater choice and flexibility in the housing market, and to contribute towards a more equitable distribution of wealth, then we can conclude that it is simply ill-considered. If, however, we assume that the perceived political advantages outweigh any real social policy considerations, then this raises more fundamental questions of the class basis of policies and the erosion of a valuable public asset which has taken 60 years to develop.

In mid-1981, unemployment is nearing three million; the level of new housing starts has declined drastically compared with the averages achieved in the 1960s and 1970s; opportunities to rent in the private sector continue to contract; mortgage interest rates are at near-record levels; severe problems of disrepair are developing, particularly in the private sector; [31] and homelessness remains severe. Is this then the right time to consider selling council houses? One of the chief advocates of sales, George Tremlett, Chairman of the GLC Housing Policy Committee, recently asserted that 'it has been known for about three or four years that there is not a substantial housing shortage in London'. [32] This knowledge does not, however, appear to be shared by the London Boroughs Association. In a recent study of London's housing needs they summarised their findings as follows:

A quarter of all homes in London are 'unsatisfactory' by the definition of the Department of the Environment. Waiting List applications at record levels: 100,000 new applications in a year.

Record numbers becoming homeless: 13,000 needing to be housed by London Boroughs in 1979/80.

Other measures of housing stress such as overcrowding and sharing persisting at far higher levels in London than elsewhere. [33]

Such a conflict of opinions is extremely disturbing if we are to believe that housing policy decisions are based on more than ideological predilections. Certainly, assertions that we have a numerical surplus of dwellings in some places tell us nothing about levels of overcrowding, housing conditions and critical questions of access. Nor is it very helpful to suggest that the houses are there but people are in the wrong place. At root there is an inevitable mismatch in a capitalist economy between investment in the built form and the volatility of investment in employment-creating activities. In the past the public sector performed a critical role in providing low-cost accommodation in areas where employment was expanding. In this context it is worth noting that, as a greater proportion of the housing stock becomes subject to market pricing, the potential barriers to labour mobility increase. Whilst bureaucratic barriers to mobility do exist in the public sector, those barriers could be reduced bureaucratically and this would not require any fundamental intervention in market processes. To institute change in the owner-occupied sector, however, would necessitate major interference in market pricing. House prices diverge considerably and, by and large, high unemployment is reflected in relatively low house prices and vice versa. Moreover the public sector tends to be smaller in more affluent areas and it is likely that it is in precisely those areas where council house sales will have greatest impact. Quite simply, how does a council tenant in a depressed area move to a more buoyant area if house prices there are high and the opportunities to rent in the public sector are further reduced?

This digression into broader social and economic concerns raises the general issue of the residualising effects of council house sales and whether public housing will increasingly represent 'welfare' housing for marginalised groups within the population. Considerations of this kind make it as important to examine patterns of movement into public housing as well as selective movement out through the sales programme. There are some examples of evidence which indicate that a combination of processes are progressively sorting out the population into two socially distinct tenures.

First, households receiving supplementary benefit have become increasingly concentrated in the public sector. In the period between 1967 and 1975 the proportion of all categories of supplementary benefit recipients who were owner occupiers remained static at 17 per cent despite the growth of house ownership in that period. Comparable figures for local authority tenants showed a rise from 45 to 57 per cent. This increase is marked in all of the major categories of recipient and in 1975 the proportion of each group of recipient who were local authority tenants was as follows: pensioners 56 per cent, unemployed 54 per cent, disabled 61 per cent, women with dependent children 71 per cent and others 68 per cent. [34] The trend reported for 1967-75 is sustained by subsequent statistics. [35]

Second, Craven's analyses of Family Expenditure Survey data show that the proportion of households in the bottom three income deciles who were council tenants rose from 26 per cent in 1963 to 41 per cent in 1972, an increase of over 50 per cent during the decade. [36]

Third, the General Household Survey shows a decrease in the proportion of households headed by unskilled manual workers living in privately rented unfurnished accommodation between 1972 and 1976 (from 20 per cent to 16 per cent). This has been matched by an increase in the proportion of the same group in the public sector (from 57 per cent to 65 per cent). While the same development is apparent among semi-skilled workers it is not apparent among other socio-economic groups. [37]

There is also evidence relating to particular social groups. For example, in England at the end of 1977, more than half of all single-parent families were public sector tenants. [38] This evidence is not conclusive but it is sufficient to indicate an increasing polarisation of housing situations. Moreover, home ownership is exacerbating housing inequalities through the opportunities it offers for wealth accumulation. This factor is evident in various studies. [39] The Royal Commission on the Distribution of Income and Wealth refers to the 'considerable and growing importance of

housing in the statistics of wealth'.[40] Estimates made by the commission indicate that the percentage of total personal net wealth
accounted for by dwellings (net of mortgages) more than doubled
(from 17 per cent to 37 per cent) between 1960 and 1975. This
aspect of home ownership provides a powerful material (as opposed
to ideological) basis to the notion of a property-owning democracy.
As is argued in Chapters 3 and 8, political resistance to council
house sales is difficult to sustain unless there are concurrent
demands for reform of subsidies in the owner-occupied sector.

These developments are of considerable social and economic significance. In view of the dominance of house property in the
assets of households, it is evident that few households who do not
own dwellings can accumulate wealth on such a scale. This is not
to suggest, however, that home owners are in any sense a homo-
geneous group. On the contrary, there is considerable different-
iation within the owner-occupied sector, and earlier in this chapter it was suggested that benefits will not accrue to all purchasers.
Nevertheless, we are likely to see a widening of the gap between
'successful' owners and public sector tenants. And this will not
be a division which relates simply to housing conditions and
opportunities. At a time when free market processes are becoming
more dominant in the determination of life chances generally, this
marginalisation of particular groups is likely to extend across
health, education, employment and housing.

There are also other issues which relate to the operation of the
housing market and, in particular, the role of public sector housing. There are demographic trends such as increased marital
break-up and the growth of elderly households. In rural areas,
the sale of council houses raises questions associated with second
homes and the relationship between housing and rural employment.[41] There are also the fundamental economic questions referred to in Chapter 3.

At a time when policy should be aiming for greater flexibility in
housing choices and opportunities, it would seem that greater
rigidity and inflexibility are being created: that the choices between renting and owning are diminishing.

It was emphasised at the beginning of this chapter that there is
nothing immutable about housing tenure; that there is nothing
sacred about the present pattern of public sector provision. No
one would deny that public housing has its imperfections. Problems associated with bureaucratic management styles, paternalism,
allocation policies and tenants' lack of freedom, which are examined in Chapter 6, will not however be alleviated by an indiscrim-
inate sales policy. Desirable changes in those areas can only be
made more difficult. Moreover, it is not even necessary to defend
the managerial practices or particular housing policies of local
authorities but rather to argue that these are not essential to the
social role of public housing. Such a role could not be performed
by the processes of private finance and control.

Amidst a number of fundamental social and economic processes
related to deindustrialisation and structural unemployment, amidst

the pervasive revival of nineteenth-century free market ideology, the sale of public sector dwellings is contributing towards a progressive widening of social divisions in housing and in other areas. As Murie has argued elsewhere: 'sales diminish the capacity to plan and control housing for social ends, reinforce social segregation and a sterile tenure system which is geared to maintaining housing scarcity. In short, a poor law service for housing.'[42]

At present, that is not yet where we are but it is the direction in which we are moving.

NOTES

1   For a theoretical discussion of this development in the context of the United States see M. Aglietta, 'A Theory of Capitalist Regulation' (New Left Books, 1979), Ch. 3.
2   J. Kemeny, Political Tenure Strategies, 'Papers in Urban and Regional Studies', no. 4 (1980).
3   'House of Commons: Official Report', vol. 952, col. 506 (21 June 1978).
4   A. Murie, Council House Sales Mean Poor Law Housing, 'Roof' (March 1977), p. 47.
5   A. Murie, 'The Sale of Council Houses', Occasional Paper no. 35 (Centre for Urban and Regional Studies, University of Birmingham, 1975), Ch. 6.
6   P. Niner, 'Local Authority Housing, Policy and Practice: A Case Study Approach', Occasional Paper no. 31 (Centre for Urban and Regional Studies, University of Birmingham, 1975).
7   Royal Commission on the Distribution of Income and Wealth, 'Third Report on the Standing Reference', Cmnd 6999 (HMSO, 1977), p. 154.
8   See, for example, J. Parker and K. Dugmore, 'Colour and the Allocation of GLC Housing: The Report of the GLC Lettings Survey, 1974-1975', Research Report 21 (GLC, 1976).
9   Murie, 'The Sale of Council Houses', Ch. 6.
10 For further discussion of resale see R. Forrest and A. Murie, 'Social Segregation, Housing Need and the Sale of Council Houses', Research Memorandum no. 53 (Centre for Urban and Regional Studies, University of Birmingham, 1975); and R. Forrest, The Resale of Former Council Houses in Birmingham, 'Policy and Politics', vol. 8, no. 3 (1980), pp. 334-40.
11 House of Commons, Environment Committee, 'Council House Sales: Minutes of Evidence', HC 535-i/1979-80, p. 10.
12 V. Karn, Pity the Poor Home Owners, 'Roof' (January 1979), pp. 10-14.
13 A. Friend, 'A Giant Step Backwards', Occasional Paper no. 5 (Catholic Housing Aid Society, 1980), p. 23.
14 Forrest and Murie, 'Social Segregation, Housing Need and the Sale of Council Houses', Appendix.
15 'House of Commons: Official Report', vol. 967, col. 80 (15 May 1979).

16 Ibid., vol. 967, col. 408 (17 May 1979).
17 F. Field, 'Do we need Council Houses?' (Catholic Housing Aid Society, 1975); and A. Murie and R. Forrest, Wealth, Inheritance and Housing Policy, 'Policy and Politics', vol. 8, no. 1 (1980), pp. 1-21.
18 Forrest, The Resale of Former Council Houses in Birmingham.
19 Forrest and Murie, 'Social Segregation, Housing Need and the Sale of Council Houses', p. 30.
20 Friend, 'A Giant Step Backwards', pp. 22-5.
21 M. Beazley et al., 'The Sale of Council Houses in a Rural Area: A Case Study of South Oxfordshire', Working Paper no. 44 (Oxford Polytechnic, Department of Town Planning, 1980), p. 62.
22 Brough, The Sale of Council Houses in Oxford City, unpublished dissertation, Oxford Polytechnic, Department of Urban Planning, (1977), pp. 18-29.
23 National Council of Social Service, 'Rural Housing in East Hampshire' (NCSS, 1980), p. 9.
24 G. Popplestone, Council House Sales: Why Some Won't Buy, 'Housing and Planning Review', vol. 36, no. 3 (1980), p. 8.
25 Conservative Central Office, 'Sale of Council Houses' (Conservative Central Office, 1979).
26 See, for example, Murie, 'The Sale of Council Houses', Ch. 6.
27 R. Forrest and A. Murie, Paying the Price of Council House Sales, 'Roof' (November 1978), pp. 170-3.
28 R. Forrest, The Resale of Former Council Houses in Birmingham, pp. 336-7.
29 H. Rossi, Adding to the Stock of Human Happiness, 'Roof' (July 1977), p. 123.
30 R. Forrest, The Resale of Former Council Houses in Birmingham.
31 For a more general discussion of developing problems of housing decay see A. Murie and R. Forrest, 'Housing Market Processes and the Inner City' (Social Science Research Council, 1980), pp. 73-6.
32 House of Commons, Environment Committee, 'Council House Sales: Minutes of Evidence', HC 535-x/1979-80, p. 289.
33 Labour Group on the London Boroughs Association, 'Capital Crisis: London's Housing Needs' (Labour Group on the LBA, 1980), p. 3.
34 Department of the Environment 'Housing Policy: Technical Volume, Part I' (HMSO, 1977), p. 80.
35 Department of Health and Social Security, 'Social Security Statistics' (HMSO, 1978).
36 E. Craven, Housing in R. Klein (ed.), 'Social Policy and Public Expenditure 1975: Inflation and Priorities' (Centre for Studies in Social Policy, 1975), pp. 119-20.
37 Office of Population Censuses and Surveys, 'General Household Survey 1976' (HMSO, 1978), Table 2.28.
38 'House of Commons: Official Report', vol. 971, col. 644 (27 July 1979).

39 See in particular A. B. Atkinson and A. H. Harrison, 'The Distribution of Personal Net Wealth in Britain' (Cambridge University Press, 1978).
40 Royal Commission on the Distribution of Income and Wealth, 'Third Report on the Standing Reference', p. 142.
41 H. Winter, 'Homes for Locals?' (Community Council of Devon, 1980).
42 Murie, Council House Sales Mean Poor Law Housing, p. 49.

5　The Demand for Home Ownership

Colin Jones

The level of home ownership in Britain has expanded rapidly since
the turn of the century. As Table 5.1 indicates for England and
Wales, just about 10 per cent of houses were owner occupied in
1914. By 1938 this proportion had risen to almost a third as a
consequence of the private housing boom of the 1930s. Today
roughly 55 per cent of the total stock of dwellings is owner occupied. There are, however, considerable regional variations in this
proportion, with Scotland having the smallest proportion at only
33 per cent. During the same period there has also been a vast
increase in the number of houses in the public sector. In 1919,
with the introduction of exchequer subsidies, the building of
council housing on a large scale was launched. It was the beginning of council housing as we know it and by the beginning of
hostilities in 1939 almost 10 per cent of all households in England
and Wales rented their home from a public authority. Since then
this proportion has tripled. Again the regional picture can be
quite different; in Scotland the majority of households currently
live in public authority housing.

The growth of the owner-occupied and council sectors has been
created largely by new building, though a substantial proportion
of houses in the former was originally privately rented. The sale
of houses into owner occupation, together with the effects of redevelopment, have been the major causes of the demise of the
privately rented sector. But the sale of privately rented housing
as a source of growth for home ownership must, by its very nature, decline with its success. If therefore the owner-occupied
sector is to continue to grow relatively rapidly - and new building
alone cannot achieve this - houses must be transferred on a substantial scale from the public rented sector. And apparently
following this logic with the Housing Act, 1980 (and the Housing
Tenants' Rights, Etc. (Scotland) Act, 1980), the government
plans to pursue further growth of owner occupation at the expense of the public sector.

The commitment to the extension of home ownership is not by
any means the prerogative of Conservative administrations; rather
it should be seen as a persistent theme of housing policy. The
Labour government in 1965, for example, stated:

> The Government strongly support the movement toward
> extended owner occupation which brings with it a standard
> of maintenance and repair by no means always found in
> privately rented houses...[T]hey will publish their plans

for bringing owner occupation within the reach of more
families.[1]

This view was reaffirmed throughout the 1970s; the 1977 green
paper, for instance, argued that owning one's own house is a
basic and natural desire.[2] This continued emphasis on home
ownership has been reflected in various policy measures. On
occasion the government has intervened in the market to reduce
the building society interest rate to borrowers and also to ensure
a steady and adequate supply of mortgage funds. Home ownership has continued to hold a preferential tax position in comparison with alternative forms of investment, and a special subsidy
scheme for first-time purchasers was introduced in 1979 under
the then Labour administration. However, there is a divide on the
issue of council house sales and this matter is discussed at length
both by Bassett and by Murie.[3]

Table 5.1: *Tenure Structure of the Housing Stock in England and Wales,
1914-75*

	Owner Occupied %	Public Rented %	Private Rented %	Total (millions)
1914	10.1	–	89.9	7.9
1938	32.5	9.6	57.9	11.4
1960	43.8	24.7	31.5	14.6
1971	52.6	28.7	19.3	17.1
1975	55.0	28.9	16.1	18.0

Source: Department of Environment, 'Housing Policy: Technical Volume, Part 1' (HMSO,
1977), Table I.23.

The purpose of this chapter is, first, to examine how political
attitudes and the current policies on housing tenure relate to the
desires of the population at large, and, second, to explore and
to quantify the constituents of the demand for home ownership.
Use will be made of a number of household surveys and studies of
housing demand. Unfortunately there is no single wholly adequate
study and as a consequence there are a number of limitations to
this approach; in particular there are some notable gaps in our
knowledge while others may be far from adequately filled. Often
it is difficult to make across-the-board comparisons between surveys owing to the variation in the questions asked and the populations sampled. It may be, for example, that recent movers will
give different responses to those of a group of long-term residents
in a given tenure. And care must be taken in any interpretation
of attitudinal responses which necessarily reflect, at least in part,
the perceived costs of different tenures. These costs in turn
reflect the level of subsidy in each tenure, which is itself not
immutable. But as a consequence it is difficult to interpret tenure

preferences because housing of the same physical quality would command different prices in each tenure. Therefore this chapter will not be constrained to a review of attitudinal surveys but will attempt to set them in the context of current market processes and the issues involved.

TENURE PREFERENCES AND THE HOUSING MARKET

At one level it would appear that government policies mirror an unfulfilled demand for home ownership. A recent national con- sumer survey for NEDO found that 69 per cent of respondents would most like to live in owner-occupied accommodation in two years time, compared with 52 per cent who were home owners in 1975.[4] As many as 40 per cent of council tenants and 36 per cent of private tenants expressed a desire to move into owner occu- pation. Other surveys have noted higher percentages; the Man- chester Tenure Mobility Study (TMS), for example, found that almost three in five of recent movers into council housing wished to buy.[5] Harrison and Lomas reported on a comparable study of moving and non-moving households in London;[6] again about three out of five public sector tenants and seven out of ten private tenants said that they preferred owner occupation. Furthermore, an analysis of council house tenants' preferences in five different estates in the inner London borough of Southwark revealed pro- portions who preferred to own ranging from 53 to 64 per cent.[7]

Part of the reason for these variations may be regional differ- ences, but caution should be taken in any interpretation along these lines. The Durham Household Survey, undertaken for the Northern Region Strategy Team in 1974, is illustrative in this matter.[8] It discovered that somewhat fewer, 24 per cent, of local authority tenants interviewed would prefer to be owner occupiers. Given that the Northern Region has a lower proportion of owner occupiers than any other English region, it is evident that we cannot presume that the highest unsatisfied demand exists in those regions where the supply is numerically smaller. Even so, in the Northern Region 57 per cent of households wanted to be owner occupiers compared with 44 per cent who actually were in this tenure.

Naturally it is important to distinguish between preferences on the one hand and actions, which are the result of the interaction of choices and constraints, on the other. In fact these stated preferences for home ownership have not been reflected in vast numbers moving from local authority housing into owner occupation. Only 11 per cent of first-time purchasers with a mortgage from either a building society, a local authority or an insurance com- pany are former local authority tenants. The major component of movement into the owner-occupied sector is new householders, comprising 43 per cent of all first-time buyers with a mortgage.[9] This picture is broadly confirmed by the Glasgow Housing Market Study (HMS).[10] A survey of first-time purchasers in the city

during 1976/7 shows that three out of every five were new householders and just under a quarter of continuing households were
formerly local authority tenants, that is about 9 per cent of the
overall total. Analysis of the Glasgow District Council Home Loans
Department records for the previous year found only 5 per cent
of first-time purchasers originated directly from the public
sector.[11] But while there is little revealed demand for home
ownership by local authority tenants in Glasgow the opposite is
true for their offspring; 36 per cent of the first-time purchasers
surveyed above were formerly living with parents in council
housing.

LOCAL AUTHORITY TENANTS AND HOME OWNERSHIP

We now turn to examine the demand for home ownership by established households in local authority housing. The present author
has drawn the following profile of moves from the public sector
to owner occupation based on data from the Manchester TMS.

> The vast majority of the heads of these households are
> manual workers and a large proportion of these households
> contain at least two economically active members. Almost
> half of these movers had spent ten years or more in rented
> accommodation and these older households tend to have
> higher incomes. In general these moves led to older terraced
> houses and a decline in housing quality (as measured in
> terms of the amenities we considered) and in some cases a
> reduction in housing size.[12]

On the other hand the Glasgow HMS observed that a high proportion of movers from council housing to owner occupation had spent
less than two years in that tenure (although a quarter had spent
more than three years as local authority tenants). Similarly the
Leeds Local Housing Study (LHS) concluded that households moving out of the public sector into owner occupation were generally
young, with more than half the heads of households (54 per cent)
aged 34 or less, and at the beginning of the family life cycle.
Again over half (55 per cent) were manual workers although the
vast majority of these, 45 per cent of the total, were either skilled
workers or foremen or supervisors. Households moved in the main
to semi-detached or terraced houses; where this could be dis-
cerned, 57 per cent of these moves led to an improvement while 36
per cent suffered a decline in physical environment.[13]
    To summarise the evidence, it would seem that council house
tenants who move to buy their home are spread over the whole
age spectrum but are generally in the first stages of the family
life cycle and are predominantly skilled manual workers. Very
often these moves lead to a decline in housing quality. But what
of those local authority tenants who want to buy a home and are
unable to do so at present? Some light is shed on this subject by

data collected for the Manchester TMS. The results here are
based on questionnaire survey material from movers into council
housing, which is not necessarily ideal since they may not be
typical of all tenants, but at least the decision to move means
that they are likely to have considered alternative tenures in the
recent past. There were 134 households in this study who were
recent movers subsequently living in local authority housing;
only 17 (13 per cent) expected to buy a house in the future and
almost half of these were actively saving for a deposit. Of the
remainder, 62 (53 per cent) would have liked to be able to buy a
house in the future, leaving 55 (47 per cent) who did not.

The majority of households who wished to buy a house were
couples with children or extended families with at least one grand-
parent living in the household. These 39 households accounted
for 63 per cent of the total, but divorced, remarried and one-
parent families also amounted to nearly one-fifth of the overall
number. Virtually all the heads of these households, as Table 5.2
indicates, were manual workers who were generally unskilled.
The annual median incomes of the heads of households and of the
whole households were in the ranges £1,041-£1,560 and £1,561-
£2,080 respectively. These medians are slightly lower than their
equivalents for households in the same sample who actually did
move to become owner occupiers. On the other hand those households who did not want to buy a house were generally older; 17
(31 per cent) were retired couples or retired single persons. A
further quarter of these households were accounted for by divorced, remarried or one-parent families. Table 5.3 shows that
these household types are reflected in low household incomes, with
median incomes for the head of household and the whole household
less than £1,000 per annum.

Returning to those households who would like to buy, Table
5.3 shows that at least 10 per cent of those households earned
more than the median income of households which had in fact
bought, and there is considerable overlap in the range of incomes.
In all, 30 per cent earned over £2,000. Table 5.4, which is derived from the Family Expenditure Survey covering all of Great
Britain, indicates that virtually a quarter of owner occupiers re-
paying mortgages in 1974 (the following year) earned between
£2,000 and £3,000.

This sort of comparison does not take into account such factors
as when these owner occupiers bought their accommodation or
regional variations in incomes and house prices; but it does seem
to suggest that at least for this top 30 per cent who want to buy,
level of current income in strictly monetary terms should not be a
barrier. If this is the situation, what are the various possible
explanations of why they have not yet bought?
(1) There may be a problem caused by the lack of a deposit.
(2) The building societies may not have a favourable attitude
towards the credit worthiness of these households; for example
their incomes may be too variable or too dependent on overtime
payments.

Table 5.2:   Distribution of Movers Who Expect to Remain Local Authority Tenants by Socio-economic Group

	Would like to buy	Would not like to buy
	No. (%)	No. (%)
Employers, managers, professionals	–	1 (2)
Intermediate and junior non-manual	4 (7)	3 (6)
Foremen, skilled workers	14 (23)	9 (16)
Unskilled workers	41 (67)	38 (69)
Not applicable	2 (3)	4 (7)
All	61 (100)	55 (100)

Source: Manchester Tenure Mobility Study Data.

Table 5.3:   Distribution of Movers Who Expect to Remain Local Authority Tenants by Income

	Would like to buy in future		Would not like to buy in future	
	Head of house-hold income	Total house-hold income	Head of house-hold income	Total house-hold income
	No. (%)	No. (%)	No. (%)	(No. (%)
£ 261-£ 520	2 (3)	–	16 (31)	8 (16)
£ 521-£ 780	9 (14)	8 (13)	19 (37)	13 (26)
£ 781-£1,040	8 (13)	5 (8)	5 (10)	7 (14)
£1,041-£1,560	22 (36)	18 (29)	6 (11)	14 (28)
£1,561-£2,080	15 (24)	13 (21)	6 (11)	7 (14)
£2,081-£2,600	6 (10)	12 (19)	–	–
£2,601-£3,120	–	4 (6)	–	–
£3,121 and over	–	2 (3)	–	1 (2)
All	62 (100)	62 (100)	52 (100)	50 (100)

Source: Manchester Tenure Mobility Study Data.

(3) The desire to buy is not strong enough to overcome the up-heaval costs of the move.

So far we have been considering the desire to buy a home, and there does appear to be an unsatisfied demand which is capable of being met if certain supply constraints were removed. As it would be widely accepted that what people want should carry consider-able weight in policy-making, and in so far as meeting the demand for ownership implies selling council houses, there is a strong argument for the present government's strategy. This conclusion must be tempered by three caveats. First, there is a cost, finan-cial, economic and social, of meeting these unmet needs, and, second, this demand is expressed within the framework of existing

Table 5.4:   Household Income by Tenure Group in 1974

Household income per annum (£)	Local authority dwellings	Owner occupied dwellings owned with mortgage	Owner occupied dwellings owned outright
	%	%	%
Under £1000	20	1	21
£1,000-£1,499	11	3	15
£1,500-£1,999	10	6	9
£2,000-£2,999	25	23	20
£3,000-£3,999	18	28	15
£4,000 and over	16	39	20
Number of households	2,098	1,841	1,404
Median income	£2,318	£3,547	£2,194

Source: Department of Environment, 'Housing and Construction Statistics', no. 16 (HMSO, 1975), Supplementary Table 3.

subsidy and taxation policies which make owner occupation very attractive. These questions are discussed in more detail in other chapters. Third, and perhaps most important of all, the demand for home ownership is not always a demand to buy council houses.

To consider this last issue further it is worth examining the motives for two of the flows into owner occupation described above. We begin with the Manchester and Leeds movers from council housing; there are two explanations for why many of these moves led to a reduction in the quality of housing.
(1) These households sought home ownership per se and were therefore prepared to forego certain housing attributes to gain others in the form of tenure rights.
(2) These movers were dissatisfied with their housing, for example they disliked living in maisonettes or flats, and there was no possibility of suitable alternative accommodation being offered. In these circumstances the only real solution to, say, the desire for a house was a move to the owner-occupied sector (or to private rented housing in some areas). This may mean the loss of some less important housing amenities. Thus, for this group, the act of house purchase derives more from dissatisfaction with the accommodation available in the local authority sector than from any desire for home ownership as a form of tenure.

Similarly, part of the explanation for the apparent growth in the demand for home ownership from the children of local authority tenants in Glasgow lies in the alternatives available to these newly married couples. As a major factor in allocation of council houses in the city was the length of time on the waiting list, and these households were generally only eligible for a house in the unpopular, low-quality council estates. In Glasgow's case this means either tenements built in the 1930s or the peripheral schemes

constructed on the edge of the city during the 1950s. And, given
the larger numbers of houses available there, most would have
been offered a house in the peripheral estates. If they were to
have accepted such an offer at that time they would have been
paying (in 1978) £32 per month in rent and rates and could not
realistically have hoped to move to another and more desirable
council house for perhaps 15 years. The alternative was to buy a
small tenement flat, perhaps a 'room and kitchen' for around
£5,000 at 1978 prices, for which the mortgage payments and rates
would have amounted to about £50 per month. In addition they
would have significantly lower transport costs, their repayments
would be relatively fixed despite inflation, they would own the
property in 15 years and they would also be able to move when
they wish. It is therefore understandable that these advantages
might be seen as outweighing possibly lower standards of internal
amenity and space. Both these examples spell out the perhaps
obvious but often forgotten notion that the demand for particular
tenures is not purely a function of tenure rights; it also derives
from the characteristics of the housing stock available in each
tenure and relative prices. Indeed, demand for housing in one
tenure, at the extreme, could simply reflect differences in house
types between tenures.

THE DEMAND FOR COUNCIL HOUSE PURCHASE

The foregoing clearly has implications for distinguishing the dem-
and for council house purchase by sitting tenants from the demand
for home ownership. The direct evidence on the former is somewhat limited but the report by the Southwark Community Development Project does provide valuable information from a survey of
183 council tenants in five estates.[14] Only one of these estates
contained any homes with gardens. Respondents in Southwark
who stated a preference for home ownership over renting were
asked, first, whether they would be prepared to consider buying
the dwelling in which they were then living and, second, if there
were any other council dwellings in the area which they would be
prepared to consider buying if they were made available. The
results are presented in Table 5.5. Just under a quarter of tenants with a preference for home ownership were interested in
buying their own dwelling (or 14 per cent of all council tenants).
And while 18 per cent were prepared to purchase other council
dwellings in the area, the great majority of these respondents had
in mind, according to the authors, only the one or two estates
nearby which contained houses with gardens as well as flats.

A more recent and extensive survey of 2,311 council tenants
has been undertaken by Glasgow District Council.[15] Nineteen per
cent of respondents stated they would be interested in buying
their house, in a local authority area where owner occupation
amounts to only 25 per cent of all dwellings. Just over a quarter
of those not interested gave as their main reason dislike of the

Table 5.5:   Attitudes Towards Council House Purchase of Council Tenants Who Prefer to Own

Whether interested in buying their own dwellings

	No.	(%)
Interested	26	(23)
Not interested	81	(72)
Don't know	6	(5)
All	113	(100)

Whether interested in other council dwellings in area

	No.	(%)
Interested	20	(18)
Not interested	76	(67)
Don't know	17	(15)
All	113	(100)

Source: Southwark CDP, 'Alternative Forms of Tenure: Preference and Cost', (Southwark CDP, 1976), Table 7.

house or the area, and so were potentially interested in other dwellings. Indeed, as many as 44 per cent were interested in buying another council house, but the vast majority qualified this response by stating that their interest depended on the area. A broadly similar picture is provided by a subsequent survey of 739 households in Dundee, a town with a similar tenure structure; 17 per cent of respondents expressed an interest in purchasing their home with 26 per cent interested in buying a council house other than their own.[16] Actual sales have so far been relatively modest in relation to the apparent level of interest in buying.

In fact Forrest and Murie have shown that in Birmingham, where 10,000 council houses were sold between 1966 and 1972, the maximum in any one ward was 6 per cent of the stock.[17] Similarly the Northern Region Strategy Team's analysis of sales in South Shields during 1971-3, when 5 per cent of the stock was sold, shows that, with the exception of one small estate, sales never rose above 10 per cent of council stock in any ward.[18] Sales in Yeovil between July 1977 and January 1980 numbered 684 and represented fractionally more than 5 per cent of the total council stock, and less than 7 per cent of the houses made available, with no marked variation in sales between areas.[19] Richmond's study of council house sales in Worcester between 1954 and 1979 reveals that 964 properties were sold but that no single area had taken more than 12 per cent of total sales. However in some cases 50 per cent of the very small estates had been sold.[20] In Bristol, another authority with a relatively long history of sales, Bassett found that 5,717 houses had been sold between 1960 and 1977, equivalent to about 9 per cent of the total dwellings.[21] In other areas sales have not been so extensive; Burns, for example, shows that sales

in the period 1972-4 amounted to little more than 1 per cent of
Edinburgh's total council stock, despite generous discounts, the
availability of 100 per cent mortgages and the fact that in many
cases repayments would have been less than rent.[22]

Perhaps the new towns have been most 'successful' in selling
off their public housing stock and, as far as Scotland is concerned,
have accounted for the bulk of sales in the past. McHugh has
shown that, beginning with a level of owner occupation in East
Kilbride of only 5 per cent in 1968, sales, including empty houses
in designated areas, by late 1976 had varied between 6 per cent
and 18 per cent of the rented housing stock in the different neighbourhoods.[23] Similarly, Truesdale describes how public housing
sales in Stevenage, amounting to 5,229 between 1969 and 1974,
raised the level of home ownership from 10 per cent to 35 per
cent.[24]

The picture is therefore generally somewhat patchy. An obvious
factor is the length of time during which council houses have been
sold in a locality and there are two closely related elements to this.
First, one would expect, given the dynamic nature of the housing
system, sales to be a continuous process and hence that greater
availability would lead to an overall increase in the total. Second,
once sales become commonplace and reach a certain threshold, and
as council house purchasers move elsewhere, one can envisage an
active resale market developing; this in turn may lead to an increase in the active demand for council house purchase. Such a
position seems to have occurred in at least certain of the new
towns. A crucial role in this process is the influence of finance,
especially that of building societies in the resale market. The
causal relationship here, however, becomes blurred as societies
will insist on some evidence of a prevailing market. Building societies will in any case be somewhat cautious, as they are generally
under strain to fulfil the demands for funds from existing supported markets. The key to extensive support from the building
society movement may lie in the possible generation of savings
funds from council tenants whose long-term aim is owner occupation. The implications of this demand for house purchase finance
are discussed in Chapter 3.

The relative cost of council house purchase compared with continuing to rent must also be an important factor. Although Burns
noted the poor response to council house sales in Edinburgh,
given the attractive nature of the financial proposition, there is
some evidence to suggest that the level of discount from the market price had some impact on the level of sales in Bristol.[25] However, it is difficult to distinguish the influence of discounted
prices from an 'announcement effect' whereby the publicity gen-
erates a high level of demand. Certainly subsequent sales in this
area after the initial few years following the introduction of a 30
per cent discount in 1971 fell back to their pre-discount level.
Allowing for this, the variation in annual sales seems to be closely
related to national economic performance, suggesting that a prime
influence is personal financial security before embarkation on house
purchase.

But perhaps the most significant factor is that the tenant's
desire to purchase his or her house is dependent on the satisfaction households derive from living in different house types
and neighbourhoods. All the studies discussed above refer to
this in some way. For example, the Glasgow District Council Survey found that households living in semi-detached houses were
two and a half times more likely to be interested in purchasing
their home than those living in tenements and high flats.[26] Similarly, more than a third of households living in the more desirable estates were interested in buying compared with just 13 per
cent in the least popular estates. Or, to take a further example,
the Leeds LHS shows that more than four out of every five council house sales in the city were semi-detached houses with gardens.[27] The pattern of sales will therefore be closely correlated
with the spatial distribution of house types, both within and
between local authority areas.

OWNER OCCUPATION AND COUNCIL HOUSE PURCHASE

Earlier we saw how the demand for home ownership from local
authority tenants was not coincident with the demand for council
house purchase, largely because of the variation in house types
between the two tenures concerned. But is making council houses
available for sale meeting a demand for owner occupation which
would have remained unsatisfied or does this at best only accel-
erate the process of home purchase for the households concerned?
To examine this issue we need to look at the characteristics of
council house purchasers. Murie has drawn the following picture
of the 'typical' purchaser based on the experience of West Midlands' local authorities.

> The householder has been a long established tenant, is in
> middle age, with a fairly large family growing up. He is
> earning above average wages, usually in a skilled manual
> occupation. The family has often reached the stage in the
> family life cycle where more than one wage earner is living
> at home.[28]

This image is virtually identical to the typical older mover from
local authority housing to owner occupation described by the
present author, but most such households tended to be younger.[29]
  A more formal comparison, however, has been undertaken by
Wilkinson between council house purchasers in Leeds and movers
out of local authority housing to buy a home in the private sector.
He notes:

> In summary, the buyers of council houses were comparatively
> older than those who were moving into owner occupation.
> They were council tenants of long standing and their child-
> ren were older or had grown up and were working. A high

proportion of wives tended to be in full-time employment
and, consequently, household income was only slightly
below that of households who made a physical move to
become owner-occupiers. Generally, therefore, these households were at a comparatively advanced stage in the family
life cycle.[30]

The evidence suggests that council house purchasers are in a
sense a special breed of purchasers, generally at later stages of
the family cycle and unlikely to have been interested in buying a
house in the private sector. And, indeed, two-thirds of the Leeds
sample said they would not have moved in order to buy a home.

The Glasgow analysis of council house tenants interested in
purchasing their home provides a similar picture. The average
age of those expressing an interest in buying was 40 years. This
interest also correlated with social class and length of time in
their present home; those who had spent 6-10 years in their home
being most likely to buy. It would appear then that there is little
difference in social (although not necessarily economic) characteristics between prospective and actual purchasers.

REASONS FOR HOME OWNERSHIP

So far we have seen how there is a large proportion of council
tenants who want to own their home, but who do not want to buy
a council house. On the other hand there is a large number of
council house purchasers who would not have moved home to buy.
Given these diverse reactions it is worth exploring in more detail
the motives of those households who prefer to own. The NEDO
consumer survey provides us with useful evidence in this respect.[31] The advantage of owner occupation most frequently cited
by this sample was that it was a form of saving or an investment
(26 per cent), followed by independence (23 per cent), freedom
to decorate as desired (22 per cent), feeling of security (17 per
cent), freedom to choose location (10 per cent), and the fact that
'it is your own' (10 per cent). Viewed from the opposite direction,
the major disadvantages of council housing as seen by this group
were that you never own your own property (20 per cent), lack
of choice (15 per cent) and the lack of freedom to decorate (14
per cent). Unfortunately the NEDO survey does not separate the
responses of public sector tenants who wished to buy (and indeed
includes owner occupiers). The Manchester TMS, however, found
that, in general, local authority tenants placed great emphasis on
the acquisition of property and the subsequent steady costs as
advantages of buying rather than renting, a view which was
largely shared across all tenures in line with the NEDO survey.[32]

Other surveys have shown a lower priority for the financial
advantages of owner occupation by public sector tenants. The
Southwark CDP survey team, for example, asked tenants who expressed a preference for home ownership to rank in order of

Table 5.6:   Relative Importance of Reasons for Preferring to Buy Expressed by Council Tenants

	Percentage of maximum possible points	*Percentage of people giving item as 1st choice*
More choice of a house with a garden	68	40
Wider choice of where to live	58	19
Controlling your own home without tenancy conditions	55	19
Absolute security of tenure	42	12
Likely increase in value of property	33	8
Income tax relief on mortgage interest	29	2

Source: Southwark CDP, 'Alternative Forms of Tenure: Preference and Cost', Table 4.

importance a number of different reasons for favouring that tenure. So as to express simply the answers to the question, points were given to each item, with six points being given for the item considered to be most important down to one for that thought to be least important. The results are shown in Table 5.6. A substantial number of tenants mentioned only two or three reasons, considering the others not important enough to rank. As many as 40 per cent of respondents gave the desire for a house with a garden as their most important reason for seeking home ownership. This response is much the most important and probably reflects the dissatisfaction of the tenants in the survey with their housing which, in the main, was flats. We can control for the level of satisfaction or dissatisfaction by focusing purely on council house purchasers who are presumably relatively happy with the housing provided for them. Wilkinson found that, when asked an open-ended question on the reasons for buying, the overwhelming emphasis of responses from council house purchasers in Leeds was economic in character. [33] Only 11 per cent of households indicated that they aspired to owner occupation for other reasons and nobody mentioned anything to do with the freedom which owner occupation confers. As far as economic reasons are concerned, 38 per cent of households instanced rising rents as important, 25 per cent regarded their purchase as a good investment, while 18 per cent thought the price reasonable and said that the mortgage repayments were less than, or no greater than, their present rent.

Examination of reasons for preferring to own reveals, therefore, the dominance of economic factors in the decision and these of course are expressed within a financial framework determined by the government. A change in the structure of housing subsidies could be expected to alter significantly the demand for home ownership, and indeed the current Conservative government's policy of increasing council house rents faster than the rate of inflation seems set to emphasise these advantages of home ownership. However, this argument cannot be fully extended to the

demand for council house purchase, given the important role that
attitudes towards house types play in determining the willingness
of tenants to buy the house in which they live. In as much as they
are dissatisfied with it, the desire of some council tenants to buy
their existing home is likely to be relatively unaffected by alterations in the relative financial attractions of the different tenures.

It should also be pointed out that the demand for home ownership stemming from the desire for more security of tenure and
control of the house environment, for example, may also be capable of satisfaction by strategies such as changes in tenancy
arrangements, the involvement of tenants in management and
other forms of tenure such as co-operatives. Indeed, the Housing
Act, 1980 (and Housing Tenants' Rights, Etc. (Scotland) Act,
1980), do make some progress in these directions. Similarly, lack
of choice may be the result of restrictive allocation policies which
are discussed in Chapter 6. The important point is that selling
council houses is not the only means of satisfying many widely-
held housing aspirations.

CONCLUSIONS

The fundamental aim of housing policy is to ensure that every
household has a decent house at a price it can afford. Any policy
which aims to influence the distribution of tenures in order to
satisfy preferences on the part of a section of the community must
subsume to this overall aim. Our discussion of the empirical evidence concerned with the demand for home ownership must be
seen in this context. However, it is important to take note of
these preferences in any policy decisions, and we now draw some
conclusions from the disparate and somewhat limited evidence
available.

First of all, many council tenants wish to be owner occupiers,
but very few households actually move from the local authority
sector to owner occupation. Indeed, the number of council tenants
who buy in any one year is a small fraction of the number who in
terms of income and age could afford to do so. Probably between
40 and 60 per cent of local authority tenants want to buy a home
of their own and a large proportion of these households would
appear to be able to 'afford' to do so. One can only surmise about
the importance of the deposit and other financial barriers, but, at
least for some, the opportunity to buy the home they live in may
be very welcome. Those tenants who wish to buy their own home
are generally families with children while, by contrast, those who
do not, probably because of the responsibilities involved, are the
old and the poor. So far the 'typical' council house purchaser
appears to be middle-aged with a family and an above-average
income. Usually two members of the family are working. It is
probable that these households would have been able to buy a
house on the private market, had they wished to do so, or if they
could have obtained a mortgage from a building society.

There is, however, a gulf between the proportion of council tenants who want to buy a home and the proportion who wish to own the home in which they are living. As a consequence the level of council house purchase is less than perhaps would be expected, reflecting the fact that many of the desirable estates contain a highly stable and consequently ageing population who because of their age are less interested in owner occupation. Having said this, there still seems some way to go before local 'saturation' points are reached, which themselves will be influenced by the threshold effect discussed earlier. And, given the ever-changing nature of households' personal and financial characteristics, a demand is always likely to exist for council house purchase.

It should, however, be remembered that a sizeable proportion of tenants wish to buy their own home to escape the house types available to them in the public sector. To achieve this goal they are prepared to take a cut in accepted housing standards. The sale of council houses to sitting tenants will do nothing to satisfy this demand, but their discontent may be allieviated by modifications to the allocation mechanisms and the level of investment within the public sector. But, for most people, the desire to own one's own home is based on economic reasons. Owner occupation has many advantages in this respect to the individual household, particularly the fact that the home is an asset. Very often it is the only way an average man or woman can save in a way that is not eroded by inflation. In addition, it also provides welcome opportunities for a householder to control his or her environment and for a degree of choice unparalleled in the public sector. Yet council housing has the important characteristic that it is available to households irrespective of income. Furthermore, although over the years rising real incomes mean that it has become possible for more and more households to enter owner occupation, it is also true that factors such as high interest rates and unemployment have made it increasingly difficult for some purchasers to remain in the tenure. The problems of low-income owner occupation have received comparatively little attention in Britain but American experience is of some relevance (see Chapter 7).

To summarise, there appears to be an unmet demand for home ownership which will not be fully satisfied by the sale of council houses. There are, however, difficulties in assessing the long-term significance of these preferences, given that they are expressed within a financial framework set by the government. As economic factors are the most significant force in determining preferences for owner occupation, government policies themselves are crucial in establishing the level of this demand. The emphasis in government policy on home ownership neglects those who prefer to rent; our evidence suggests that even among those who could afford to buy many, especially older, households do not want the responsibilities of owner occupation despite the financial attractions noted above. The conclusion must be, therefore, that policies which place almost exclusive emphasis on home ownership in general and the sale of council houses in particular can at best only be partially successful in meeting the housing aspirations of households in a wide variety of different circumstances.

NOTES

1 'The Housing Programme 1965-1970', Cmnd 2838 (HMSO, 1965).
2 'Housing Policy: A Consultative Document', Cmnd 6851 (HMSO, 1977).
3 K. Bassett, The Sale of Council Houses as a Political Issue, 'Policy and Politics', vol. 8, no. 3 (1980), pp. 290-307; A. Murie, 'The Sale of Council Houses: A Study in Social Policy', Occasional Paper no. 35 (Centre for Urban and Regional Studies, University of Birmingham, 1975).
4 National Economic Development Office, 'BMRB Housing Consumer Survey' (HMSO, 1977).
5 C. A. Jones, J. Parry Lewis and S. Gudjonsson, 'Movers and Nonmovers' (Centre for Urban and Regional Research, University of Manchester, 1976).
6 A. Harrison and G. Lomas, Tenure Preference: How to Interpret the Evidence, 'CES Review No. 8' (Centre for Environmental Studies, 1980), pp. 20-3.
7 Southwark Community Development Project and Joint Docklands Action Group, 'Alternative Forms of Tenure: Preference and Cost' (Southwark CDP, 1976).
8 Northern Region Strategy Team, 'Housing in the Northern Region', Technical Report, no. 15, vol. 2 (NRST, 1976).
9 Department of the Environment, 'Housing Policy: Technical Volume, Part II' (HMSO, 1977).
10 D. Dawson, C. A. Jones, D. Maclennan and G. A. Wood, 'The Glasgow Housing Market Study' (Scottish Economic Planning Department, 1980).
11 C. A. Jones, Population Decline in Cities in C. A. Jones (ed.), 'Urban Deprivation and the Inner City' (Croom Helm, 1979).
12 C. A. Jones, 'Household Movement, Filtering and Home Ownership', Discussion Papers in Urban and Regional Studies, No. 23 (University of Glasgow, 1976), p. 8.
13 R. K. Wilkinson, 'The Characteristics of the Movers Out', Leeds Local Housing Study, Project Paper VII (University of Sheffield, 1976); see also R. K. Wilkinson, How People Value Their Housing: Some Factors in Tenure Choice, 'Housing Review', vol. 25, no. 1 (1976), pp. 11-14; and R. K. Wilkinson and I. A. Law, The Analysis and Forecasting of Housing Requirements: Tenure Switching in a Local Housing Market, 'Environment and Planning, Series A', vol. 13, no. 1 (1981), pp. 57-64.
14 Southwark CDP, 'Alternative Forms of Tenure'.
15 Glasgow District Council, 'The Sale of Council Houses in Glasgow' (Glasgow DC, 1977).

16 Dundee District Council, 'Council House Sales in Dundee' (Dundee DC, 1980).
17 R. Forrest and A. Murie, 'Social Segregation, Housing Need and the Sale of Council Houses', Research Memorandum no. 53 (Centre for Urban and Regional Studies, University of Birmingham, 1976).
18 Northern Region Strategy Team, 'Housing in the Northern Region'.
19 P. Malpas, Council House Sales in Yeovil District, 'Policy and Politics', vol. 8, no. 3 (1980), pp. 308-15.
20 P. Richmond, Council House Sales in Worcester, 'Policy and Politics', vol. 8, no. 3 (1980), pp. 316-7.
21 K. Bassett, Council House Sales in Bristol, 'Policy and Politics', vol. 8, no. 3 (1980), pp. 324-33.
22 J. T. Burns, House Sales to Council Tenants: the Situation in Edinburgh in J. English and C. A. Jones (eds.), 'The Sale of Council Houses', Discussion Papers in Social Research no. 16 (University of Glasgow, 1977).
23 E. A. McHugh, The Sale of Rented Housing in East Kilbride New Town in English and Jones, 'The Sale of Council Houses'.
24 D. Truesdale, House Sales and Owner Occupation in Stevenage New Town, 'Policy and Politics', vol. 8, no. 3 (1980) pp. 318-23.
25 Burns, House Sales to Council Tenants; and Bassett, Council House Sales in Bristol.
26 Glasgow DC, 'The Sale of Council Houses in Glasgow'.
27 R. K. Wilkinson, 'The Buyers of Council Houses', Leeds Local Housing Study, Project Paper XIX (University of Sheffield, 1977).
28 Murie, 'The Sale of Council Houses', p. 103.
29 Jones, 'Household Movement, Filtering and Home Ownership'.
30 Wilkinson, 'The Buyers of Council Houses', p. 4.
31 NEDO, 'BMRB Housing Consumer Survey'.
32 Jones, Parry Lewis and Gudjonsson, 'Movers and Nonmovers'.
33 Wilkinson, 'The Buyers of Council Houses'.

6 Ideology and Housing Management

Pam Gallagher

This chapter reviews the history and practice of housing management and demonstrates how nineteenth-century attitudes towards applicants and tenants have helped to shape current values and practices. Management 'problems', as defined by managers and would-be housing management reformers, are analysed and the potential for change is examined.

What is housing management? According to veteran housing managers Macey and Baker:

> Good management may be defined as the application of skill in caring for the property, its surroundings and amenities, and in developing a sound relationship between landlord and tenant, and between tenants themselves. [1]

Housing management is an integral part of housing policy, yet there has been little discussion on the subject until recent years. [2] The ways in which council houses are let, repaired and the rents collected have been matters for local discretion and the effects of administrative decisions have not been fully explored. It is fashionable to argue that housing management is suffering from an excess of paternalism. But 'paternalistic' is not a true description: 'oppressive' and 'regulatory' would be more accurate. Management policies are divisive and individualistic and, whilst purporting to be for the good of the majority, do in fact assist the 'respectables', and discredit and stigmatise the less fortunate. Problems are defined bureaucratically and the response is management-oriented. Whilst it is possible to discover individual authorities that have adopted good practices, underlying assumptions and the basic values of housing management are common to most local authority landlords. The dominant ideology favours owner occupation whilst housing management is left to pick up those who cannot compete in the market and, in so doing, confirms the image of council housing as a residual 'welfare' sector.

HISTORICAL FOUNDATIONS

An examination of the historical foundations of housing management demonstrates that its roots can be located in nineteenth-century philanthropy and Victorian ideological assumptions about 'control' of the working class.

One middle-class response in the nineteenth century to the

132

growing unease about the connection between bad housing conditions and disease, together with fear of revolution amongst the
masses, was to put sound capitalist principles to philanthropic
use. Some enlightened industrialists and charitable housing societies provided housing for the industrious poor. The societies
offered a 5 per cent return on money invested and tried to ensure
that only the deserving became tenants. Strict regulations concerning the occupancy of these model dwellings were enforced,
and, as will be seen later, these regulations provided a model for
the first public landlords to adopt.

A parallel influence in the development of housing management
was the work of one woman who attempted to help a class lower
than the skilled workers being housed by the philanthropic societies. Octavia Hill set out to demonstrate that through education
(and arguably coercion) she could guarantee a landlord 'good'
tenants. In the latter half of the nineteenth century she acquired
slum properties and improved them to a basic standard (for example, one tap per landing), whitewashed the walls, and patched
the roofs and windows. She then tried to show that, with close
supervision, tenants would pay their rents and care for the property, thus ensuring a return for the enlightened landlord. [3]

Wohl sums up her contribution to the solution of housing problems: 'Her schemes, so endearingly personal, were hopelessly
insular. Her activities, so sound, so altruistic, and godly, tended
to push into the background the real crises which had to be met...
[H]er contribution was, after all, a negative one.' [4] Wohl fails,
however, to stress the very real influence that Octavia Hill had
over contemporary housing management philosophies or to show
how her ideas have been used and built on for over 100 years.
He comments:

> In her determination to convert the working class houses
> under her control into homes of bourgeois respectability,
> and to instil in the working classes a sense of self-respect,
> independence and pride, and above all in her insistence upon
> the virtues of punctuality, cleanliness, order and discipline,
> she began to assume the role almost of an enlightened, all-
> seeing, but omnipresent, ruler. [5]

Octavia Hill's emphasis on improving the life style of her working-
class tenants, through constantly interfering with their lives,
organising activities, advising on curtains and furniture, and
discussing their finances, established a basic principle of housing
management – that tenants could, and should, be trained: model
tenants for model dwellings. Those who could not live up to
Octavia Hill's expectations were evicted. Today, the 'less respectable' tend to be rehoused in the worst accommodation, though
judgemental attitudes are only one reason for this.

Octavia Hill concentrated her work in small groups of properties
owned by private landlords but was eventually asked to manage
Church Commissioners' houses. She trained other volunteer women

workers and the idea that property management could be a positive contribution to the solution of housing problems gained wider
recognition. By the 1914-18 war, the number of trained women
managers was such that an Association of Women Housing Workers
had been formed. The Ministry of Munitions employed some of
these women to manage the housing that was built for munitions
workers. No doubt they were guided in this decision by the recommendations of the Church Commissioners who, referring to the
Octavia Hill system of management, stated:

> The following beneficial results are experienced:
> Practically no losses of rent and no arrears;
> Steady continuance of tenancies;
> Repairs and redecorations moderate;
> Character and conduct of tenants good;
> Absence of quarrels over user of joint rights, eg stair-
> cases, yards.
> Tenants contented and taking pride in the appearance of
> their dwellings;
> Education influence beneficial. [6]

The promise of well-behaved tenants must have been very attractive.

Returning to the work of the charitable trusts, it will be noted
that the principle of philanthropic capitalism dictated their attitudes towards their tenants. In parallel with the influence of
Octavia Hill it can be seen that the management practices of these
societies were of an oppressive and regulative nature, and they
survive today in public housing management. One society, the
Metropolitan Association, had strict rules regarding rent payment,
carefully screened applicants and allowed sub-letting to relatives
only. As many of the working class needed to sub-let to pay the
higher rents of 'model' dwellings, this limitation was particularly
severe. The Peabody Trust was also careful in selecting its tenants: ' "Only those who will conform to certain rules may become
tenants", and the dirty and dissolute were dismissed immediately
their failings were detected.'[7] The trust's regulations provided a
model that has been followed by local authorities ever since. Indeed, some of the regulations could easily be found in current
tenancy conditions, examples of which will be discussed later in
this chapter. The importance of these rules in tracing the history
of the oppressive nature of housing management is such that it is
useful to quote some examples:

1. No arrears of rent will be allowed.
2. The passages, steps, closets, and lavatory windows
   must be washed every Saturday and swept every morn-
   ing before 10 o'clock. This must be done by tenants in
   turn.
3. Washing must be done only in the laundry. Tenants will
   not be permitted to use the laundries for the washing of

any clothes but their own. No clothes shall be hung out.
4. No carpets, mats, etc., can be permitted to be beaten or
    shaken after 10 o'clock in the morning. Refuse must not
    be thrown out of the doors or windows.
5. Tenants must pay all costs for the repairs, etc., of all
    windows, keys, grates and boilers broken or damaged
    in their rooms.
6. Children will not be allowed to play on the stairs, in the
    passages, or in the laundries.
7. Dogs must not be kept on the premises.
8. Tenants cannot be allowed to paper, paint, or drive nails
    into the walls.
9. Disorderly and intemperate tenants will receive immediate
    notice to quit. [8]

Tenants of charitably provided housing and, later, council housing have thus found themselves subjected to strict rules. These
reinforce the notion that the 'respectables' readily accept and
welcome tenancy conditions but the 'disrespectables' must learn
to conform or be evicted. In the nineteenth century, the sifting
of applicants attempted to keep out those unlikely to prove 'good'
tenants. Thus, the very poor and those in irregular employment
were denied access to the new, improved dwellings. Victorian
capitalist ideology underpinned the values of the philanthropic
societies.

In 1920 the Ministry of Health recognised the role of management in the provision of public housing and, borrowing from the
experience of Octavia Hill and the housing societies, advised local
authorities in its short-lived housing periodical:

Whatever system is adopted arrangements will have to be
made for carrying out the following objects:
1. The careful selection of tenants;
2. The elimination of unsatisfactory tenants;
3. Constant supervision of the property and its occupants
    by officials directly employed and paid by owners;
4. Systematic and punctual collection of rents. [9]

Sixty years after the publication of this advice local authorities
still operate these policies even if they are sometimes implicit in
practice rather than expressly stated. The other noteworthy comment in the Ministry of Health statement refers to the necessity
for local autonomy in management matters. Later government
advice to housing authorities through the Central and Scottish
Housing Advisory Committees has continued this tradition, [10] thus
leaving the way open for widely differing practices, whether good
or bad, liberal or illiberal.

These early influences are apparent in a reference to the role
of management in the 1946 Scottish Housing Advisory Committee
Report 'Housing Management in Scotland':

The primary duty of the housing manager is the collection of rent, but under the Octavia Hill system this is more than a mere business transaction. The housing manager tries to create a sense of responsibility in the tenants, a realisation that the punctual fulfilment of his obligations is ultimately in his own interest as a member of the community.

An analysis of these government reports reveals a reflection of nineteenth-century attitudes towards the deserving and undeserving. The divisive and individualistic approach of housing management is exposed in a consideration of 'problem families'. The 1938 report on 'The Management of Municipal Housing Estates', commenting on the rehousing of families displaced by slum clearance, states:

Bad habits are not easily broken and when these habits govern the behaviour of a small community, such as sometimes exists in a slum street, they persist for want of better alternatives. The bad tenant will learn more readily by eye than by ear... [W]e therefore favour the principle of separating unsatisfactory tenants from one another.[11]

This report was produced at a time of large-scale slum clearance in the 1930s. Damer has shown that the 1920s council estates were largely let to the highest paid workers, owing to high rents and strict selection policies.[12] These estates were of a higher standard than the later slum clearance schemes. Slum dwellers, assumed to be 'rough', were given more basic housing, with less space and a bleak design. The 1930s estates were, in part, a reflection of the prevailing political and economic situation, but lettings policies and official attitudes towards those rehoused clearly mirrored nineteenth-century ideology.

HOUSING MANAGEMENT TODAY: POLICIES, PRACTICES AND PROBLEMS

As tenancy conditions reflect the nature of the relationship between landlord and tenant, these will be examined first.

Ward, in calling for tenant control, demonstrates the 'serfdom' of a council tenancy.[13] He points out that it is 'the lords of the municipal manor who call the tune'. The tenancy conditions generally contain a list of do's and do not's, and rarely show the landlords' responsibilities. Even the landlords' statutory repairing obligations are conveniently left out. The National Consumer Council drew attention to some of the common conditions in tenancy agreements which included the following:

The tenant shall: Obey the caretaker, inform the council of a death or confinement, oil hinges, furnish windows with clean curtains in good condition whilst

The tenant shall not: Be a nuisance to neighbours, hang
washing on balconies, beat carpets at inconvenient hours,
drive nails into walls, allow wood chopping on the premises,
bribe servants of the council, use front garden for vege-
table growing, clear the chimney by setting it on fire.[14]

Actual tenancy agreements usually continue with another list pre-
faced by 'The tenant shall not without permission'.

The government's response in 1977 stressed the need for a fundamental change in the relationship between landlord and tenant,
including a review of tenancy conditions. The report of the Housing Services Advisory Group concluded that tenancy agreements:
'are unnecessarily restrictive...do not express clearly, if at all,
the obligations of the landlord...and contain somewhat incompre-
hensive legal phraseology'.[15]

Some local authorities accepted this criticism whilst others
argued, as they always have, that tenants want these restrictive
conditions in order to protect themselves from their neighbours.
One of the legacies of nineteenth-century individualism has been
the definition of tenants by other tenants as 'good' and 'bad'.
Housing management methods and regulations serve this purpose
well. Tenants can be readily defined as unsatisfactory by reference to the tenancy conditions and other tenants perpetuate myths
about the 'rough end of the estate'.[16] If paternalism means bene-
volent rule, then tenancy conditions cannot always be termed
paternalistic. They are oppressive and regulatory by nature.

The effects of capitalist ideology - the individualistic approach,
the division between the deserving and undeserving - can be
clearly seen in three interrelated areas of management policy:
allocations, 'difficult' tenants and difficult-to-let estates. The
method of allocating council housing - the rationing of a scarce
resource - has always played a dominant part in management policies. Despite certain legal requirements relating to allocation,
central government has insisted that individual councils are
in the best position to decide the type of selection scheme most
appropriate for their area. But guidance on selection of tenants
and allocation priorities has been given to local authorities by
circular, and through the Central and Scottish Housing Advisory
Committees.[17] This guidance has concentrated on 'primary'
rationing - on the different schemes that can be used to decide
who becomes a council tenant, that is, how to assess who is in the
greates housing need to ensure that they receive priority. Many
authorities have in the past entirely prevented access to council
housing for some groups by placing restrictions on admission to
the waiting list such as residential or age qualifications. (Local
authorities in Scotland and London are now obliged to open their
lists to anyone living in the area.) Apart from such restrictions
the system still requires skilful negotiation by waiting-list applicants if they are to be allocated a house.[18]

Perhaps of greater importance has been the question of who gets
what. There is now a wide range of council housing in terms of its

accessibility to transport and shops, standards of space, amenity and maintenance, and general attractiveness. Many local authorities have, in the past, operated grading schemes, attempting to 'match' applicants with houses. For example, only a 'good' tenant with a clear rent record and clean house would be offered a new house on a well-planned estate. Recent reports have condemned this practice and fewer authorities now operate an explicit grading scheme. However, poorer-standard housing still goes to those who are already disadvantaged in the housing system. There are two possible explanations. An important factor is the waiting time. Within the same area there may be a large difference in waiting time for popular and for less attractive estates. Those who are not in great housing need can afford to wait for a good house whilst the homeless and those in desperate need cannot wait and accept the first offer.[19] Amongst those who are allocated the worst housing are ethnic minorities, one-parent families and low-income families. But differential waiting time is not the only factor. Many housing management staff would say that high-standard housing should only go to families who have already proved themselves to be capable of looking after a home and paying their rent. Clearly, to housing staff, this 'standard' cannot be achieved by the homeless, one-parent families and the other disadvantaged groups. This 'secondary' rationing reflects the dominant ideology that is summed up by Burney: 'a clean person gets a clean house and a dirty person gets a dirty house'.[20] In any case, because housing management is concerned with 'good' management practice, which means minimising problems for the department, it makes sense to offer the worst housing to the most desperate – no one else would take it.

Related to the values implicit in the allocation of council housing is the attitude towards those tenants who subsequently prove to be 'difficult' or 'anti-social'. Tenants who fail to pay their rent, upset neighbours and neglect their homes and gardens are defined as management problems. In 1955 the Central Housing Advisory Committee Report, 'Unsatisfactory Tenants', concentrated on those tenants whose attitudes and life styles did not conform with those of managers, and the other tenants who did conform to expected norms. The report adopted a 'blame the victim' approach, assuming that the tenants' difficulties were self-made. Whilst the punitive measures advocated may not be adopted today, nevertheless the tone of the report is echoed in the practices followed by many authorities. Macey and Baker's suggestion that difficult tenants need training is a reminder of the continuing influence of Octavia Hill.[21] Their attempt to divide unsatisfactory tenants from the 'real problem families' demonstrates the constant ideological pressure to individualise all problems so that even tenants with problems are divided amongst themselves.

The question of tenants with problems is one that has not been widely discussed, apart from rent arrears, and there is relatively little literature on the subject when compared to allocations. Difficult tenants, however, are the bread and butter of much housing management, whether it is a case of vandalism, noise, cooking smells or rent arrears. The housing manager has to decide the extent of his or her involvement and it seems that this can be an impossible task.

> Whatever they do about difficult tenants they are likely to evoke criticism. If they sanction a stern approach to any offensive behaviour, they risk the charge of being author-itarian or of lacking compassion. But if they go for patience and understanding, they risk alienating those who have to suffer the consequences of any difficult tenant's behaviour and they will be accused of encouraging difficult tenants in their irresponsible ways. [22]

The problem is a sensitive one but it is an integral part of hous-ing management. If standards are to be set, then they must be upheld. Difficult tenants are defined, generally, by other tenants, and local councillors support the complaints as they need the votes of the 'respectables'. The action taken regarding complaints is likely to reflect the attitude of officers towards different estates. One housing manager 'implied that tenants from different estates would be treated differently when he said his first consideration was to protect the good estates'. [23]
Rent arrears is one of the problems that difficult tenants (as defined by managers and other tenants) very often face. Macey and Baker are quite clear about arrears policies and state:

> It is not in the best interests of the tenants that too lenient or complacent an attitude should be adopted by the housing authority. Such an attitude brings two results in its train. The bad payer is not checked until he has a millstone round his neck, while the general body of tenants gradually adopts a negligent attitude and the number of arrears cases in-creases quite unnecessarily. [24]

In 1976, the National Consumer Council examined the problems facing low-income tenants and stated that their survey 'did not discover tenants who can well afford the rent but refuse to pay it'. [25] Like the 1980 Scottish Office study, [26] the report demon-strated that many tenants need personal contact with housing staff who can advise them on welfare benefits and rebates, and that procedures for the recovery of arrears need to be improved. These reports are looking for appropriate management responses to what they reveal is, basically, a problem of poverty.
'Difficult' tenants, people in rent arrears and disadvantaged groups such as one-parent families and blacks, are to be found disproportionately on what are now termed 'difficult-to-let' estates. These undesirable estates were once referred to as 'sink' estates but, as this implied deliberate dumping policies on the part of the local authority, a more acceptable phrase is now in official use. A 1975 Shelter report emphasised that, although all council estates

carry a social stigma, there is an internal hierarchy with some
estates having a particularly bad reputation.[27] The reasons for
this are complex. Relative acceptability within an area rather than
absolute standards is important and a difficult-to-let estate in a
provincial town might be quite popular in a city. Design and age
of the houses is only one factor. Estates built to replace slum
dwellings in the 1930s are often today's stigmatised estates,
whereas those built for general needs in the previous decade are
generally popular. Poor maintenance and lack of modernisation are
contributory causes, together with the use of cheap materials and
poor building methods. The Benwell Community Project refers
to 'slums on the drawing board'. Describing the Noble Street
Estate, the report states:

> Disasters like this are not accidental, Noble Street was not a
> mistake; it was consciously and deliberately designed to con-
> form with a widely held view of council housing; that it should
> be economical - which is to say, cheap.[28]

Noisy and lacking privacy, with large numbers of children in flats
and often located away from shops and social facilities, these
council schemes are let to those people already designated by
management as unrespectable. 'They say the flats are full of problem families - but we're sure of having problems when they move
us here.'[29]

Reference has been made to the fact that poor maintenance con-
tributes to the difficulties facing tenants on problem estates. More
generally, the National Consumer Council's study of the repair,
maintenance and improvement of council housing from the consumer's viewpoint identified certain key problems.[30] These included
the high costs of maintenance services and poor communications
between management departments. Tenants were often given little
information and experienced long, unexplained delays. The study
states that extensive changes in the organisation of housing departments are needed, and it recommends more tenant involvement
to ensure that tenants, as consumers, know what they can do to
improve their houses and what action to take if the council is not
providing an adequate service.

It is possible that these estates are sometimes deliberately neglected. It is more satisfying for management to keep reasonably
good housing in repair than to spend time and money trying to
maintain estates that were shoddily built or suffer from basic design faults.

THE ORGANISATION AND STAFFING OF HOUSING MANAGEMENT

A consideration of housing management must include a discussion
of both the organisation of housing departments and their staff.

As was seen above, the first government advice to the new
local authority landlords in the 1920s was based on the experiences

and ideas of philanthropic housing management, but at the time
housing functions were distributed amongst existing departments.
The view that all functions of housing management would be more
efficiently organised within one department was not accepted by
the majority of councils until local government reorganisation in
the 1970s (although there are still a few authorities without a
housing department). Despite government advice that there should
be a unified system of management,[31] it was the dual influence of
the demands for a comprehensive approach to housing and the
opportunity offered by the creation of larger housing authorities
with reorganisation that achieved change.

The aim of a comprehensive housing service should be to provide an efficient service - oriented towards the client and seeking
to cover all aspects of housing in the public and private sectors.[32]
This move away from the 'waiting list mentality' coincided with
the introduction of corporate management into local government.
Prior to reorganisation, the Maud Report had urged local authorities to rethink their management structures, and the Bains Report (Paterson in Scotland) outlined structures and procedures for
the implementation of management reforms.[33] This provided an
opportunity to up-grade the housing service by linking it with
the new management-oriented approach to local government. The
Housing Services Advisory Group recommended principles to guide
local authorities 'who take a comprehensive view' and implied that
those using the housing service would benefit by an integrated
approach.[34]

At the same time, the need to train staff was emphasised if the
new approach was to be successful. The lack of qualified staff
had been highlighted by research at The City University in 1977.[35]
The research revealed that only about 3.5 per cent of housing
staff held a professional housing qualification and another 4 per
cent held other professional qualifications. Very few non-qualified
staff went on training courses of any kind and only five departments had housing training officers. The Housing Services Advisory Group report on training suggested that 'an improvement
in the standards of housing management is unlikely to be achieved
unless better training facilities can be provided'.[36]

The lack of training in basic communication skills and insufficient
knowledge of the work of housing departments are given as major
deficiencies in the service provided by housing staff. However,
perhaps more important is the following comment:

> The conflict between public service and private attitudes is
> often crucial in a housing department which is, after all,
> staffed by human beings who have faults, views and pre-
> judices. Attitudes are particularly difficult to define and to
> deal with. Nevertheless they cannot be ignored especially
> because much current criticism is often of the attitudes of
> housing staff. Not only are moral judgements towards public
> tenants...frequent causes for disquiet but there is an
> occasional corresponding resentment of councillors.

'Undeserving tenants' and 'interfering councillors' are two
common examples which affect how housing work can be
disrupted unless the staff can be made to be part of the
system. [37]

This paragraph is worth quoting in full as it demonstrates three
points. First, the recognition that housing staff make moral judgements and reflect the wider values of society in defining the 'undeserving'. Second, the fear that the attitudes of staff will dis-
rupt the service and create yet more management problems. And,
finally, the assumption that there is a conflict between 'public
service and private attitudes'. Perhaps the staff are simply dis-
playing the attitudes that are implicit in all aspects of housing
management and the notion of a 'public service' attitude is quite
misleading.

Another important aspect of the staffing of housing management
is that it is a male-dominated profession. Despite the work of
Octavia Hill and her successors in the Society of Women Housing
Managers, today the top posts in local government are almost all
taken by men. Women are to be found in the lower grades doing
clerical and counter work. Women also constitute the majority of
housing visitors. Their current role in housing management reflects the 'welfare' approach that was associated with Octavia Hill
and the first lady rent collectors. They are supposed to soften
the oppressive aspects of management. However, owing to low pay,
which affects recruitment, and to lack of training, many of these
women continue to reinforce the notions of the deserving and undeserving. They tend to take the side of the tenants who do not
cause management any problems. The male-dominated hierarchy is
often more concerned with career progression and advancement in
the professional organisations, and rarely questions the values
perpetuated by the bureaucracy under its control.

THE POTENTIAL FOR CHANGE

The last ten years have seen various changes in the organisation
and practices of housing management, partly as the result of
recent legislation. This has, for the first time, attempted to dic-
tate certain management policies to local authorities in what had
always been a matter for local discretion. It is necessary to examine these changes and other proposals to discover how far they
are likely to achieve any real improvement in housing management.
The pattern of response to allegations of inequitable treatment,
poor maintenance and harsh practices has been a management-
oriented one. Problems are bureaucratically defined and solutions
are sought that, as far as possible, have few resource implications.
These answers relate to the organisation of housing management
and to policies affecting the rights of tenants. The following organisational responses will be examined: the comprehensive approach,
neighbourhood management, tenant participation and training of

staff. Then policy changes will be discussed together with other resource implications.

The move towards a comprehensive housing service only serves to erect more barriers for those seeking access to public sector housing. A housing advice service may have as its aim assistance to everyone about all their housing problems, be they landlords, tenants or applicants, but in reality it acts as a buffer for the housing department, sifting enquiries and, wherever possible, relieving the public sector of the need to rehouse. Lambeth Housing Advice Centre, one of the first to be set up, asked people as they came in for help 'do you need to continue living in Lambeth?'[38] In a letter to local authorities, the Minister for Housing and Construction was quite explicit about the aims of such a service:

> A housing aid centre can bring several important benefits...
> [I]t will lead to the best use being made of our stock of
> rented housing, both public and private. In fact it will save
> an authority money by sometimes finding solutions [such as]
> helping people to move to other areas or to buy a house of
> their own.[39]

The comprehensive approach to housing services, in attempting to look at housing in both the private and public sectors, is part of the image of corporate management that local government has tried to cultivate. However, it has been shown that, just as corporate management cannot counteract the effects of external factors (such as unemployment or cuts in the rate support grant), so comprehensive housing departments cannot influence other agencies.[40] In Lambeth, the constraints imposed by the market system for housing and land, and the impact of central government policies led to a 'disorganisation of housing'.[41] Harloe, Issacharoff and Minns show that local authorities are unable to intervene effectively in the distributive processes of the market and it is naive to think that this is possible. The extent and nature of public housing is still, in the final resort, dictated by the capitalist market.

Comprehensive approaches can do little to improve the quality of housing management apart from, perhaps, bringing all aspects of housing management within one umbrella department. Theoretically, at least, it should improve communications between different housing functions. However, communications with tenants have not improved. With the increasing size of housing departments there has been a consequent lack of contact between officers and tenants caused by the trend towards centralisation. Many large authorities have decentralised management functions to area offices but these offices can often have responsibility for a number of properties equivalent to a small district council.

One major response to difficult-to-let estates and poor communications with tenants on high-density schemes has been to set up neighbourhood management schemes. Neighbourhood management takes the principle of decentralisation one stage further and involves the establishment of local management offices on large estates. These offices deal with all management and tenant 'welfare' matters, and have a technical officer and small maintenance staff working only in that area. The DOE Housing Development Directorate Report on up-grading problem estates considers that 'local management offices almost immediately restore relations with tenants and improve workers' morale'. [42]

Whilst this management initiative means an improvement in communications between housing management and tenants in those areas where neighbourhood offices operate, as a general prescription for change it is not always appropriate. There are staffing and other resource implications, and small authorities with scattered properties could not easily justify the additional expenditure. There are limitations even when the proposal is applied to difficult estates: 'The "dump" or "sink" estates are often considered undeserving by local councillors, while they require substantial sums to make an impact.' [43] The question of resources is a vital one. Without sufficient money, repairs still will not get done and modernisation schemes will be delayed. Neighbourhood management brings housing departments closer to the realities of council housing and may elicit more sympathetic responses from the staff concerned, but it cannot actually tip the balance of power in favour of the tenants.

The legitimisation of tenants' struggles through the recognition of tenant participation schemes has been another recent management response. The Housing Act, 1980, requires local housing authorities to consult tenants on housing management matters. (Note that the equivalent Tenants' Rights, Etc. (Scotland) Act, 1980 has no such provisions.) This provision does not go as far as the original proposal of the previous (Labour) government in their consultation paper, but it does recognise the role that tenants' associations have played in the management of their estates. It is also a response to pressure from large groups of tenants' associations such as the National Tenants Organisation.

Ward has been one of the chief advocates of tenant participation. His anarchic approach is really demanding co-operative housing as an alternative form of tenure. Whilst co-operatives have been set up, using the provisions of the Housing Rents and Subsidies Act, 1975, of more interest to local authorities has been the idea of management co-operatives. These organisations do not take over ownership from the authority but carry out specified management and maintenance functions. The National Consumer Council issued a warning of the consequences of such policies: 'In the present climate of "economic restraints" we feel there would be considerable reservation and resistance by consumers to be entangled in a policy of day-to-day management of their estates.' [44] The council's comment on consultation is also relevant: 'We are well aware of the depth of suspicion of many tenants' associations to the development of "consultation schemes" as a device for local authorities to shed some of their management responsibilities.'

Much of the official literature about tenant participation has

tended to concentrate on managerial issues. For example. a
Housing Development Directorate paper asks the following
questions:

What sort of questions are discussed by participants...and
are they the most appropriate issues for tenant involvement?
Who raises most of the issues (ie councillors or tenants) and
is the balance of initiators a desirable one?
Are the tenants representatives adequately reflective of
general tenant opinion?[45]

Management, represented by councillors in this instance, is looking for the right kind of tenants for participation; in other words,
those not readily labelled as 'disrespectable' or 'disruptive'.

Tenant participation schemes legitimise the conflict between
tenants' organisations and their landlords by selecting issues for
discussion and involving managers. The Housing Act, 1980,
allows local authorities to decide which issues are discussed
and specifically excludes rents. In this context tenant consultation becomes a management tool and a diversionary issue. The
interests of tenants as a class are not served by such management
responses.

The failure of housing management, ineffective communication
with tenants and the public, and bad relationships with councillors
have all been attributed to a lack of training. Reference has
already been made to the findings of the major housing training
research project at The City University. One of the main recommendations was for the establishment of a centrally-funded training organisation which would also have responsibility for professional examinations. The political and resource implications of this
proposal were too demanding and no central government initiatives
were taken (except in Scotland where the Scottish Development
Department have funded a housing training officer for a temporary period). The Local Government Training Board set up its own
Housing Service Training Committee in 1979 and allocates limited
resources to it.[46] So far the emphasis has been on the development of courses without formal qualifications but from 1981 the
committee is funding a research project looking at the professional
examinations of the Institute of Housing.

Karn considers that housing management has had a low status in
local and central government and this, in part, reflects the lack
of 'professionalism'.[47] The difficulties faced by the Institute of
Housing are considerable; it lacks resources to organise training
itself, and assesses graduates and non-graduates who are study-
ing, for the most part, by correspondence course or day-release
class. But even if more staff are qualified in housing management,
does an increase in 'professionalism' really mean a better service?
At an individual level more sympathetic managers may help to
improve communications with tenants. More importantly, 'professional' senior housing officers could argue more effectively with
other local government professionals for financial and staffing

resources. However, too many professionals today are opportunist managers who become entangled in corporate management structures and pursue 'professionalism' for its own sake. If examples are taken from related disciplines such as architecture or planning, it is evident that professionals can 'tend to be trapped by their occupational context into working to serve the dominant interests of society'. [48] The ideology of management is the dominant value. Simmie states that town planning is essentially a political activity; 'It is much less an altruistic and rational policy making and implementing exercise.' [49] This view can be adopted in a housing context and it challenges the apparently neutral role of professional housing managers.

Much emphasis is placed on the training of non-professional staff. How effective is this training and can it really achieve the changes in attitude and improved efficiency as suggested by its supporters? The National Consumer Council recommends more in-service training, and suggests that the 'potential of skills amongst tenants... has not yet been tapped'. [50] A particularly relevant suggestion is that housing departments should encourage the recruitment of tenants if only on a part-time basis. Training cannot always work wonders - it depends on the raw material. Recruitment policies of housing departments have not been researched but, if staff are employed who already 'have hardened attitudes and preconceived ideas', [51] training cannot be very effective. Some attempt to assess the validity of attitude training has been carried out in relation to housing training and race relations, but, as yet, there are no firm conclusions. [52] A report on a course for counter staff summarises some of the difficulties encountered by the trainers:

> Staff declared their ignorance of Departmental policy...
> [S]ome of this ignorance may be 'self-inflicted' as a basis
> of self-defence. By 'playing' ignorant staff can avoid
> escalating conflict with clients, avoid having to say 'no'...
> Other self-defence mechanisms were apparent... unfavourable
> stereotyping...traditional classification of 'deserving' (eg
> the elderly) and 'undeserving' (eg one-parent families)
> clients...effectively blocking access to information in order
> to protect themselves from further enquiries and demands...
> blaming the victim...Staff tended to feel threatened by the
> training course...participants denied the validity of many
> comments made by almost anyone - lecturers, senior managers,
> the personnel officer. [53]

Counter staff lack status within a housing department and are at the end of a long line of communication. Can they be expected to respond to training when, in reality, they are reflecting the values of senior managers and sometimes councillors? An officer, quoted in the report above, who said 'it's alright with the nice ones', is summarising the attitudes expressed both implicitly and explicitly in housing management practice since the 1920s.

This section of the chapter has so far concentrated on organisational issues which have been strongly emphasised in pre-
scriptions for change. However, there have been some policy
changes, in the areas of lettings and tenancy conditions, partly
brought about by legislation.

The statutory duties contained in the Housing (Homeless Persons) Act, 1977, are probably the most influential provisions
affecting local authority lettings policies. The act obliges housing
departments to house all those within specified 'priority groups'
(such as families with children or pregnant women) who are not
intentionally homeless. Prior to the act, in many local authorities
provision for the homeless was still the responsibility of the
social services departments which had no permanent accommodation. Since the act, some local authorities have demonstrated
that they find the prospect of having to house the 'unrespectables'
quite unpalatable. The homeless have often been regarded as inadequate, or even 'scroungers and scrimshankers',[54] and many
authorities have shrunk in horror from fulfilling their duties. 'The
act embodies the basic principle that housing should be available
for all, a concept which grates on those brought up with the attitude that housing has to be earned at the very least by serving
time on a waiting list.'[55] Authorities have grudgingly accepted the
responsibility, but in many cases it is an opportunity to fill up
some of the empty properties in difficult-to-let estates. As one
government report states:

> Concentration of homeless families give an estate a bad name
> because flats are accepted out of desperation as a last resort
> rather than choice, and because 'problem' families are pushed
> into the homeless category as they are evicted down the
> housing ladder, thereby causing 'homeless' and 'problem' to
> become synonymous.[56]

Thus an apparently 'liberal' policy to help the homeless is used by
management as a deterrent by a refusal to offer them good houses,
so as to warn other families of the stigma attached to being homeless.

Reference to allocation policies was made earlier in this chapter.
Some changes have been made, such as a move away from explicit
grading schemes. The need for greater publicity and more information for applicants has been acknowledged in the Housing Act,
1980, which requires local authorities to publish their allocation
and transfer schemes. In Scotland, the Tenants' Rights, Etc.
(Scotland) Act, 1980, has removed residence qualifications with
the aim of increasing mobility amongst council tenants. All these
provisions are essential and they attempt to improve access to
council housing. However, knowing the rules for eligibility is not
synonymous with actually getting a council house, especially a
good quality one. An applicant still has to compete with homeless
families, urgent medical cases and people being rehoused because
of public developments. Legislation is unable to ensure that all

applicants are treated fairly in terms of the quality and location of house allocated. Though a dwelling of some sort may be readily available in most areas, there is severe competition for popular council housing, and this competition is carefully controlled by management.

Recent publications urge local authorities to look at the needs of special groups, including single-parent families, the handi-capped, battered women and ethnic minorities.[57] They imply that their special needs, neglected in the past, must be the concern of housing management now that general needs have been met. This raises two issues. First, there is an assumption that only when traditional and respectable families have been housed should local authorities make the extra effort needed to house these difficult groups. Second, it is implied that to define special needs means actually helping these groups. Lack of resources and political will, as well as secondary rationing, all influence the housing chances of special need groups. They must still compete with more accept-able groups for access to better quality housing.

The other major area of policy change has been in the conditions governing the landlord-tenant relationship. The changes have been introduced as a direct result of the 1980 legislation, and the rights introduced (together with the provision for tenant consult-ation) have been generally referred to as the 'tenants' charter'. The previous government had published consultation papers on 'A Tenants' Charter' and these included all of the provisions introduced in 1980 by the Conservative government. The stated aims of the 'charter' are to

> provide public sector tenants for the first time with a full
> framework of statutory rights to match their responsibilities
> under their tenancy agreements. At the same time the
> Charter recognises the need for public authorities to be
> able to manage their dwellings efficiently, economically and
> fairly.[58]

The major 'rights' covered in the legislation are: security of ten-ure and rights of succession on death; the right to take in lodgers and sub-let; the right for tenants to improve their homes; in England, the right to be supplied with information about contract-ual and statutory rights and obligations; and in Scotland, the right to a written tenancy agreement.

The response of the housing management profession, as evi-denced in discussions at seminars on the legislation, has been predictably management-oriented.[59] Managers have expressed resentment at the imposition of more work on already hard-pressed departments. The view has been continually expressed that hous-ing management is liberal and fair, and that tenants are not un-justly treated. The administrative work and legal advice are seen as additional and unnecessary burdens. The Chartered Institute of Public Finance and Accountancy observed that 'the proposals entail a new series of administrative procedures which... have significant manpower and financial implications'.[60]

Of greater importance than these bureaucratic responses to the tenants' charter is the 'right to buy' provision in the 1980 legislation, which is likely to overshadow any positive effects of the charter. At an Institute of Housing Conference in June 1979 the Secretary of State for the Environment, Michael Heseltine, expounded at length the benefits of owner occupation. Whilst Heseltine went on to say that the tenants' charter was an opportunity to give tenants a feeling of pride in their homes, he clearly saw this as a consolation prize. He stated that council tenants have no comparable benefits to that of home ownership in increasing personal wealth and that 'the control of council housing hampers people's ability to move'. Clearly the government's view is that council tenants are worse off than owner occupiers. This statement is a logical progression from the capitalist ideology of the nineteenth century through years of oppressive regulation and individualistic management approaches. To the shortcomings and divisive policies of housing management have been added the government policy of 'buy or be damned'.

CONCLUSIONS

This review of the development and current state of housing management and of recent policy changes has sought to demonstrate how ideological assumptions pervade housing practice. These assumptions and values effectively block radical proposals for change and improvement. The reforms that have taken place over the last ten years and the implementation of the Housing and Tenants' Rights Acts have only a limited potential for securing any real improvement in housing management.

A major limitation on change relates to ideological assumptions about home ownership. Whilst owner occupation is held to be a 'natural' desire, somehow innate and satisfying, council housing will always be regarded as second best. Those responsible for public sector housing, whether councillors or professionals, will continue to discriminate so that the better designed and maintained estates are allocated to the more able and affluent tenants. Tenants themselves will continue to defend their own estates or streets, anxious that the label 'problem' should not be attached to them, and buying if at all possible to rise to the expectations of prevailing government ideology.

Cullingworth argues that 'only incremental change is practicable. ..thus one comes sadly to the conclusion that there is little alternative to...the package of limited proposals'. [61] The current debate on issues such as tenant consultation, the identification of special needs, rent arrears policies and training are diversionary as they imply the possibility of significant change. This will be far from easy in the absence of much more fundamental reform.

Whilst improving communications with tenants and more liberal policies are an essential first step towards freeing council tenants from past oppressive practices, these changes do not fundamentally alter the nature of the relationship between local authorities and their tenants. The entrenched privileged status of owner occupiers is not threatened and council tenants remain second-class citizens. As Pinker states, 'the ideology of self-help and individualism receives powerful support from the continuing dominance of market values in our lives'. [62] Because of the existence of a large private housing market, this ideology pervades the council sector. Current reforms do not take account of the inequities in housing and in access to housing which cannot be easily resolved within a capitalist economy.

So what can be done to achieve even incremental change? In Chapter 2 of this book the effects of public expenditure cuts on housing are examined, and it is not proposed to repeat the arguments but rather to make a plea, perhaps somewhat simplistic but impassioned, for a massive injection of capital investment to enable more and better council housing to be built and extensive modernisation programmes to be carried out. However, this must not be at the expense of central government support for increased revenue expenditure on maintenance, and on the selective employment of more and better-trained staff.

Finance will not prove a panacea for the ills of housing management but over a sustained period it could help to eradicate scarcity and to improve existing estates so that council tenants have a real choice. Major reforms in the financing and taxation of owner occupation would also help to redress the balance so that council housing becomes a genuine alternative to owning a house. Sympathetic and efficient housing management would also have a positive role to play.

In summary, housing management currently reflects the dominant capitalist values of our society. As a local government profession it responds to the demands of state capitalism and is subservient to individualistic ideologies. Instead of 'blaming the victim' and individualising problems, housing management must serve the collective needs of council tenants. Given adequate resources and political will, estates can be improved and tenants given real control. Housing managers would then work for tenants rather than against them.

NOTES

1   J. P. Macey and C. V. Baker, 'Housing Management', 3rd edn (Estates Gazette, 1978), p. 4.
2   See, for example, a series of articles in 'Roof' (January, April, May, July and September 1978); and F. Gray, Consumption: Council House Management in S. Merrett, 'State Housing in Britain' (Routledge & Kegan Paul, 1979).
3   For a full discussion of Octavia Hill's work see M. Brion and A. Tinker, 'Women in Housing' (Housing Centre Trust, 1980), Chs. 6 and 7.
4   A. S. Wohl, 'The Eternal Slum' (Edward Arnold, 1977), p. 169.

5 Ibid., p. 189.
6 Quoted in Brion and Tinker, 'Women in Housing', pp. 61-2.
7 'Journal of the Royal Statistical Society' (March 1891), quoted in Wohl, 'The Eternal Slum', p. 159.
8 Referred to by Wohl, 'The Eternal Slum', pp. 159-60.
9 Ministry of Health, 'Housing' (19 July 1920), p. 189.
10 See, for example, Central Housing Advisory Committee, 'Councils and their Houses' (HMSO, 1959); and CHAC, 'Council Housing: Purposes, Procedures and Priorities' (HMSO, 1969).
11 Central Housing Advisory Committee, 'The Management of Municipal Housing Estates' (HMSO, 1938), para. 27.
12 S. Damer, Moorepark: A Study in the Political Economy of Slum Rehousing in Glasgow, unpublished PhD thesis, University of Manchester, 1979.
13 C. Ward, 'Tenants Take Over' (Architectural Press, 1974).
14 National Consumer Council, 'Tenancy Agreements' (NCC, 1976), Appendix 2.
15 Housing Services Advisory Group, 'Tenancy Agreements' (Department of the Environment, 1977), p. 2.
16 Damer examines the attitudes of tenants to other tenants in Moorepark.
17 Particularly, Central Housing Advisory Committee, 'Selection of Tenants' (HMSO, 1949); CHAC, 'Council Housing: Purposes, Procedures and Priorities'; and Scottish Housing Advisory Committee, 'Allocation and Transfer of Council Houses' (HMSO, 1980).
18 P. Niner, 'Local Authority Housing Policy and Practice', Occasional Paper no. 31 (Centre for Urban and Regional Studies, University of Birmingham, 1975).
19 J. English, Access and Deprivation in Local Authority Housing in C. Jones (ed.), 'Urban Deprivation and the Inner City' (Croom Helm, 1979).
20 E. Burney, 'Housing on Trial' (Oxford University Press, 1967), p. 71.
21 Macey and Baker, 'Housing Management', Ch. 23.
22 G. Popplestone and C. Paris, 'Managing Difficult Tenants', Centre for Environmental Studies, Research Series no. 30 (CES, 1979).
23 Ibid., p. 19.
24 Macey and Baker, 'Housing Management', p. 327.
25 National Consumer Council, 'Behind with the Rent' (NCC, 1976).
26 C. Wilkinson, 'Rent Arrears in Public Authority Housing in Scotland', Scottish Office Social Research Studies, Scottish Office Central Research Unit (HMSO, 1980).
27 P. Griffiths, 'Homes Fit for Heroes' (Shelter, 1975).
28 Benwell Community Project, 'Slums on the Drawing Board', Final Report Series no. 4 (BCP, 1978).
29 Ibid., p. 14.

30 National Consumer Council, 'Soonest Mended: a review of the repair, maintenance and improvement of council housing' (NCC, 1979).
31 Central Housing Advisory Committee, 'Management of Municipal Housing Estates'; CHAC, 'Councils and their Houses'; and Scottish Housing Advisory Committee, 'Housing Management in Scotland' (HMSO, 1967).
32 'Committee on Local Authority and Allied Personal Social Services' (Seebohm Report), Cmnd 3703 (HMSO, 1968), p. 124; and 'The Comprehensive Housing Service: Organisation and Functions' (Institute of Housing, 1972).
33 Committee on the Management of Local Government, 'Report on the Management of Local Government' (Maud Report) (HMSO, 1967); Study Group on Local Authority Management Structures, 'The New Local Authorities Management and Structure' (Bains Report) (HMSO, 1972); and Scottish Development Department, 'The New Scottish Local Authorities: Organisation and Management Structure' (Paterson Report) (HMSO, 1973).
34 Housing Services Advisory Group, 'Organising a Comprehensive Housing Service' (Department of the Environment, 1978).
35 Education and Training for Housing Work Project, 'Housing Training' (The City University, 1977).
36 Housing Services Advisory Group, 'Training for Housing Work: A Consultative Document' (Department of the Environment, undated).
37 C. Legg, M. Brion and M. Bieber, Time for a Great Leap Forward, 'Roof' (May 1978).
38 M. Harloe, R. Issacharoff and R. Minns, 'The Organisation of Housing: Public and Private Enterprise in London' (Heinemann, 1974).
39 Quoted in D. Fox, 'Housing Aid and Advice' (Department of the Environment, 1973).
40 See C. Cockburn, 'The Local State: Management of Cities and People' (Pluto Press, 1977).
41 Harloe, Issacharoff and Minns, 'The Organisation of Housing', p. 172.
42 Department of the Environment, Housing Development Directorate, 'Priority Estates Project: up-grading problem council estates' (DOE, 1980), p. 13.
43 Ibid., p. 12.
44 National Consumer Council, 'Housing Management: A Tenants' Charter' (NCC, undated), p. 15.
45 Department of the Environment, Housing Development Directorate, 'Tenant Participation in Council Housing Management', HDD Occasional Paper 2/77 (DOE, 1977).
46 For a discussion of the use of these resources see P. Gallagher, The Objectives of Training, 'Municipal Journal' (6 June 1980).
47 V. Karn, The Newest Profession, 'Roof' (November 1977).
48 J. Darke and R. Darke, 'Who Needs Housing?' (Macmillan, 1979), p. 120.

49 J. M. Simmie, 'Citizens in Conflict: The Sociology of Town Planning' (Hutchinson, 1978), p. 127.
50 National Consumer Council, 'Housing Management', p. 14.
51 P. Gallagher, Management Responses: First Catch Your Staff, 'Roof' (September 1978).
52 The Housing Training Project, 'Developing Training for Housing Work in Multi-Racial Areas' (The City University, 1980).
53 P. Gallagher, Report on Training Course for Counter Staff from Nottingham City Council Housing Department, unpublished paper, 1980.
54 W. R. Rees-Davies, MP, quoted by A. Arden in Homelessness: A New Criminal Offence, 'New Law Journal' (24 November 1977).
55 N. Finnis, The Heartless and the Homeless, 'Roof' (September 1978), p. 138.
56 Housing Development Directorate, 'Priority Estates Project', p. 12.
57 CHAC, 'Council Housing: Purposes, Procedures and Priorities'; and SHAC, 'Allocation and Transfer of Council Houses'.
58 Department of the Environment, 'Legislation on Housing: Tenants' Charter Provisions – Consultative Paper' (DOE, 1979).
59 Series of seminars on the Tenants' Rights, Etc. (Scotland) Act, 1980, held by the Institute of Housing, Autumn 1980; and Housing Centre Trust seminar on Management Implications of the Housing Act, 1980, December 1980.
60 The Chartered Institute of Public Finance and Accountancy, 'Housing Bill Consultative Papers: The Institute's Observations' (CIPFA, 1979).
61 J. B. Cullingworth, 'Essays on Housing Policy: The British Scene' (Allen & Unwin, 1979), p. 166.
62 R. A. Pinker, 'Social Theory and Social Policy' (Heinemann, 1971), p. 201.

7   Private Housing at All Costs: Some Lessons from America

Valerie Karn

The aim of this chapter is to highlight the advantages of the British and continental European systems of socially owned and managed rental housing by examining an alternative approach to housing policy, namely the manipulation of the private market to try to induce it to meet the needs of lower-income households. This is the method upon which housing policy in the USA essentially relies. The US Housing Act, 1949, expressly declared as a statement of policy that 'private enterprise shall be encouraged to serve as large a part of the total need [for housing] as it can'.[1] The chapter explores parts of this partnership between government and private industry, and shows that while it serves private interests well, it imposes heavy social and economic costs on lower-income households.

THE AMERICAN APPROACH TO SOCIAL POLICY

In the political climate of the USA the boundaries of what are considered acceptable policy approaches are very different from those in Britain or in, say, Sweden, the Netherlands or Germany. In essence most Americans are more wary of too much government than of too little government. The fear of loss of freedom is a very real one in a country which shook off an exploitive colonial government, to which so many immigrants fled from oppressive governments and in which the individual effort of pioneers opened up the continent to settlers. So valued is freedom that if it clashes with any other objective of social policy, notably equality, then that other objective has to be dispensed with.

This concept of freedom, often used interchangeably with individualism, is very much one of freedom from outside, particularly government, intervention in a family's private affairs, and is close to the approach of the present Conservative government in Britain. The notion that freedom is something that government can actively promote by creating greater economic opportunity for poorer people is not one that is commonly considered in the USA.

However, in practice, American social policy falls far short of the non-interventionist, liberal ideal, because in a democratic state of great affluence people expect to share in material benefits. Only government measures can enforce any degree of redistribution or ensure that people do not fall below a minimum living standard. Nevertheless, the liberal philosophy pervades the style of intervention, in that it is a style designed to minimise the

154

problems said to be associated with substantial government activity, namely that it undermines incentives, is wasteful of resources, promotes economic inefficiency and obliterates individual freedom. Fear of these harmful effects has a number of impacts on the style of policy adopted. First, policies are designed so that, preferably, people do not have their work incentive undermined by coming to expect benefits as of right, but may have them as a safety net if their own efforts fail. Second, to prevent waste of resources, social benefits should be as small as possible, highly selective and tightly targeted to only the most needy groups or areas. Where possible, smaller amounts of government help should be used to stimulate larger amounts of private sector activity (commonly called 'leveraging'). Third, to avoid economic inefficiency, public ownership should be avoided and instead use should be made of private institutions to supply and manage services, even if these have to be subsidised. It is felt that economic efficiency will be better ensured through the profit motive, even if that profit is artificially created and sustained. It is also axiomatic that public programmes should not compete with the private market. Fourth, individual freedom should be protected by minimising government activity, maximising choice in the marketplace and giving legal safeguards to the public.

THE AMERICAN APPROACH TO HOUSING POLICY

The market approach to housing policy has been much more evident than in other areas where the service to be provided is not a physically defined commodity, for instance education or income maintenance. The approach to housing is more similar to that towards health care, where provision is made by the private sector but government helps to reduce costs to the consumer. In housing, though, government help is more limited, because there is no housing programme of anything like the same scale or coverage as Medicare and Medicaid. But, as in all areas of policy, there has not been a static approach to housing policy. There have been two periods of more active central government intervention in housing and other areas of social policy; these were the depression, when house-building and mortgage insurance were used to stabilise the economy, and the late 1960s, when concern about inner cities and racial conflict led to increased federal activity. Outside these two periods the approach has been much more market-oriented. Even during these periods the emphasis was still on government stimulus of the private sector rather than on direct government activity, but, as we will see, it was during these periods that public housing received its greatest encouragement.

The experience of the private sector, as much in the USA as in Britain, is that profits cannot be made from housing low-income people in good accommodation unless governments provide some sort of subsidy or tax incentive, so that landlords or builders can make a profit out of what is really a loss-making enterprise.

In Britain the method adopted has been to let builders make
profits out of construction of property for poor people but to
leave the distribution of that housing to the public sector, using
subsidies to absorb the difference between the capital and running costs on the one hand and the tenant's ability to pay on the
other. The USA has instead used financial incentives to try to
persuade the private sector to undertake both the supply and
distribution of housing, inviting landlords, developers and investors to provide housing for low-income people to rent or, less
commonly, to buy.

This is the general picture, but not the total one for, while the
private sector has taken the lion's share of government funds,
there has been some limited-profit and non-profit rental housing
and some public housing. Public housing has been largely of two
types: first, conventional purpose-built public housing and,
second, private properties leased to the public housing agencies
on scattered sites. Essentially, however, the American philosophy
on the role of government in social policy has been incompatible
with the effective development of public housing. Since this philosophy is very similar to that of the Thatcher government, it is
illuminating to see precisely how and why the development of
public housing has been undermined in the USA, and what the
impact has been on tenants and potential tenants. In Britain
efforts are being made to reduce in size a large public sector,
whereas in the USA there is long-standing opposition to the build-
up of more than a very small one. But the differences are a matter
of degree rather than kind, and the lessons are not less valid
because problems occur in more extreme form in the USA than
would be likely to happen in the short term in Britain, even with
a single-minded pursuit of market principles in housing policy.
But the American experience provides a salutary warning of what
could happen in the longer term.

AMERICAN PUBLIC HOUSING

Public housing in the USA started with the Housing Act, 1937. It
was introduced in the depression to stimulate the building industry
when the private sector was in disarray. It began, as did British
council housing, with a rather up-market working-class image.
There was careful screening of applicants and emphasis on housing those in work or, a very American concept, the 'temporarily
poor'. This image was reinforced during and after the war when
servicemen's families, war-industry workers and those hit by the
post-war housing shortage moved into public housing. But despite its apparent respectability public housing was not provided
on any scale. It was always kept very short of funds, which
reflected the fact that 'too many in Congress viewed the program
with suspicion and even hostility. Public housing never arrived
politically. Its very existence was an annual political cliffhanger.'[12]
When public housing started, the question was even raised as to

whether it was unconstitutional. It was regarded by the public as a 'kind of socialist conspiracy'. [3]

After the war the position became even worse. During the Eisenhower presidency, public housing was lucky to be allowed to build 25,000 units a year. In some years it was given no money at all. It has become irrelevant to the style of housing strategy being adopted. The Housing Act, 1949, enshrined this new approach, in the same way that in Britain the Housing Act, 1980, enshrines the Conservative government's new approach (Chapter 2). First, measures were introduced to liberalise insured lending for home ownership and thus encourage financial institutions to lend more readily to workers who wanted to purchase their homes. Second, new insured and subsidised loan programmes were introduced for private landlords. Third, measures were introduced to ensure that public housing should not compete with privately rented housing. Tight income limits were set on eligibility so that the level of rents and incomes at which public housing operated was at least 20 per cent below the lowest level at which a substantial supply of private subsidised housing was available in the area. At the time these limits were imposed, Senator Allen Ellander prophesied correctly that public housing would become a 'poorhouse' in many cities. Fourth, large slum clearance programmes were initiated but, in contrast with Britain, no equally massive public housing construction accompanied them. Essentially the private sector was supposed to provide for the majority while the public sector acted as a safety net. In fact, the public sector was overwhelmed with demands for rehousing. Fifth, because public housing was to be kept only for the really poor, it was felt that housing could be of only a very basic standard. Fears were voiced that 'penthouses for the poor' would be built. So housing was sanitary, but rudimentary, in quality. 'Luxuries' such as lavatory seats and cupboard doors were omitted. There was also increasing public hostility to the location of public housing near to other residential properties, particularly owner-occupied property. Because of these attitudes and the desire to reduce costs, public housing was increasingly constructed as high-rise apartment blocks, whereas in the inter-war period there had been considerable building of terraced housing.

The impact on public housing of all these measures was rapid and acute. Better-off tenants were required to move out, leaving behind women on their own with children, the unemployed and the old and sick. Increasingly the poor in the Northern cities were black, as were many of the families dispersed in slum clearance programmes. So public housing began to be more and more black and segregated. Subsidies and rent-paying ability, already low, fell further so that it became impossible to meet management costs. Public housing, in larger cities particularly, plunged into worse and worse difficulties of racial segregation, deteriorating environment, crime and insolvency.

Ironically, as is happening now in British council housing, while the housing service was deteriorating the rents needed to meet costs were rising. With no rent rebates this created growing hardship for poorer households. So the Housing Act, 1969, and subsequent amendments, introduced a new arrangement under which tenants should pay no more than 25 per cent of their incomes in rent. This reform was to be accompanied by increased subsidies but, because of political opposition in Congress and a retreat from the more interventionist governmental style of the late 1960s, these largely failed to materialise. The result was increased financial crisis in many public housing agencies. This pattern of pressure on rents created by the concentration of poorer and poorer tenants in public housing has also been experienced in Australia where sales of public housing have so reduced the public sector stock that a very large proportion of tenants have to receive rent rebates.[4] In far less extreme form, council housing in Britain is experiencing the same trend as increases in rents are reflected in increases in rebates and supplementary benefit rent payments to the growing proportion of non-earning tenants.

At the time that these new rents and subsidies were introduced in the USA, an attempt was also made to tackle the problem of resistance to the construction of new estates and the ghettoisation and stigmatisation of estates. A programme was introduced under which public housing agencies could lease privately rented properties and pay rent assistance. This programme was relatively successful but in 1973 Nixon put a moratorium on all housing programmes. Since then there has been little public sector building except for the elderly and no leased housing. Public housing still accounts for only 1.5 per cent of the total US housing stock.

So, because of the decision not to allow public housing to compete with private landlords, it was designed to be given only to the very poorest. As a result it has become stigmatised, segregated and difficult to manage. Because it has such poor tenants, it needs large subsidies but has received only meagre ones. This has led to insolvency, deterioration of maintenance and management, and a tendency to avoid the worst management problems by moving towards housing the elderly rather than families. Apart from its use for the elderly, public housing now has almost no political support because it has such a bad image. Even the low-income housing lobby has switched its allegiance to housing allowances or subsidised owner occupation. Yet public housing has not been nearly as unsuccessful as it is painted, especially considering the odds against which it has struggled and the fact that, alone of all the US housing programmes, it has been housing the poorest. In New York, public housing stands out as islands of stable, occupied and well-maintained housing in a sea of private sector abandonment. In small towns there is much good low-rise development. There are some appalling estates in most cities. But is public housing in the USA, in general, worse than the worst 4 per cent of council housing in Britain, with which it should be compared? Apart from the crime rate, which in America is not unique to public housing, the answer is that it is not.

Given that the public rental sector was maimed if not stifled at
birth, it could be argued that in the American context there was
no need for such a tenure at all but that the stated goal of 'a
decent home in a suitable living environment for all Americans'
could be and was being achieved through the use of the private
sector.[5] To consider this proposition the American approach to
private sector provision will now be examined.

THE PRIVATE SECTOR

In the USA, as in Britain, lower-income households, apart from
the elderly, tend to rent rather than own their homes. In rural
areas the widespread ownership of shacks and mobile homes by
low-income families modifies this picture. The tenure pattern in
urban areas, where in 1977 only a third of those with incomes
below $4,000 owned their homes, is not very different from that
in Britain. Home ownership has been regarded as the ideal tenure
and much emphasis has been placed on stimulating demand for it.
Nevertheless, policies specifically for the poor in the USA have
been aimed at improving the supply of private rental housing,
rather than helping more lower-income families to buy. There are
some exceptions to this, which are of particular interest and which
will be examined later. However, we need first to consider the
state of the private rental sector, to see whether private landlords in the USA really do provide a good, stable supply of housing that the poor can afford, something their brothers in Europe
have signally failed to do.

The Private Rental Sector

Traditionally, American housing subsidies have been linked
to the construction of new units. Builders or contractors
have undertaken to build new units or rehabilitate existing
units substantially with the assurance that the federal government would provide sufficient subsidies in addition to the
rents the low income occupants could afford to assure the
builder or developer a fair rate of return.[6]

The means by which these subsidies have been paid have varied,
but the most common in the past were reduced interest loans for
developers, provided both by the federal and state governments.
The current major form of rental subsidy, 'Section 8', introduced
in the Housing Act, 1974, represents a departure from previous
patterns in that it subsidises consumption. Under Section 8, payments are made to landlords to meet the difference between market
rents and the rents paid by tenants. The latter are fixed at 25
per cent of tenants' incomes (recently raised to 30 per cent).
However, Section 8 is not a general entitlement programme. It is
still tied to supply by being used basically for new or substantially
rehabilitated projects, with only a limited amount of existing rental

property being subsidised. Because of the financial problems of tenants and landlords, there is pressure to increase the programme for existing dwellings. A compromise has been introduced, namely the introduction of a programme for modestly, rather than extensively, rehabilitated property.

In addition to these special subsidy programmes, landlords of all types of rental developments qualify for income tax shelters and depreciation allowances. In many cities, notably New York, there have also been special schemes which fully or partially exempt projects from property taxes. Many of these have been for middle-income rental property. Finally, in addition to subsidies, the federal government gives 100 per cent mortgage insurance to encourage lending to developers of both subsidised and unsubsidised developments.

So on the private rental side there is a range of types of inducements to developers and landlords to supply housing for low- or middle-income tenants. These range from insured loans and tax relief, through reduced interest loans, to Section 8 subsidy. However, there is no general entitlement housing or rent allowance programme. The result is that only a small proportion of tenants receive any subsidy at all. The greatest problem of the private rental sector is the very high rents being borne by lower-income tenants, combined with the rising costs faced by landlords.

In the period 1967 to 1977, the costs of maintenance and repairs for rental housing rose 100 per cent, and the cost of fuel oil and coal rose 151 per cent (Table 7.1).

Table 7.1: Increase in Operating Costs of Multi-family[a] Housing in the USA, 1967-77

	%
Housing maintenance and repairs:	100
Fuel oil and ~~repairs~~ coal	151
Electricity	78
Property taxes	67
Water and sewage charges	89
Increase in rents	45
Increase in cost of living	71

Note: a. Multi-family housing is rental housing containing more than 4 units which constitutes about 39 per cent of the US rental housing inventory.
Source: US Department of Labor, Bureau of Labor Statistics, The Consumer and Wholesale Price Index, Annual Averages and Changes, 1953-1976, 'Monthly Labor Review' (December 1977).

In the same period, landlords were able to raise their rents by only 45 per cent compared with the 71 per cent increase in the overall cost of living. The reason for this is that private landlords are increasingly finding that tenants cannot meet the rents if they are raised. Cities, too, have reacted to protect tenants

against increases by imposing rent control. In mid-1976 there
were 230 communities, containing about 14 per cent of the urban
population of the USA, which operated rent controls and the
number has grown since.[7] The fact is that many tenants are
already paying very large proportions of their income on rent. In
1975, 26 per cent of all tenants paid more than 35 per cent of
their income in rent.[8] The problem of a high rent-to-income ratio
is worst for the poorest tenants; nearly 30 per cent of Hispanic
and black tenants paid more than 35 per cent of their income in
rent. So did almost 40 per cent of all unsubsidised black central-
city renters, including 22 per cent who were spending more than
half.[9]

These trends have produced what Downs calls a 'double squeeze'
on the rental sector,[10] in that it is caught between increasing
costs and tenants' inability to pay more. Even the projects included in the subsidy programmes have not escaped the problem.
Many projects have foundered because the size and type of subsidies failed to deal with the rising costs facing landlords. The
initial reduction in interest on loans was not sufficient to offset
these and, until Section 8 was introduced, no provision for further subsidy was made.

So just as the solvency of public housing has been hit by the
inability of poor tenants to meet operating costs, private landlords are meeting the same problem. At the same time that they
are experiencing rising costs, they are losing their better-off
tenants to owner occupation. Inflation has been making owner
occupation more attractive because houses have appreciated in
value while mortgage payments on old debts have fallen in relation
to incomes. In the past, most mortgages in the USA have been at
fixed interest rates, so the advantages of inflation for existing
owners have been even more marked than in Britain. These advantages of rising values have been increased by the tax arrangements, which, again as in Britain, have given tax relief on interest payments and effectively waived capital gains tax. (There is
capital gains tax for those under the age of 55 in the USA but
only if the seller fails to repurchase a house or buys a cheaper
one. Both actions are naturally avoided.)

So landlords, even those affluent enough to benefit from tax
shelters, find themselves offering a less and less popular product,
at lower and lower profit. One effect has been that new investment in rental housing has fallen. In 1980 some 80 per cent of new
rental housing was built under Section 8 subsidies (though this
is more a reflection on the small size of the building programme
than the large scale of Section 8).[11] In addition to falling new
investment, the value of existing rental property has dropped.
'Multifamily values, which have been declining since the nineteen
sixties, reflect the markets' increasingly dismal evaluation of the
long-term earnings prospects of this class of properties.'[12] In
New York, although in 1960 multi-family properties were being
traded at six times their current rent rolls, in 1975 the gross
multipliers were as low as one or two. 'In money terms average

sales prices of New York City elevator buildings fell by close to 20 per cent from the latter half of the sixties to the first half of the 1970s. In real terms, prices have fallen by 65 per cent.'[13]

With an asset that is falling in value, costs that are rising and rents that are fixed or rising only slowly, the natural reaction of the landlord is to withdraw investment. At the top end of the market, the most common strategy adopted by landlords has been to sell the property for conversion into a 'condominium', that is effectively owner occupation. This has met the demand of many tenants to share in the financial gains from home ownership and has relieved the landlord of an increasingly unprofitable investment. However, these condominium conversions have fallen hard on lower-income tenants, who have found their outgoings greatly increased or who have had to move out because they cannot afford to buy their apartment. Because of these problems, states and cities and the federal government have acted to control conversions and protect sitting tenants. When condominium conversion has not been possible, many landlords have resorted to passing more and more of the costs of management on to the tenants, leaving them to meet utility costs, service charges and so on.

At the bottom end of the market the position is very much worse. As the value of stock and profits fall, so property tends to come into the ownership of a more marginal class of investor. These investors tend not to have the skills or resources necessary for adequate management of multi-family rental property even when the financial climate is good. On one side are non-profit groups stepping in to try to preserve homes and the community, but they lack expertise and resources, and tend to experience even higher rates of foreclosure than the private landlords. On the other hand many private landlords merely come in to 'milk' the property of any rent revenue they can for the minimum of expenditure. But even good, long-standing landlords find that the only strategy available to them apart from selling to these marginal investors is to make economies in the quality of maintenance and management.

> When landlords begin to recognise that they cannot profit-
> ably manage their buildings, they defer or eliminate routine
> maintenance, do not replace failing systems, cut corners on
> providing heat and hot water, and fail to pay mortgage
> charges, taxes and city water and sewer charges. The
> result is that the quality of housing diminishes rapidly.
> Tenants, realizing that services are not being provided,
> may withhold rent payments, or pool their funds to make
> their own repairs and purchase their own fuel and utilities
> or they may simply move out.[14]

In the case of foreclosures, those properties for which the Department of Housing and Urban Development (HUD) has insured the mortgage pass to the department, which has to pay off the investor's insurance and then decide whether to try to sell the property or to take over the mortgage (accept assignment) and continue to service it as a 'Secretary-held mortgage'. In 1978, nationally, HUD owned 2,280 repossessed or assigned rental projects, containing about 245,000 rental units;[15] of these 10,000 were in Detroit alone. In all, between 15 per cent and 24 per cent of rental properties insured by HUD under a variety of programmes have suffered foreclosure or assignment.

The other type of recipient of failing rental property is the city government which receives it as a result of tax arrears. In 1979, New York City repossessed 4,100 buildings as a result of tax delinquency. These, though often partially or totally vacant, still housed 35,000 tenants, about 2 per cent of all tenants in New York. The occupied and vacant units represented 5 per cent of all rental units. In addition there were 45,000 buildings, containing 550,000 tenants, on which no taxes had been paid for at least three quarters (repossession is permitted after one year's tax arrears). 'Taken together, properties currently In Rem [repossessed for tax arrears] and those at risk... represent 8.4 per cent of the total number of properties in the city and 20.9 per cent of the total rental units.'[16] The blight affects certain areas more heavily than others. In 1979 in eight community districts 61 per cent or more of the total units were either already repossessed or at risk. In one area of the Bronx the figure was 95 per cent.

The main cause of abandonment is population decline in the inner areas of the Northern and North Eastern cities, but, contrary to the views of those who regard it as successful 'filtering', the process is not a tidy withdrawal from the worst areas leaving them available for redevelopment. Though the lowest-quality housing is the worst affected, surrounding areas also suffer. Typically one area will be 70 per cent abandoned, another 30 per cent and another 10 per cent. Good housing is affected as well as bad. Abandoned property affects the value of surrounding property, however good, and then this enters the process of disinvestment already described. In this way much good property as well as bad is abandoned, vandalised and demolished. (80 per cent of units abandoned in New York City during 1968 were in buildings classified only three years earlier as sound, or deteriorating but not dilapidated.[17])

Dramatic and visible though the collapse of the rental market is in New York, Detroit, St Louis and the other North Eastern cities, it is arguable that the plight of the low-income renter is as bad, if not worse, in the areas of tight demand and high prices, where landlord disinvestment takes a different form. In California, and other high-demand areas such as Washington DC, the problem is of erosion of the rental stock through condominium conversions (and the purchase of single-family rental housing for home ownership), and of high rents and restrictions on lettings to families with children. Indeed, the New York market is more complex in that it combines in different parts of the city the symptoms of high demand (South Manhattan) and of abandonment (North Manhattan, South Bronx and Brooklyn).

Gentrification, or as it is called in the USA 'displacement', is another problem, added to those of scarce accommodation and high rents, which lower-income people face in the high-demand areas. This phenomenon is particularly noticeable in city-centre areas which are becoming popular again with the white middle classes. Without publicly or socially owned rental housing there is no protection for poorer tenants when better-off families start to compete. Many communities see special help for low-income home ownership as a defence against displacement, since owners enjoy security of tenure. But, of course, the process of displacing poorer families is only postponed until occupants leave or die. Only some form of non-market, non-profit rental can permanently prevent gentrification.

Both the high- and low-demand market situations therefore illustrate the failure of private rental housing in providing for lower- or even moderate-income families. This failure has been all too familiar in Europe but its wholesale appearance in the USA has been postponed by a generous system of tax incentives, historically low building costs, the relative youth of the rental stock compared with Europe, and lack of competition from publicly owned and subsidised housing. However, now the effects of an ageing stock, inflation, rising land and building costs, and the competition of owner occupation have brought rental housing to a crisis. The symptoms can be summarised as follows:

(1) A failure to build new rental housing without subsidy and hence an ageing rental stock.

(2) Economic rents outpricing those needing rental housing.

(3) The failure of landlords at the bottom end of the market to maintain and manage their properties satisfactorily.

(4) Even at middle-income levels, the unwillingness of landlords to let to the type of households which involve higher management costs (notably those with children).

(5) The conversion of much rental housing to home ownership and generally disinvestment by landlords and investors.

(6) A net decline in the number of low-rent units available.

(7) The growing introduction of rent control which, while it has the immediate effect of retaining a scarce stock of private rental housing within the range of lower-income families, in the longer term adds one more disincentive for private landlords.

At present, Section 8 subsidies are the federal government's only policy measure designed to tackle the problems of the private rental sector. Because it is based on market rents, which are allowed to rise, the subsidy formula, unlike earlier ones, can take into account landlords' rising costs. However, as a solution it has considerable defects. First, though a relatively large programme by American standards, and with a large coverage of new rental production, it covers only a very small part of the existing rental stock which is where most of the problem arises. Second, Section 8 subsidy is expensive per unit of stock subsidised. The subsidy arrangements are that tenants should pay not more than 30 per cent of their income in rent. The difference between this and the

market price is paid direct to the landlord by the federal government. The high cost of the project arises largely because of the
use of 'market rents' which, by definition, tend to be high and
rising. This contrasts with European housing allowance programmes, which are all subject to some type of non-market rent
formula, and where in some cases, such as Sweden, rents are led
by the public rather than by the private sector. In addition, for
new and substantially rehabilitated projects, 'market rent' equates
with the cost of loan repayments on capital costs, plus normal
rates of profit. This means that there is every incentive to make
the project an expensive one, within the limits set for the programme. Moreover, in all three parts of the programme (new construction, rehabilitation and existing housing) there have been
problems of collusion between landlords, tenants and officials
over the income levels declared and the rents agreed. The very
formula upon which the programme is based leads to collusion and
to expense, because it relates only to income and therefore gives
tenants no incentive to bargain about rents.

In all, Section 8 is a far more expensive programme per unit of
housing provided than is public housing. It will remain so because,
whereas public housing is owned by government agencies, in the
private sector all the advantage of historic costs accrues to the
landlord, not the tenant or the state.

But this brings us to another problem about Section 8. The
property is not only built largely by private developers; it is
allocated and managed by private landlords and managing agents.
These landlords naturally want to maximise profits by receiving
all the financial guarantees but at the same time minimising their
management costs and problems. As a result landlords have
remained unwilling to provide Section 8 rental housing for families
with children, particularly large families. They have preferred to
build for the elderly who present fewer management problems and
cause less wear and tear on the property. In addition, typically,
landlords have selected the most 'respectable' poor, and have
required bank references and security deposits from incoming
tenants. This reaction has very much harmed the ability of government to target Section 8 to the most needy groups. Also conventional public housing has been harmed yet again because it has
been left to house the people who cannot obtain Section 8 allocations. The attraction of Section 8 developments vis-à-vis public
housing is all the greater because, while public housing standards
are deliberately kept very basic, in Section 8 the combination of
the subsidy and rent formulae has encouraged high standards.
The rent formulae for the two types of housing are, however, the
same (30 per cent of income), so there is no saving for a tenant
by staying on in the inferior surroundings of public housing.

Not only do developers of subsidised rental housing try to let
it to the same sorts of tenants as those to whom they would have
let unsubsidised housing, but under previous low-interest loan
programmes there has been a marked tendency for landlords in
buoyant rental markets to withdraw from the scheme as soon as

permitted, having already benefited, of course, from the supply
subsidy. Under Section 8 there is less incentive to do this because
the subsidy is paid continuously. But in high-rent areas there
will still be this tendency, encouraged by the high standards to
which many of the projects have been built. To stop too rapid a
draining away of subsidised stock in the areas where it is most
needed, the Section 8 rules have been changed to increase the
minimum participation period from five to twenty years.

In effect the selection procedures adopted by Section 8 developers bring the programme close to the sort of activity which
landlords would have carried out without the subsidies, though it
is questionable whether they would have built anything at all without it. The justification is then that it is better to get any new
rental housing, even if it is not for those in most urgent need,
than none at all. Another argument, strongly put, is that new
housing should not be built for the poorest, but that they should
be housed through the filtering down of second-hand property.
But, as the National Commission on Urban Problems has said,
filtering 'falls short of supplying enough housing for low income
families, principally because: (1) the availability of the lowest
cost housing is not always where the poor can get to it, and because (2) so much of the cheapest available housing is substand-
ard.'[18] Or as Anthony Downs, a member of the Commission, more
forcefully put it, 'for the poor it is a disaster'.[19]

From this discussion of the private rental sector, we have identified a number of problems associated with the use of private
landlords to house poorer families.

First, only if developers, landlords and lenders can make a
profit will they either provide new housing or continue to manage
and finance the existing stock of houses. The fact that a landlord
can no longer make a profit on letting a property may have no
relationship to the need of tenants to continue living there. Similarly, the reluctance of developers to build new rental housing
for families does not mean that there are not families in the area
needing rental housing.

Second, to maximise their profits, developers and landlords
often pocket the incentives but try to minimise the risks or costs
by deflecting the programme from its stated aim or target group.
Provision of so much Section 8 housing for the elderly is the
classic example.

Third, the types of agency involved in the management of property have not always been suited to the needs of poorer families
or sympathetic to them. Government has concentrated on stimulating the production of housing but has neglected its continuing
management and financing; in other words the whole consumption
side of housing.

Fourth, in areas of high demand, lower-income households find
it difficult if not impossible to compete for decent housing, even
with subsidies. Moreover, in such areas particularly, there is no
guarantee that rental housing produced under a particular subsidy arrangement will remain available to the poor once the period
of control has expired.

Fifth, at the other extreme, when demand is very slack and depends on lower-income households, the result has been severe dislocation of the local housing market because rents have had to fall to enable poorer families to afford them. Falling rents mean falling values which in turn mean reluctant and worried lenders and owners. In extreme cases, for landlords to continue meeting mortgage repayments and taxes becomes a matter of sending good money after bad. Tax and mortgage arrears increasingly lead to foreclosure and abandoned property because sales will not cover the outstanding debt. The effect is contagious, so that whole areas of cities become much more blighted than loss of population alone would have produced had the property been publicly owned. Moreover, the blight reinforces the exodus of population.

Sixth, in both high-demand and slack markets, landlords are faced with high and rising costs of repairs, maintenance and utilities. Current subsidies to existing rental housing, except for the very limited Section 8 programme, fail to cover the costs of repairs and maintenance. This is causing landlords to disinvest by, in low-demand areas, neglecting the property, failing to meet taxes and mortgage repayments, and finally abandoning it. In high-demand areas they disinvest by selling flat blocks for conversion to owner occupation.

Seventh, the devices used to stimulate private rental activity tend to be very expensive per unit because of the need to provide what the private sector considers adequate return for engaging in troublesome activities. As a result rents will remain high and so will the subsidies. In contrast, in the public sector loan repayments on many projects are now nearly complete, so that rents and subsidies have to cover little more than the cost of management and maintenance.

There are other general points which could have been raised, but we will delay discussion of these until the end of the next section, which considers American government policies towards the low-income home owner.

Policies for Lower-income Home Owners
Though more low-income households in the USA own their homes· than they do in Britain, this is not the result of more generous subsidy arrangements in the USA for low-income owners. Subsidy to home owners there, as in Britain, is essentially through tax relief and this gives least help to the poorest. The high rate of lower-income ownership is explained partly by rural ownership and lower land and construction costs, and partly by a generally higher standard of living and larger per capita expenditure on housing. However, the government has encouraged lower-income ownership through guaranteeing loans, as it does for landlords. In addition, between 1968 and 1972 HUD operated a highly subsidised programme (Section 235) for lower-income buyers in inner cities. (Section 221d(2) and Section 223e). The Department of Agriculture also has a subsidised loan programme for house purchase in rural areas, the Farmers' Homes programme. An exam-

ination of the guarantee schemes, when used for lower-income
households, and the subsidised loan programmes provides some
interesting insights into the difficulties of using owner occupation
as a mechanism through which to house the poor.

In 1934 the Federal Housing Administration (FHA) was founded
to stimulate the flow of private capital into long-term loans for
house purchase and construction. Up until then most loans had
been very short-term 'balloon' mortgages, which had created high
rates of repossession during the depression. FHA changed this
by granting 100 per cent insurance on long-term loans. This was
coupled with the creation of another government agency, the
Federal National Mortgage Association (FNMA), which could buy
loans on the secondary mortgage market. Unlike public housing,
this programme took off on a vast scale. Between 1934 and 1974
FHA insured eleven million mortgages for the purchase or construction of owner-occupied homes and over two million for rental
homes. Until about 1950 it insured between a quarter and a third
of all new construction, substantially financing the building of
the suburbs created in that period. However, from 1950 its role
for owner occupiers declined, essentially because it was no longer
needed. Savings and loan associations and commercial banks had
moved into giving long-term loans, in conjunction with private
mortgage insurance firms. Ordinary buyers therefore had little
need of FHA, while those prospective buyers who needed extra
financial help, because of low incomes, found no assistance, because there was no subsidised loan programme. In 1961, FHA
introduced a very small subsidised loan programme for lower-
income buyers, but it was not until the late 1960s that it really
changed direction towards helping lower-income buyers.

In 1968, during a period of more active government presence in
social policy and after the riots in many American cities, the US
government decided that the extension of home ownership to
larger numbers of inner-city blacks would create a greater sense
of personal investment in neighbourhoods and hence reduce the
likelihood of renewed violence. To this end FHA was required,
partly through changing the operation of existing loan schemes
and partly through new legislation, to direct its attention towards
providing subsidies and guarantees for lending to lower-income
families, particularly in the inner city. Under the subsidised programme buyers were to pay 25 per cent of their income on the
mortgage or pay a 1 per cent interest rate, whichever was the
higher. The group of people who qualified for the subsidy were
somewhat better off than public housing tenants, or tenants of
subsidised rental properties, but they were considerably poorer
than the usual FHA buyers.

The unsubsidised schemes were aimed at helping lower-income
buyers by encouraging institutions to lend in previously 'redlined'
areas and by effectively eliminating the need to have cash for a
down-payment or for fees. To facilitate this, 100 per cent loans
were given covering all costs including fees. In other words, easy
loans were the order of the day, a far cry from FHA's traditional

conservative attitude to inner cities and particularly to black areas and black buyers (towards whom its policies had been openly discriminatory in the past).

The scheme immediately ran into difficulties. Whereas the savings and loan associations had been happy to take 100 per cent insurance when they had needed it to fund the expansion of the white suburbs, they were now largely uninterested in moving back into the black inner city, or in lending on lower-income suburban developments, even when the insurance arrangements seemed completely to safeguard them against loss. There were two main reasons for this. First, most had plenty of business in the white suburbs without bothering about troublesome lending elsewhere. Second, even those operating in the cities found the bureaucratic systems of the scheme irksome and the regulations inappropriate.

Who then was to lend if the conventional lenders would not? In Britain, local authority lending was extended to fill this gap. Although it proved unable to reach the very bottom of the owner-occupied market whilst retaining the safeguards of a conventional lender, it did have a 'social' approach to lending, in that in the competition for funds inner-city buyers were given preference. In the USA the decision went a different way. Direct lending could have been introduced along the lines of the very successful Farmers' Homes Loan Scheme of the Department of Agriculture. Instead, in urban areas what happened was that the programmes for lower-income buyers and inner cities were effectively taken over by a type of institution known as mortgage bankers. These mortgage bankers are really closer to being mortgage brokers than banks. They usually have little capital themselves. They operate by borrowing capital, lending mortgages out, assembling the mortgages into packages and then reselling these packages on the secondary mortgage market. They make their profit largely out of fees for initiating loans and out of the profit on selling mortgages to investors. When they have sold the mortgage, they usually continue to service it for a fee from the investor. The government insures the investor against loss of any of the capital lent and up to one year's arrears of interest payments. In other words, a government gives otherwise unsaleable mortgages an exchange value by translating them into a marketable commodity on which the mortgage banker can make a profit. In addition, government has set up its own secondary market investor, the Government National Mortgage Agency (GNMA), as successor to FNMA (it had become a private profit institution), which does not need to make a profit and can even write off losses as a matter of policy, in order to guarantee a market for these mortgages. They thus become a 'liquid' investment.

So the mechanism of providing mortgages to lower-income people has been to create an artificially supported market and hence to create the incentive for mortgage bankers to provide them. Has this been as successful a method of helping lower-income owners as it was of developing middle- and higher-income owner occupation between 1934 and 1960?

There is general agreement that the use of very easy lending and 100 per cent insurance, in conjunction with relying on mortgage bankers as the main lenders to lower-income first-time buyers in inner-city black areas, has proved catastrophic. The rates of foreclosure under the lower-income lending programmes were 20 per cent for the subsidised scheme and 24 per cent for the main unsubsidised schemes. This compares with only 4 per cent for the ordinary middle-income FHA insurance programme (section 203b) and for direct lending through the lower-income Farmers' Homes lending programme. [20] The chief causes of this extraordinary failure rate were the particular character of mortgage banks combined with the type of inducements government devised, the character of housing stock in inner cities, lack of preparation for setting up the programmes, lack of government control over what was happening, and a drive to increase the scale of lending at any cost. In this section we are concerned particularly with the characteristics of the mortgage bankers because they epitomise all the characteristics of private institutions which are harmful to the poor. The nature of the incentives offered under the programmes and the problems of control will be considered later.

On average, mortgage banks foreclose on a higher percentage of their serious default cases and tend to have higher overall foreclosure rates than other FHA insured lenders operating in the same locality. In 1970-5 the foreclosure rate on FHA loans for mortgage banks was twice that of banks, savings and loans or savings banks. [21] Some of this is explained by the safer type of lending done by savings and loans even with FHA insurance, but there is much more to it than that because not only do mortgage bankers have much higher average foreclosure rates but there is also extreme variability between one banker and another.

While higher foreclosure rates would be expected for the sort of lending being carried out under the new programmes, one all-important reason for the particularly high and variable foreclosure rates of mortgage bankers appears to be the poor quality of servicing. Most companies operate nationally and have few local field officers with responsibility for carrying out loan servicing as opposed to loan initiation. The tendency at all times is for servicing to rely heavily on computerisation and punishments, such as charges for late payment, which merely exacerbate the problem. There is little tolerance of arrears. What are called 'forebearance' arrangements, for instance interest only or additional monthly payments to reduce arrears, are not uniformly made.

Because the fees for servicing are modest, mortgage bankers have little incentive or staff resources to 'nurse' a difficult account along. Instead their tendency is to go for rapid foreclosure to cut their potential servicing losses. A controversial but common practice is the refusal of partial payments, reminiscent of the activities of London landlords in the Rachman era. With fixed mortgage interest rates, lenders have every incentive to foreclose loans, in order to lend out the money at a higher rate to someone

else. Although the last point would also apply to savings and
loan associations and banks, they tend to have a more socially
and locally responsible attitude to borrowers. A study in Philadelphia found that mortgage bankers were four times more likely
to foreclose on a mortgage if it once fell into arrears than were
savings and loans or commercial banks. [22]

The other apparent reason for high foreclosure rates under the
low-income insurance programmes was careless assessment of the
houses and the buyers. Much of the second-hand property bought
was overpriced, overvalued and in a poor state of repair. Much
of the newly constructed property was shoddily built on poor
sites considered unsuitable for better-off buyers. Many buyers
found themselves unable to meet the repair and heating bills and
property taxes, even if they could meet the repayments. But why
should lenders have been willing to lend in such a rash way and
to accept such high foreclosure rates?

The reason essentially is that the programme arrangements
allow mortgage bankers to make the overwhelming proportion of
their profits out of the origination of loans rather than their servicing. They charge fees for the origination of loans and this,
along with profits from sales of guaranteed mortgages to the
secondary mortgage market, is their main source of income. They
have an inbuilt incentive to make large numbers of loans as quickly
as possible, because that produces more origination fees and because they need to consolidate loans into large enough packages
to sell. Most mortgage bankers have too little capital to be able to
retain mortgages for long. It is often more important to make a
quick loan to complete a package for resale than to ensure that
the borrower is going to be able to keep up the repayments. This
tendency is strengthened because investors in FHA-insured loans
are not really concerned whether the loan is kept up. They are
100 per cent insured against any capital loss, and also against
one year's arrears of interest payments. Within limits, therefore,
investors are unlikely to be concerned about the quality of the
screening that mortgage bankers carry out on buyers and properties. It was this that led to the worst abuses of the scheme.

The picture is then that the creation of this risk-free artificial
market for mortgages to low-income, often inner-city and predominantly black buyers of overpriced, poor-quality houses, did
nothing to change the essentially risky nature of the activity. The
type and scale of incentives to mortgage bankers and other
dealers in the market encouraged massive production of what in
the real world remained a very dubious product. The scandals
associated with the programmes, which involved the arrest of
many HUD officials, coincided with Nixon's decision to have a
moratorium on housing programmes. Section 235(1) did not survive the moratorium. It reappeared but converted to a small programme for middle-income buyers. Sections 223e and 221d(2) were
reduced to a fraction of their former size and more conventional
assessments of risk were adopted. However, the 100 per cent
mortgage insurance was retained and so was the role of the

mortgage banks. It has been suggested that the most sensible move would have been to introduce 80 per cent insurance, more comparable with private (75 per cent) insurance, so that the mortgage bankers would have had to accept 20 per cent of all losses. But they would not or could not accept the 20 per cent liability. Because they do 80 per cent of HUD-insured lending, and there are such close relationships between HUD and mortgage bank staff, the change was rejected.

External regulation of mortgage bankers also remains weak. Only two states, Illinois and Florida, have regulatory legislation covering mortgage bankers, unless they are subsidiaries of commercial banks which are themselves regulated. The federal government in the form of HUD has a Review Board whose task is to discipline lenders. A study of its activities concluded, however, that it has 'more holes than net'. [23]

But even if substantial improvements were made in the statutory regulation of mortgage bankers, the structure of the housing and home finance industries is still likely to be particularly resistant to control. Mortgage bankers are only one set of agencies involved; there are also builders, speculators, brokers, real estate agents and other lenders.

> The industry remains heavily localized and fragmented. It is a potpourri of economic units - individual firms, subindustries - heterogeneously distributed in relatively isolated noncompetitive markets and submarkets. [24]

This means that both internal and external enforcement of standards of behaviour are very difficult to achieve. In low-income home ownership programmes this is of the utmost importance because so much of their actual running was handed over to private agencies.

> [T]he major responsibility for informing the public of the existence of the Section 235 program fell upon members of the real estate industry. Local Federal Housing Administration Insuring Offices did not advertise the 235 program nor did they seek out potential eligible buyers. Rather they informed participants in the real estate industry, brokers, builders and mortgage lenders of the terms of the program and waited for them to bring in applicants for 235 mortgages. [25]

Some brokers, particularly those who also speculate in residential property, saw the 235 programme as a golden opportunity to make money.

> A salesman for a St Louis broker, who as a speculator sold 21 per cent of the houses in the Commission's St Louis sample, told [The Civil Rights Commission] staff members that his firm mailed out about 12,000 post cards to potential 235 buyers after the program began. [26]

The lower-income buyers involved were extremely vulnerable to
such heavy sales tactics. 'Some brokers commented on how easy
it was to sell a house to a 235 buyer.'[27] As Silverman writes, 'As
compared with most unsubsidized consumers purchasing a similarly priced house, the 235 purchaser may be housing-poor,
"house-hungry" and particularly susceptible to...sales tactics.'[28]
They were also almost completely unprotected. As Representative
Widnall has said:

> While much attention has recently been focused on the area
> of consumer protection in the borrowing of money and the
> purchase of retail goods, little or no attention has been paid
> to the need for consumer protection in house buying... I
> think it is safe to say that few home buyers enter the housing
> market on an equal bargaining position with those selling the
> house, be it used or new.

In the US inner cities, speculators or brokers are almost invariably involved in sales, which makes this problem even worse than
in Britain.

> If the consumer's interest is in general absent from the home-
> buying field, it is particularly absent from the FHA-subsidised
> home buyer program... In most instances these buyers are
> people who have had no previous exposure to the phenomenon
> of home-ownership and all the problems and responsibilities
> that go with it... This program has injected into a complex
> market an extremely unsophisticated buyer and HUD owes a
> special duty to see that he is treated fairly.[29]

These comments might equally well be applied to many of the families buying deteriorated housing in Britain's inner cities. Policies
to encourage more poorer people to buy should at least be accompanied by greater measures of protection against loan sharks,
unregistered estate agents, bogus home-improvement firms, and
all the agencies whose social attitudes and practices have played
such a large part in creating racial segregation in the USA and
Britain.[30]

If we compare HUD's programmes with the Farmers' Homes programme, we are immediately struck by the totally different emphasis. Farmers' Homes has the same subsidies as Section 235(1)
but is a direct government loan scheme. It is a 'supervised credit'
system with a heavy emphasis on local office contact with buyers,
careful screening of applicants, credit counselling and trying to
help people remain home owners as well as to buy initially. The
effect of this has been low default rates and few scandals about
poor standard construction. Farmers' Homes has normally catered
for buyers with incomes below those of HUD's insured buyers.
But these incomes have to be seen in a rural context. More important, the income level of borrowers is drifting up from the lower-
to the middle-income bracket as the rising costs of construction,

repairs, maintenance and utilities make it increasingly difficult
for poorer people to meet the costs of owner occupation even with
a subsidy down to a 1 per cent interest rate on their mortgage.

Because of this cost problem, coupled with the acute difficulty
of providing rental housing in isolated areas, the Department of
Agriculture is trying to launch a 'Homeowner Assistance Programme' (HOAP). Under HOAP low-income families would pay only
15 per cent of gross income towards their total housing costs,
including principal and interest, property taxes, insurance,
utilities and maintenance. Farmers' Homes would meet the difference between the family's payments and total cost. So far the
programme has met too much political opposition to be funded
even in pilot form. Nor has anyone explained how the subsidy
would be operated or the costs of maintenance and so on assessed.
These are not trivial questions. What is involved is the feasibility
of a subsidy which could provide genuine home ownership for all.
The proposition is technically interesting but politically it is a
non-starter.

To sum up, Farmers' Homes and Section 235 present two sides
of the same coin. Easy lending to the poor (Section 235) on bad
properties with irresponsible lenders produces massive default.
Careful lending to the poor on good properties produces a tendency for lending to creep up-market as the costs of construction,
repairs and maintenance increase. If we recall, too, the problems
of the private rental sector, it is clear that the common factor is
that there are many people whose incomes are too low to meet the
costs of decent housing of whatever tenure; some cannot even
meet the costs of maintenance, taxes and heating alone. None of
the private sector subsidy arrangements fully caters for this
situation.

A number of lessons about housing policies for lower-income
households emerge from these examples of attempts to extend
home ownership. First, it is clear how much better suited has
been a socially-oriented government agency to low-income lending
than private agencies. This is not because all private agencies
are irresponsible but because the most responsible and conventional agencies tend not to be attracted to such programmes even
by strong financial incentives. The programmes may not accord
with what they see to be their interests or image; this may include
having more than enough business elsewhere. Second, the type
of agency that is attracted to the programme is likely to be
entirely influenced by financial incentives and have no interest in
the social aims of the programme or the well-being of clients. This
is the more serious when clients are as vulnerable as the Section
235 buyers were and when the activities of dishonest middlemen
are at the same time so easy and so disastrous. Third, regulation
of such private agencies is extremely difficult, either internally
or externally, partly because they are so many and varied but
mainly because the threat of control is likely to be countered with
a threat to withdraw from the programme entirely. Fourth, the
incentives designed to attract agencies may be such that they

undermine the very viability of the programme, for example in
this case the 100 per cent insurance. Yet it may be impossible to
change these arrangements and retain the interest of any private
agency in the programme. Fifth, easy lending on cheap, deteriorated houses in poor inner-city environments does not make the
properties any better, nor does it increase the ability of the
owners to improve them. All it does is give poor people heavily
mortgaged ownership of an asset so dubious that no one else
would buy it. Sixth, the low-income lending programmes originally involved HUD only as guarantor of the mortgages and the
source of subsidies. But, ironically, the high levels of default
led ultimately to HUD being both a direct lender, with thousands
of 'Secretary-held' mortgages, a landlord of repossessed property
let back to the original owners and an estate agent trying to sell
empty property. Seventh, the whole experiment proved extremely
expensive in terms of damage to the housing stock, cost to the
government and disruption of the lives of many hard-pressed
families. Between 1969 and 1979, HUD paid off insurance claims
on 134,000 repossessed owner-occupied homes insured under
Section 235(1) and Section 223e,[31] and a further 149,000 between
1960 and 1979 under Section 221. It lost on average $12,000 on
each, at 1980 prices. In Detroit alone 13,400 were demolished
because they were too vandalised to sell. The financial institutions
lost little or nothing.

LESSONS FOR THE FUTURE IN AMERICA AND BRITAIN

In all but one respect, namely the benefits accruing to market
institutions, the outcomes of these programmes (and those for the
rental sector) must be seen as failures in terms even of the aims
of the US government. The anti-collectivist philosophy requires
that such government programmes as are necessary should be
designed to be highly selective and targeted to specific groups of
the population, should minimise expenditure and should avoid
unnecessary extension of government activity. In reality the
approach adopted has resulted in the selection of subsidy recipients by private sector agencies, often randomly and with great
inequity between those with similar incomes. The very poorest
have seldom been the beneficiaries. In addition, the programmes
have been expensive and wasteful of resources, and have involved government not just as a guarantor but also as a landlord
and lender of last resort, and ultimately as an estate agent. For
all these roles government agencies have proved reluctant, un-
prepared and, at federal level, fundamentally unsuitable.

These results are not an accident of poor programme design.
They arise out of the very nature of the approach. First, adverse
attitudes to large-scale government intervention, coupled with
very expensive programmes per unit, result in very small-scale
programmes. Second, the nature of the programmes is to give
inducements to the private sector to meet the needs of all groups.

As we have seen, sometimes no inducements are of any avail. On other occasions the conventional private sector agencies are uninterested but other fringe agencies are, and so take over the role without being suited to it. At other times inducements are accepted but the programme becomes diverted to, for instance, a different client group. With private agencies selecting clients for very small programmes the benefits are bound to become a lottery or, worse, the subject of corruption. Lastly, once private agencies have taken their profits they have no motive for retaining management of properties. Government mortgage guarantees merely facilitate the process of moving investment elsewhere.

Invariably it is not long before Congressional hearings reveal that programmes are costly and are missing their target. The programme is usually abandoned and replaced with another. As a result, American housing policy is characterised by what Downs calls 'compulsive innovation', [32] the constant introduction of new programmes. The new ones, however, often closely resemble the old. The lobbies see to that.

Unfortunately for the future chances of federal housing programmes and their recipients, it is upon government administration and upon the fecklessness of tenants and home owners, not upon the use of private sector agencies, that public blame falls for the failures. One of the dilemmas of the style of housing programmes operated in the USA is that it is extremely easy for critics of government policy to point, quite correctly, to how expensive per unit and how ineffective in targeting are the housing programmes. It is simultaneously true that housing programmes for the poor are too small and underfunded and are too expensive and wasteful. What is needed is not more of the same but less dependence on for-profit housing institutions. Because this different approach is not currently acceptable, the end result of the present style of programme is that all housing policy for poorer people becomes discredited and solutions are regarded as unattainable. It becomes easiest to blame the victims.

But the growing crisis of the lower-income rental market and declining home ownership rates amongst the poor make one wonder how long such attitudes can continue. To someone from Euope it appears inevitable that some sort of non-market rental sector will have to be established. Already, in a society in which systematic and explicit municipalisation or nationalisation would be out of the question, city governments like New York and Baltimore and the federal government (HUD) are, de facto and by default, municipalising huge amounts of rental property. But the processes through which cities and HUD acquire and manage this housing are totally unsatisfactory since they are not accompanied by subsidies for the management, improvement and maintenance of the property. Thus the emphasis is still on trying to return property to the private sector. In effect, public ownership is just not seen as a policy solution.

Though it would not seem possible to ignore the crisis for ever, the cost implications of any real solution are enormous. As Downs has written:

Pressures will rise for the Federal government to adopt new
policies responsive to this situation, but the real costs of
coping with it effectively are too great to be politically
acceptable. Hence a few token expansions of existing housing aims or symbolic adoptions of new ones will be the main
federal policy reactions.[33]
The effect will be that
much of the American rental housing sector - especially the
low-income end - will experience declining average physical
quality standards, increased crowding, higher real rent
burdens and generally tightening market conditions throughout the 1980s.[34]

It is no wonder then that those Americans who understand the
dynamics of the private rental and low-income home ownership
markets should view with amazement Britain's masochistic attempts
to starve and maim its public sector, all in the name of economy,
freedom of choice, individualism and competition. The public
sector in Britain is by no means perfect, but it is still large,
stable, relatively good-quality, relatively well managed, relatively
solvent and, not least, publicly accepted.

The fundamental question which must arise in relation to the
type of housing policy adopted in the USA and favoured by the
present British government is which agency, if any, has responsibility for making sure that the most vulnerable people are housed.
A private landlord, even a subsidised landlord, has no such obligation, nor does a lending agency. Even if the government rec-
ognises an obligation, how is it to be implemented?

The Housing Act, 1949, presented a national goal of a 'decent
home' for all Americans but, as Wolman says, 'Unfortunately, it is
not clear what interpretation to put upon this statement. Was it
meant to be a commitment for government action or merely a pious
expression of desire?'[35] Whatever the intention, there has been no
systematic government approach to implementing that goal. In
Britain, until the present Conservative government changed the
emphasis, there was in contrast considerable consensus between
the parties on the responsibility that government has for meeting
the housing needs of the population. Despite differences of political opinion, there was also wide agreement on the need for substantial public rental sector to achieve housing policy goals. The
Housing (Homeless Persons) Act, 1977, represented a culmination
of the approach which puts an obligation on government to see
that everyone is housed.

In the USA, on the other hand, public housing was never allowed
to develop into the sort of institution conceived by its early ex-
ponents. Once full employment returned, public housing, having
served its economic purpose, was starved of resources and stigmatised into a residual welfare sector. Despite a short-lived
reprieve in the late 1960s it has never recovered. Now its bad
image presents an impediment to the acceptance of further publicly
owned or even non-profit rental housing, just when America really
needs to develop something of this sort.

All this is of the utmost relevance to Britain because it explodes the prevailing myth that there is something uniquely sensible, logical and successful about market approaches to housing policy. On the contrary, the experience of the USA has been that government help to one private sector, home ownership, is undermining the other, the private rental market, without replacing its role. Britain is currently allowing home ownership policies to do the same thing to council housing. Clearly, too, in the USA the concentration of the private agencies and government programmes on the profits to be made from the production or transfer of housing from one person to another lead to neglect of the simple fact that people need to live in the homes once they are produced, let or sold. In assessing the success of a policy one has to ask for whom it is successful, whether for private market institutions or for lower-income households. As Eugene Meehan writes of the post-war public housing programme:

> The principal beneficiaries of the housing program, the designers and planners, construction companies and construction workers, building supply companies, those who sold their land to the Housing Authority at inflated prices, and some of the earlier tenants, obtained their benefits at the outset of the program. The losers, federal taxpayers, tenants, and the collectivity, plus all of those unfortunates who were denied cheap and decent housing over the long run because of the destruction of the concept in the ill-conceived policy matrix of the 1950s, were not handed their losses until the winners had departed.[36]

With the addition of 'better-off owner-occupiers' this description would apply to any of the housing programmes used in the USA. And in Britain today Meehan would see most of the same losers, and the same winners, with the addition of the recipients of council house sales. The degree to which sales and financial cuts are used to destroy the economic and social viability of council housing will determine whether the Housing Act, 1980, is allowed to destroy the concept of publicly owned housing in Britain, in the same way that similar ill-conceived policies did in the USA after the 1949 Act. That concept will be harder to revive than to destroy. And, as America's crisis-ridden rental market and failed experiments with low-income home ownership show, it will be even harder to replace it with a workable alternative.

NOTES

1   (US) Housing Act, 1949, tit.I, ch. 338, para. 2.
2   M. C. McFarland, 'Federal Government and Urban Problems' (Westview Press, Boulder, Colorado, 1978), p. 133.
3   Ibid.
4   J. Kemeny, 'The Myth of Home-Ownership' (Routledge & Kegan Paul, 1981), Ch. 7, p. 112.

5 Preamble to (US) Housing Act, 1949 (reaffirmed in Housing Act, 1968).

6 H. Aaron, Policy Implications of the Housing Allowance Experiment: A Progress Report, unpublished paper, The Brookings Institution, 1981, p. 33.

7 M. A. Stegman, Trouble for Multifamily Housing: Its Effects on Conserving Older Neighbourhoods in 'Occasional Papers in Housing and Community Affairs, Vol. 2' (Department of Housing and Urban Development, Washington DC, 1978), p. 243.

8 Ibid., p. 261.

9 Ibid., p. 243.

10 A. Downs, The Future of Rental Housing in America, unpublished paper, The Brookings Institution, 1979, p. 1.

11 V. A. Karn, 'The Position of Lower Income Households in the Owner-Occupied Housing Market in the USA and Great Britain' (Urban Institute, Washington DC, 1980), p. 15.

12 Stegman, Trouble for Multifamily Housing, p. 244.

13 E. Tobier et. al., Mortgage Financing and Housing Markets in New York State: A Preliminary Report, unpublished paper, presented to the New York State Legislature, May 1977, p. 111.

14 The City of New York, 'The In Rem Housing Program: First Annual Report 1978/79' (Department of Housing Preservation and Development, New York, 1979), p. 1.

15 C. Wye et al., HUD's Insured Multifamily Housing: The Problems of Financially Troubled Subsidised Projects in 'Occasional Papers in Housing and Community Affairs, Vol. 2' (Department of Housing and Urban Development, Washington DC, 1978), p. 170.

16 The City of New York, 'The In Rem Housing Program', p. 8.

17 US Congress, 'Housing and Urban Legislation of the 1970s', Hearings before the Senate Committee on Banking and Currency, 91st/92nd Congress (US Government Printing Office, 1971), p. 807.

18 Quoted in McFarland, 'Federal Government and Urban Problems', p. 100.

19 A. Downs, The Successes and Failures of Housing Policy, 'The Public Interest', Winter 1974.

20 Karn, 'The Position of Lower Income Households'.

21 J. Zinsmeyer et al., 'Opportunities for Abuse: Private Profits, Public Losses and the Mortgage Banking Industry' (Neighborhood Revitalization Project, Center for Community Change, Washington DC, 1977).

22 B. Callaghan, 'Bad Money After Good: Change in Mortgage Lending Patterns in Lower Germantown' (Institute for Study of Civil Values, Philadelphia, Pennsylvania, 1975), p. 26.

23 P. L. Maier et al., 'More Holes Than Net' (Center for Study of Responsive Law, Washington DC, 1977).

24 R. H. Silverman, Homeownership for the Poor: Subsidies and Racial Segregation, 'New York University Review', vol. 38 (1973), p. 101.

25   US Commission on Civil Rights, 'Home-Ownership for Lower
      Income Families: A Report in the Racial and Ethnic Impact of
      the Section 235 Program' (The Commission, 1971), p. 45.
26   Ibid., p. 46.
27   Ibid., p. 45.
28   Silverman, Homeownership for the Poor, p. 92.
29   Evidence by Representative Widnall: see US Congress, 'HUD
      Investigation of Low and Moderate Income Housing Program',
      Hearings before the House Committee on Banking and Cur-
      rency, 92nd Congress, 1st Session (US Government Printing
      Office, 1971), p. 3.
30   Commission for Civil Rights, 'Home-ownership for Lower
      Income Families', pp. 47-8; and D. Collard, Exclusion by
      Estate Agents - An Analysis, 'Applied Economics', vol. 5,
      no. 4 (1973), pp. 281-8.
31   Karn, 'The Position of Lower Income Households', p. 104.
32   Downs, The Successes and Failures of Housing Policy.
33   Downs, The Future of Rental Housing in America, p. ii.
34   Ibid., p. 57.
35   H. Wolman, 'Housing and Housing Policy in the US and UK'
      (Lexington Books, 1975), p. 18.
36   E. J. Meehan, Looking the Gift Horse in the Mouth: The Con-
      ventional Public Housing Program in St Louis, 'Urban Affairs
      Quarterly', vol. 10, no. 4 (1975), pp. 460-1.

8 The Choice for Council Housing

John English

In examining the future of council housing in Britain this book
has so far looked at its development and at various aspects of the
present position of the tenure. Particular attention has been
given to issues raised by the sale of council houses, both because
sales are important in themselves and because they crystallise
differing views about the desirable balance between housing tenures. This chapter is not intended to summarise the book as a
whole, but rather to draw out some of the implications of the discussion. Whereas previous chapters have had a comparatively
narrow focus, and have looked into the future to only a limited
extent, the present one is more wide-ranging and speculative in
its approach. Some of the ways in which public sector housing
may develop and alternatives for policy are examined.
    Council housing is now at something of a crossroads: after more
than half a century of at least fairly steady development (Chapter 1), during which it has grown to nearly a third of the total
stock in Britain, there is a strong possibility that it is about to
enter a period of sustained decline. A major factor in any decline
may be the sale of council houses on an unprecedentedly large
scale which is being promoted by the Conservative government
elected in 1979, with the tenant's statutory right to buy at a discount. But as well as sales there is the level of new building in
the public sector; it has already fallen very steeply and even
greater reductions are implied in the government's public expenditure plans (Chapter 2). Neither of these influences will immediately transform the position of the public sector; their effect will
be incremental. Expenditure cuts might be reversed within a few
years and sales looked on with less favour; in any case the popularity of council house purchase is uncertain. If, however,
present policies were to be maintained, in, say, 20 years or so at
the turn of the century it is likely, not just that the size of the
public sector will have been substantially reduced both as a proportion of the housing stock and absolutely, but that its role in
the housing system will have been much altered if not transformed.

TWO VIEWS OF COUNCIL HOUSING

It is probably fair to say that the bigger the public sector has
grown the less coherent has been discussion of its overall objectives or role. Essentially there has been a series of changing short-
term objectives: to add to the general housing stock in the 1920s,

to rehouse people from the slums in the 1930s, to allocate desper-
ately scarce accommodation to those in need after 1945 and so on.
Perhaps the nearest approaches to a long-term strategy for
council housing were John Wheatley's 15-year building programme
of 1924 and Aneurin Bevan's support for the public sector after
1945; each was intended to provide good quality housing for at
least a broadly-defined working class (Bevan went beyond this),
and each was aborted by political changes. At the present time,
however, it is possible to discern in the welter of political controversy about housing policy two broad views about the proper
role of the public sector vis-à-vis owner occupation.

First, there is what may be called the 'residual' view of council
housing: that owner occupation is the 'normal' tenure which can
best meet the requirements of most of the population and that a
small public sector should cater only for 'special' needs. (Outside
the realm of political rhetoric the contribution of the private landlord must now be largely discounted, so that the choice is essentially between the two main tenures.) Second, there is the view
that a public sector of more or less its present size should co-
exist with owner occupation, a separate but equal tenure catering
for substantial numbers of people who do not have a particular
necessity to rent but may prefer to do so. It is on this group that
controversy centres, in the sense that it is not seriously disputed
that the public sector will in any case have to house groups such
as the elderly, the handicapped and the poor. (A third view,
exemplified, for example, in some Community Development Project
publications,[1] that council housing is such a superior tenure that
it ought to be very substantially expanded at the expense of
owner occupation, may be discounted for practical purposes.)
Although these contrasting views of the future of council housing
are widely held, their far-reaching social and economic implications have rarely been explored.

Owner occupation has grown even more rapidly than council
housing since the First World War, until it now constitutes well
over half the housing stock in Britain. In addition to new building,
a major source of expansion has been the transfer of formerly
privately rented dwellings, but this process is nearing exhaustion.
Owner occupation and council housing together account for between eight and nine out of ten dwellings. The contribution of new
building is minimal in comparison to the size of the housing stock;
even if concentrated in the private sector, it could not sustain the
historical expansion rate of owner occupation, and would take
years substantially to alter the overall balance of tenures. In
short, council house sales are a necessity if the growth of owner
occupation is not to be severely checked. On average (the argument cannot realistically be applied to all localities) the public
sector has grown too large for determined proponents of owner
occupation to be content with simply halting its further expansion.
Extension of owner occupation and residualisation of the public
sector have become, in effect, different aspects of the same policy.

If the foregoing is the background to the case put forward by advocates of a residual public sector, a range of more specific arguments have been used by them. Though these arguments will be examined chiefly in the context of council house sales, many of them apply equally to the balance of new construction. Indeed, supporters of council house sales can be expected also to favour a low level of public sector construction. It is possible to do otherwise but this would, in effect, be to accept local authorities as suppliers of new housing for purchase in direct competition with private developers; such a position would not fit in with the general political orientation of the majority of those concerned. Building for sale by local authorities has in fact never enjoyed more than limited political backing.

The chief argument used in favour of selling council houses seems to have been the alleged financial advantages of the policy; though to a considerable extent it is a convenient rationalisation of an underlying ideological position. The crude version of the financial case, which enjoyed a wide currency until fairly recently, is that sales (and any extension of owner occupation) benefit both the individual householder on the one hand and the taxpayer and ratepayer in their role as suppliers of subsidies on the other. It would have been wonderful were that the case but, as has already been demonstrated in detail (Chapter 3), this is at best an extremely doubtful proposition. The advantages which the individual owner occupier can expect to enjoy at a time of inflation are undoubted: declining real housing costs and the acquisition of an increasingly valuable asset. Given these gains, a loss to the community is almost inevitable. Though a case for benefits to the public purse beyond the short term can be made out, as in the recent Department of the Environment appraisal, the calculations have to be based on consistently extreme assumptions (about future real rents, maintenance costs and so on) and lack plausibility. A subtle shift appears to have taken place in the attitude of government spokesmen, for instance, which reflects more realistic appraisals of the financial effects of sales which are gaining currency. The Secretary of State for the Environment was reported as stating early in 1981 that his 'principal motive for encouraging the sale of council houses was to reverse the polarization of society between home owners and council tenants. That was far more important than any savings that might accrue to taxpayers and ratepayers'.[2] Less is being said about alleged advantages to the community, but the financial benefits gained by buyers are still, quite realistically, emphasised.

A further set of financial considerations which undoubtedly carry weight in government circles, especially when the overriding preoccupation is the reduction of public spending, is that the cost of income (and other) tax reliefs, by which owner occupation is subsidised, are not counted in the total. The absurd convention whereby 'tax expenditures' are seen as being somehow different from direct spending may be slowly breaking down (witness the tentative inclusion of the cost of allowances and reliefs in public expenditure white papers), but this artificial distinction is still

sufficiently accepted to make owner occupation appear attractive.
And, in so far as the distinction is accepted by the general public, it is possible to present owner occupiers as paying their own
way in contrast to uniquely subsidised council tenants.

The non-financial arguments used in favour of council house
sales and the growth of owner occupation are more diffuse and,
being based primarily on a particular set of value judgements
rather than on technical analyses, are harder to evaluate. The
arguments typically centre on claims that, for example, home
ownership is more 'natural' than renting, it increases freedom, it
reduces the role of the state, and it encourages a sense of civic
responsibility. These claims can be examined on two levels. First,
there is the question whether they imply intrinsically desirable
objectives. Some objectives, like the enlargement of freedom, are
in themselves unexceptionable but this is not true of them all, for
example reduction in the role of the state. Second, it can be asked
whether the policy will in fact foster the achievement of the objectives. Many of the claims are oversimplified or operate at the level
of unsupported assertion. There is little hard evidence on the
enhancement of civic responsibility; this popular notion is perhaps
based on naive comparisons of different populations living in different tenures. A related consideration for the Conservative
Party itself, if not an argument which can be much used in public,
is the belief that owner occupation engenders sound political attitudes, leading to self-reliance and a rejection of socialistic nos-
trums. Assertions about increased freedom beg all kinds of
questions concerning what is meant by the term and whether the
term and whether the enlargement of some people's freedom dim-
inishes that of others. The notion that owner occupation is in
some sense 'natural' is really a sort of metaphysical statement
about which it is difficult to say anything useful, though it is
certainly not reinforced by the experience of Sweden, Switzerland
and West Germany where the tenure is comparatively small.

One argument in favour of increased owner occupation which
has some substance relates to mobility of labour. But even here
the argument tends to be overstated, in as much as the considerable barriers to mobility in that sector, caused by regional variations in house prices and by transaction costs, are commonly
ignored. Nevertheless, a weakness of the public sector has been
its failure to allow tenants to transfer readily between different
local authority areas. There is no reason in principle, however,
why council housing should not be able to meet demands for long
distance moves even more effectively than owner occupation. While
the National Mobility Scheme which has recently been set up
through the initiative of the government would seem to be too
limited to do this, there has in the past been little enthusiasm
from local authorities and it is a step in the right direction.

It would be more accurate to argue that, although owner occupation does have real advantages for the individual (though much
more doubtfully for the community), in the main these advantages
are not intrinsic attributes of the tenure but are conferred upon

it by specific housing policies. By the same token, therefore, the growth of owner occupation at the expense of council housing is not necessarily preferable to reforms in these policies.

The arguments deployed by opponents of the residualisation of council housing tend to be both more negative and narrower than those of its advocates. This is because the opponents' case rests primarily on attacking that of the other side; less is said about the positive virtues of the public sector and least of all in the way of direct criticism of owner occupation. The case tends to be mainly concerned with council house sales, particularly forced sales under the right to buy, rather than with a coherent view of what would be a desirable balance of tenures. Much therefore of what has already been said about the case for sales applies, *mutatis mutandis*, to the other side.

The alleged financial advantages of sales to the community have been questioned with success; indeed, as has been pointed out, there are signs that this argument is being tacitly abandoned. Financial advantages to the individual, on the other hand, are undeniable, and it is a major weakness of the pro-public sector lobby that the Labour Party has been unwilling seriously to consider altering housing finance and taxation in order to make the position of owners and tenants more equal (this important issue is examined later). Other arguments in favour of sales (such as reducing the role of the state) tend to be ignored; they may indeed be simplistic or involve unacceptable assumptions but the opposition case is too often allowed to go by default. Opponents of sales do emphasise the near certainty that the quality of remaining council housing as well as the size of the public sector will be reduced, thus making the meeting of urgent housing needs more difficult. More positively, they have also emphasised the desirability of measures to improve the position of the council tenant (albeit generally from a non-financial point of view), such as legally enforceable security of tenure and a right to consultation.

There are, however, major problems associated with the residualisation of council housing, and the concomitant extension of owner occupation, which so far have received surprisingly little attention. First, there are the implications for the repair and maintenance of the housing stock. Despite the widespread assumption that home owners take exceptionally good care of their property, there is evidence, notably from the national House Condition Survey,[3] that the growing problem of disrepair is more serious in the owner-occupied than in the public sector. Second, and closely related, there are the problems of low-income owner occupiers which will undoubtedly increase as government policies draw in more and more economically marginal purchasers. Neither they, nor the growing number of elderly owners, are likely to have incomes that are adequate to enable them properly to maintain their homes. The cost of necessary repairs and maintenance tends to be postponed by many owners (not always because they have low incomes) without immediate inconvenience, but the resulting deterioration in the housing stock has later to be made good. The gradual abandonment of Schedule A tax (through a failure to use updated property values) and its final abolition in 1963, by removing a financial incentive to undertake maintenance (the cost of which could be offset against tax liability), can only have made the problem worse. The response by successive governments of increasingly liberal grants, first for improvement and later for repair, while further subsidising private housing at public expense, have been far from completely successful. Another emerging problem is mortgage default by economically marginal purchasers, with its consequences for homelessness. [4] It must be wondered how many beneficiaries of the right to buy will return to local authorities in order to be bailed out by the public sector which they had abandoned.

Third, and perhaps most serious of all, are the financial and economic costs of owner occupation to the community (Chapter 3). Under existing taxation and subsidy arrangements the long-term cost to the taxpayer of an owner-occupied house can be expected substantially to exceed that of a similar council house. But the costs of the tenure in terms of economic inefficiency must be a matter of even greater concern. The physical deterioration of owner-occupied housing has already been mentioned. Home ownership is a uniquely attractive way for most people to hold savings so that they maintain (or increase) their real value. This results in the overconsumption of housing, with low densities of occupancy, because it is purchased as an investment over and above the extent to which it would be bought merely for use. Owner occupation has a seemingly insatiable demand for mortgage funds which competes for savings and drives up interest rates. This use of more and more funds, the bulk to finance the exchange of existing houses rather than fresh investment, increases the cost of capital for investment by productive industry. [5]

Finally, the non-financial advantages of rented housing (actual or potential) tend to be ignored. There is no doubt that many people welcome the opportunity provided by owner occupation to invest time and effort in the alteration and improvement of their homes, something which it would be difficult fully to emulate in rented housing. On the other hand, not all householders are in a position to deploy do-it-yourself skills of real value and would equally welcome an efficient repair and maintenance service, as well as the absence of transaction costs on movement and other advantages that rented housing can provide. Too often, of course, the public sector has failed to provide these advantages, but this does not mean that its destruction is preferable to improvements in its administration.

PARTY POLICIES AND HOUSING TENURE

The arguments which are deployed in support of different views of the proper role of council housing have been outlined only briefly, but they provide some background to the different approaches identified above. It is now necessary to examine the policies of the main parties towards the public and private sectors. The first thing which should be said is that the two sides are not, as it were, fighting on the same terms. The advocates of a residual public sector, who may be broadly identified with the Conservative Party, are defending a comparatively coherent position; they are eager to fight for the expansion of owner occupation at the expense of council housing up to the point at which the latter caters only for narrowly defined 'real needs'. Their logical opponents, the straightforward advocates of council housing, are too few significantly to affect the battle. Their actual opponents, who may be identified with the bulk of Labour Party opinion, are unsure of their aims and are fighting something of a phoney war.

Conservatvies are clear that council housing is a second-class tenure for second-class people (though naturally they tend not to make their attitude too explicit). A residual public sector will be second-class housing from a physical point of view; as has been pointed out (Chapter 4), there can be little doubt that sales will be heavily concentrated among more attractive housing, leaving behind a preponderance of flats and less popular accommodation. [6] Only very unconvincing attempts have been made to deny that this will be an inevitable outcome of extensive sales. But such a result is unlikely to worry advocates of a residual public sector: implicit in their approach is that it is sufficient that adequate housing - adequate on basic criteria of appropriate size, internal amenities and so on - should be provided. In other words, council housing should be concerned with meeting officially defined minimum needs, and not with meeting individual preferences and tastes. The public sector is already second class from the point of view of the financial attractions of the different tenures. Though much of the present system of subsidies and taxation, at least in the private sector, owes more to accidents of historical development than to conscious design, it serves well enough. These arrangements fit in with the Conservative approach to housing, though they are being strengthened by the reduction in general assistance to council tenants through a policy of increasing real rents, with greater reliance on rebates for the poor.

It is perhaps a little brutal to describe the users of a residual public sector as second-class people, though the classical formulation of the deserving and undeserving poor is certainly appropriate. The deserving users of council housing will be those groups, such as the elderly, the handicapped and (possibly) the single, who through no fault of their own will often have incomes which are inadequate to enter owner occupation. Their reliance on the public sector will inevitably be increased by their special needs for sheltered accommodation and expensive adaptations that usually only it can provide. Then there are the undeserving poor, those without specific special needs or justification for lack of independance: low wage earners, the unemployed, the thriftless and other unfortunates. Conservative attitudes have, of course, been presented here in a stark fashion and it would be many years before they could have their full effect. But it clarifies the arguments if the potential implications of the residualisation of council housing are made clear.

Before moving on it is useful to point out a paradox in the Conservative position. The government places a high priority on reducing public expenditure and claims that the sale of counqil houses assists the achievement of this objective. It may do so in the very short term, but the government is storing up increased demands on the exchequer for the future by encouraging owner occupation while doing nothing to curb its cost to the taxpayer. The implication must be that an even greater priority is placed on the alleged advantages of owner occupation than on limiting the cost of housing to the exchequer.

The Labour Party, to put the matter succinctly, is trying to sit on the fence as far as housing policy is concerned; as well as being undignified, its position is increasingly uncomfortable and precarious. The party has traditionally been strongly in favour of council housing but its difficulties arise from a terror of offending actual or intending owner occupiers. This is understandable: owner occupiers are numerous, they include many floating voters and there is no doubt that political opponents would seize upon anything which could be represented as an attack on their interests. Offending council tenants, by contrast, does not hold such dangers for the Conservatives: there are both fewer of them and they tend to be thought of as irredeemably Labour in allegiance. The realities of the Labour Party's position were demonstrated in the Housing Policy Review in 1977,[7] which was widely condemned for its conservatism in the field of finance. The contradictions of Labour housing policy are demonstrated in its attitude to council house sales. This is confused enough in itself, ranging from outright opposition to the half-hearted acquiescence of recent Labour governments. But the main point is that opposition to sales, in the absence of radical changes in other aspects of housing policy, is not in the long term a politically viable policy. Though sales may be opposed at particular times, the attractions of owner occupation, particularly the financial attractions, are so great that they cannot be resisted indefinitely.

To put the point another way, while owner occupation continues to benefit from policies which make it such an attractive tenure for most people, not to sell council houses is likely to lead to the building up of intolerable pressures in the housing system. This is certainly likely to happen in areas with large public sectors, with a growing disparity of the balance of supply and demand in different tenures. But the right to buy is predicated on the assumption - in a sense the reasonable assumption - that, given the overwhelming (and increasing) advantages of owner occupation, any council tenant should be allowed to purchase his house. The government has allowed the right to buy to be limited only by very exceptional considerations of the adequacy of the public sector stock in an area, a politically unavoidable outcome once the

gains to individual purchasers had been so much emphasised. It
has been established for some time that the characteristics of
council tenants are changing; no longer is the public sector well
up the hierarchy of housing, underpinned by a large privately
rented sector of cheaper and inferior dwellings. But this applies
to the stock of existing tenants; when the flow of new tenants is
examined the trend is shown up even more clearly - newcomers
to council housing are very markedly different from their now
middle-aged and elderly predecessors.[8] The point has already
been made (Chapter 5) that the sons and daughters of council
tenants are tending to opt for owner occupation. In short, the
average council tenant is of falling socio-economic status and,
quite apart from the active promotion of sales, council housing is
being residualised by default.

There is another weakness of Labour policy concerning subsidies. It is widely accepted at a theoretical level that there are
strong arguments for altering the relationship between subsidies
to the consumption of housing and the level of capital investment,
so that a greater amount of investment in both the public and
private sectors could be accommodated within a given level of
public expenditure. But, if nothing is done about subsidies to
owner occupiers, increases in council rents in real terms are
bound to be resisted on grounds of equity. (Equity between different tenures is not an issue for Conservatives, apart from anything else because the tenures are each intended to cater for
different categories of people.) The result is that Labour governments have tried to restrain the level of rents and found the
current expenditure implications of new building unacceptable;
this (as well as reductions in capital spending as such) has led
to investment being cut back, as happened in the late 1970s. It
does not follow that it is desirable to push up rents so that council housing makes large profits; but the lack of a sound rationale
for rent levels, which allows them to fall in real terms (below
long-run costs), will stifle investment in new building and
improvement, and ensure that the public sector is reduced to the
role of welfare housing.

A further point may be made about the difficulties of the Labour
Party in defending the public sector. Many of the arguments in
favour of council housing, and especially those against sales, are
concerned with what may be called public benefits: for example
that good quality accommodation should be available according to
generous criteria of need. The benefits of increased owner occupation, by contrast, are to a large extent enjoyed privately by
individuals, especially the financial ones. Regrettably the prospect of private advantage probably has greater political salience
than that accruing to the community as a whole.

The Conservative Party has a fairly coherent policy in the
sense that it will lead eventually to the residualisation of the public sector. There is little need therefore to examine changes in
policy which might better achieve its narrow objectives for council
housing. (The policy is far from coherent in other respects:

reference has already been made to the costs of residualisation in
the context of existing taxation and subsidy policies, in terms of
the deterioration of the stock, public expenditure and overconsumption of housing.) The Labour Party, on the other hand, has
failed to develop comparable policies which could support the continued existence of a large public sector, providing high-quality
housing for a wide section of the community. The remainder of
this chapter will explore some of the measures which will be necessary if in due course Britain is not to have a public sector that
increasingly assumes the limited role of welfare housing.

THE ALTERNATIVE TO RESIDUALISATION

Despite the shortcomings and unpopularity of some council housing, the public sector has enjoyed major achievements; it has
been the means by which a great deal of good quality housing has
been provided and by which the housing conditions of many ordinary people have been improved. It is sometimes claimed that, in
the absence of rent control and competition from council housing,
adequate provision would have been made by private enterprise.
But it is unprofitable to speculate about what might have happened under very different conditions; and, in any case, actual
experience before 1914 shows no evidence of this. As it is, much
council housing is unproblematic, attractive and popular; and
sales are likely to be concentrated in this part of the stock. The
shortcomings of council housing, which do make the tenure unat-
tractive to many people, are really of two kinds. First, there is
the regime of subsidies and taxation which makes owner occupation
financially attractive. Second, there are a range of problems with
the public sector housing stock itself and its management. If
council housing is not to move towards a purely residual role,
measures will have to be sought which will counter both kinds of
shortcoming. What follows is an attempt to indicate in outline the
possible nature of some of these measures.
   The financial attractions of owner occupation to the individual
are mirrored in its financial and economic costs to the community.
In the public sector these advantages and disadvantages are
essentially reversed, and the question is how these differences
can be reduced if not eliminated. This is obviously an issue for
the advocates of council housing, looking at the matter from the
point of view of the householder, but it ought also to be an issue
for advocates of increased owner occupation if their policy is not
to be costly for the nation.
   The notion of a precise equality of treatment of individuals in
the different tenures is something of a chimera. Nevertheless,
this does not mean that a broad equality of treatment is not both
desirable - if council housing is not to move inexorably towards a
purely residual role - and achievable; the hopeless defeatism of
the Labour government's Housing Policy Review on this issue
should not be taken as the last word. Attention tends to be focused

on the income tax relief on mortgage interest enjoyed by owner
occupiers; and it is indeed costly, futile, inequitable and counter
productive. It is costly because the subsidy is not related to the
cost of construction and occasional major improvement (as in the
case of council housing) but to a periodically revalued market
price every time a house changes hands. It is futile to the extent
that tax relief is capitalised and therefore reflected in higher
prices rather than in lower mortgage costs. It is inequitable
because it gives the greatest assistance to those with the highest
incomes (especially those paying higher marginal tax rates) who
can afford the most expensive houses. It is counterproductive in
that it encourages the overconsumption of housing space in competition with more economically and socially productive investment.
The Labour Party seems to be seriously considering limiting relief
to the basic tax rate but this change could not have more than a
slight effect on the attractions of owner occupation. Even the
complete abolition of income tax relief would not transform the
situation, owing to the other tax benefits enjoyed by owner
occupiers.

At the present time the most important reason for the financial
attractiveness of owner occupation is inflation (and the exemption
of capital gains from taxation). If the rate of inflation was to be
very much reduced the balance of advantage between tenures
would be radically altered. The best comment on inflation is that
it may be substantially and permanently reduced but that it would
be foolhardy to proceed on the assumption that this will happen.
New owner occupiers suffer initially high housing costs (particularly through the effects of high interest rates, a major cause of
which is inflation); but the bulk of their outgoings, which reflect
the capital element in housing costs, are fixed in nominal terms
and fall in real terms (unless they choose to trade-up). Owner
occupiers also obtain a valuable asset and, while in practice its
value cannot be easily realised, it should not be ignored: at the
time of a move a proportion of receipts can be spent on consumption. [9] Also a house can be used as security for a loan or to
provide an income in old age through a 'home income plan' as well
as a valuable bequest to heirs.

The council tenant enjoys few of these advantages, in essence
because he does not own the equity of his house but merely hopes
to benefit from possible falls in the real cost of the local authority's stock of housing. It is true that inflation does reduce the
real burden of local authority housing debt, which could result in
lower real rents, but, unfortunately for existing tenants, councils
continue to build. The new houses increase the average debt on
the whole stock and counteract the beneficent effects of inflation.
On past experience council tenants can expect to pay broadly
constant real rents throughout their lives and, of course, do not
gain a capital asset. (The position of low-income tenants is rather
different in as much as they can claim rent rebates or supplementary benefits, and are therefore likely to have lower housing costs
in the public sector than as owner occupiers. But obviously this

consideration can really only carry weight with advocates of a residual public sector.)

A number of measures are possible to move towards greater financial parity between council tenants and owner occupiers but none has been satisfactorily worked out in detail. It is only possible here to give a general indication of what might be done. In essence the need, if financial parity is to be approached, is to counter the effects of inflation. Capital gains tax could be applied to owner-occupied houses; but it would probably be necessary to permit gains to be rolled over during lifetimes (sellers of houses usually also have to buy at current prices though part of the proceeds of sales are often realised). Alternatively, some form of index-linked investment could be made available, possibly through the National Savings machinery, to tenant householders. At present, with near zero or even negative real rates of interest on savings media available to most people, house purchase is a uniquely attractive investment. Whereas a capital gains tax on owner-occupied housing would undoubtedly be represented as an attack on home ownership, an index-linked investment would not share such a political drawback. Yet such a scheme would have major disadvantages: policing access to an attractive investment, the limits on which would necessarily have to be substantial, would not be simple. But, above all, it could prove expensive to the exchequer, whereas an extension of capital gains tax would bring in additional revenue besides curbing over-consumption of housing to the benefit of the economy. It is perhaps not unfair to say that the choice would be between buying an easy solution in the short term and following a harder path which makes greater financial and economic sense.

A further way in which tenants are at a disadvantage is in the non-taxation of imputed income from owner occupation (since the final abolition of Schedule A in 1963); someone who puts his savings into financial assets rather than an owner-occupied house is taxed on the interest and must pay rent out of taxed income. Furthermore, an effective tax on imputed income would provide an incentive for the proper maintenance of owner-occupied housing. Here again, particularly given the history of past controversies, it is easy to imagine the political minefield that would be created by such a measure. None of these possibilities, or other measures to equalise the financial attractions of different tenures, is likely to be either politically or administratively straightforward to introduce; yet they are indispensably necessary if council housing is not to be residualised.

Moving from subsidies and taxation to the problems of the public sector stock and its management, the measures which could make council housing more attractive are not easy to summarise. The shortcomings of council housing have been extensively discussed elsewhere,[10] though it must be emphasised that serious shortcomings affect only a limited part of the stock. This is not the place to discuss how the differential quality of council housing interacts with the allocation process and results in the most

disadvantaged applicants often getting the worst accommodation. [11]
The issue is a major one for council housing and there is an
urgent need for very substantial expenditure on difficult-to-let
estates. The concern here, however, is with tenants who could
realistically enter owner occupation and at the present time are
in any case generally allocated far from the worst council housing.
How council housing can be made more attractive to them is a much
wider problem than that of difficult-to-let estates. There needs to
be a higher level of investment in improvement and better standards of maintenance; yet both are now being cut back under the
effect of expenditure restrictions. Then there is the need for
much more effective arrangements to facilitate the mobility of
public sector tenants both within and between authorities; the
potential here is surely for council housing to surpass owner
occupation with its large transaction costs.

Housing management in the public sector today has its origins
in the paternalistic provision of housing for the poor and these
origins have still not been entirely shaken off (Chapter 6). The
level of training and standing in the local government hierarchy
of housing management staff are both comparatively low; unpro-
fessional and judgemental attitudes remain. [12] It might indeed be
said that the traditions of housing management would equip it well
to preside over a residual public sector.

It would probably assist the effectiveness of housing management if the different aspects of its work were more clearly defined.
On the one hand, it will in any case have a growing welfare
function as more vulnerable and poorer people become council
tenants. This role can perhaps be seen as a modern equivalent of
the Octavia Hill tradition of management, if not of the work of
Miss Hill herself with her insistence on a business-like relationship with tenants. [13] In a residual public sector it would dominate
housing departments. On the other hand, in a large public sector
at any rate, the great majority of tenants can look after their
affairs and their houses perfectly well; they want not paternalism
but efficient and courteous administration of generally routine
functions such as allocations and transfers, rent collection and
repairs. Different tenures do have intrinsic attributes (though
far fewer than are commonly attributed to them), and those of
rented housing have positive attractions for substantial numbers
of people. It is up to the housing management profession to seek
to provide good quality, trouble-free and economical accommodation
for those who prefer to rent. Better housing management cannot
by itself create the conditions necessary for the maintenance of an
attractive public sector catering for a wide range of tenants; but
it is essential for the achievement of that goal.

PROSPECTS FOR THE FUTURE

It is difficult to avoid the conclusion that council housing faces
a bleak future, and two recent publications provide only slight

grounds for optimism. After long deliberation a majority of both
Conservative and Labour members of the House of Commons
Environment Committee managed to agree on a final report on
council house sales.[14] It is undoubtedly significant that
Conservative MPs were willing to recognise that sales are likely to
have costs as well as benefits, that much of the DOE appraisal
was of questionable validity and that the effects of the right to
buy should be monitored. But the report fails to put sales in
context and to discuss the policies which in any case are leading
to a residual public sector. There is no doubt that a Labour Party
discussion document,[15] originating from a working group
appointed by the National Executive Committee, fully supports
council housing. Many proposals are made for its improvement,
covering issues such as physical conditions, tenants' rights and
allocations. But it does not make any major recommendations for
the reform of housing finance, the most crucial issue of all. It is
true that another working group is to consider housing finance,
but unless the party does tackle this issue it should recognise
the limitations of its support for the public sector and come to
terms with the inevitable decline of the tenure.

The expansion of owner occupation at practically any cost,
together with the residualisation of the public sector, is the
cornerstone of Conservative housing policy. The Labour Party
does not have a coherent alternative. The Liberals and Social
Democrats talk about radical housing policies but, if they were to
gain a position of power, they would then have to face the vested
interests represented by owner occupation. Without accepting the
wilder claims which are made for owner occupation, there is no
doubt that its growth will be to the real benefit of many people
under present conditions. Those who oppose the move towards
residual council housing point out, first, that many of the
attractions of owner occupation stem not from the inherent
attributes of the tenure but from advantages conferred upon it by
housing policy; second, that rented housing has, or could have,
important attractions of its own for at least some people who have
a genuine choice of tenures; and, third, that a radical change in
the balance of tenures could have substantial social costs.

As well as the enormous problems of welfare housing for the
poor, there are the difficulties of attempting to extend owner
occupation to low-income groups and of using subsidies to achieve
specific objectives through the private sectors: the experience of
the United States (Chapter 7) should act as a salutary warning.
One of the most ignored virtues of council housing is its efficiency
in utilising subsidies as an instrument of policy with the minimum
of waste and harmful spill-over effects; its record in this respect
has been far better than that of owner occupation.

This book has sought to highlight the many inefficiencies and
inequities of housing policy as it affects the public sector; many
of these failings are of long standing though they have been
exacerbated by the policies of the Conservative government since
1979. Both the strengths and failings of council housing have been

explored as have the prospects for its future. The inescapable conclusion is that if there is not to be a steady drift towards a residual public sector, serving only the disadvantaged and those accepted as having special needs, changes must be made in policy which will affect owner occupation as well as council housing. Its supporters, if they are to be taken seriously, must seize the main issues. They must not, like the last Labour government, be side-tracked by a rhetoric of choice and search for 'alternative tenures' into ignoring them. Policies which are as forthright as those of the present Conservative government must be developed. It may be that such policies are not now politically feasible; if this is so then the sooner the implications of the transformation of the public sector into welfare housing are recognised the better. Clarification of the choices involved may at any rate encourage a more realistic discussion of housing policy in Britain.

NOTES

1 See, for example, Community Development Project, 'Whatever Happened to Council Housing?' (CDP, 1976).
2 'The Times', 13 February 1981.
3 Department of the Environment, 'English House Condition Survey 1976' (2 Parts, HMSO, 1978 and 1979).
4 V. Karn, Pity the Poor Home Owners, 'Roof' (January 1979).
5 B. Kilroy, Housing Finance - Why So Privileged?, 'Lloyds Bank Review', no. 133 (1979), pp. 37-52.
6 J. English, Council House Sales: What Will Be Left?, 'Housing Review', vol. 26, no. 6 (1977), pp. 136-7.
7 'Housing Policy: A Consultative Document', Cmnd 6851 (HMSO, 1977); and 'Scottish Housing: A Consultative Document', Cmnd 6852 (HMSO, 1977).
8 V. Karn, Public Sector Demolition Can Seriously Damage Your Wealth, 'Roof' (January/February 1981).
9 Department of the Environment, 'Housing Policy: Technical Volume, Part II' (HMSO, 1977), p. 116.
10 See, for example, Department of the Environment, 'An Investigation of Difficult to Let Housing: Volume 1 General Findings', Housing Development Directorate Occasional Paper 3/80 (HMSO, 1981).
11 J. English, Access and Deprivation in Local Authority Housing in C. Jones (ed.), 'Urban Deprivation and the Inner City' (Croom Helm, 1979).
12 V. Karn, The Newest Profession, 'Roof' (November 1977).
13 M. Brion and A. Tinker, 'Women in Housing: Access and Influence' (Housing Centre Trust, 1980), Ch. 6.
14 House of Commons Environment Committee, 'Council House Sales', HC 366-I/1980-81.
15 Labour Party, 'A Future for Council Housing' (Labour Party, 1981).

Appendix

REPORT OF THE HOUSE OF COMMONS ENVIRONMENT
COMMITTEE ON COUNCIL HOUSE SALES

The final report of the Environment Committee's enquiry into
council house sales* was published in June 1981 after the main
text of the book had been completed. The committee's standing
and ability to call for a range of evidence beyond the resources of
other bodies are likely to give its report an authoritative stamp.
Evidence, both written and oral, was taken from local authorities,
construction companies, credit institutions, pressure groups,
professional bodies, academics and volunteers, and was supported
by eight impressive memoranda from its specialist advisers. This
note on the report has therefore been included.

Allowance must be made for difficulties such a body has in
dealing with an issue of such party-political sensitivity. In the
event, the committee's fourth draft secured a bipartisan majority
(voting was 5-4) which was unequivocally critical of sales at
discounts in respect of all the main implications which were
investigated. It was severely critical of each of the DOE's
arguments. It felt that forward thinking by housing authorities
about sales was less than adequate.

Impact on the local authority housing stock. The committee felt
that a likely volume of sales of around 100,000 per year would
over a decade reduce the stock of council houses (as distinct
from flats) by nearly one-third. Sales would be disproportionately
of houses and indeed of the better quality houses. The committee
felt that the claim by the Secretary of State and his department
that the consequent loss of relets would be 'minimal' was based on
a false premise in the DOE's 1980 appraisal. In fact, over 30
years 78,000 relets could be lost per 100,000 dwellings sold, and
26,000 over the first ten years. This would cause substantial
harm to lettings and transfers (including those to families now
living in tower blocks) and so exacerbate housing need. This
misjudgement by the DOE added a further reason for reconsidering
the reduction in public expenditure on housing. Capital receipts
(varying widely from area to area) would be equivalent to no more
than an average of 10 per cent of sale values because outside
finance would not be available. Therefore the offsetting benefit
to investment funds from sales was small.

Although specially adapted dwellings are excluded from the
right to buy, the committee was concerned that the housing

prospects of the elderly and other disadvantaged groups would be damaged by the sale of non-specialist properties. Misgivings were also expressed about the general effects of sale on rural areas, notwithstanding the designated area exemptions. Equally, sales in outer urban areas were likely indirectly to increase the housing stress of inner urban areas.

Impact on private housing. The committee had few immediate fears because the proportion of sales financed privately was likely to be small. Otherwise, the effects on mortgage costs could be significant. In the medium and longer terms, the financing of resales could become significant and some destabilising effects on the housing market could occur.

Impact on public finance. The committee felt that the DOE's appraisal was unrealistic and unduly favourable; that its assumptions on future rent income were improbably low; and that some assumptions on management and maintenance savings, on improvement costs and on rent rebate costs were questionable. It commented: 'Our adviser, applying the same analytical techniques as those used in the Department's Appraisal, but with some alterations to the assumptions, concluded that, whilst the financial effect remained favourable in the short term, the 20-year appraisal contained both losses and gains and over a 50-year period every variant, under the assumptions used showed a loss'. Therefore a comprehensive reply from the DOE was necessary. Fears were expressed that the treatment of receipts from sales under the new subsidy system would channel resources away from the areas of need.

Equity between individuals. The committee recognised the advantages to tenant purchasers, both financial (net mortgage outgoings could even be sometimes be less than council rents) and non-financial. However, the redistribution of wealth involved would be to purchasers 'likely to be better off than the majority of council tenants'. Therefore, the committee recommended that the Secretary of State should delay adding further to the range of finance concessions to purchasers.

Effect on the economy. The committee felt that the possible benefits of sales locally (extra mobility and retention of skilled groups through greater opportunities for owner occupation) would be slight and carry offsetting risks. Indeed, most beneficial effects could 'be achieved by other means at a much smaller cost to public funds'. The wider national economic effects, such as the leakage of funds and the diversion of resources away from investment, were the subject of an adviser's memorandum on which the committee declined to comment.

In spite of the criticism and an urgent call for further monitoring of the effects of sales, the committee's analysis followed a reactive

pattern, closely influenced by the DOE's policies and appraisal.
Policy alternatives, even suggesting reasonable norms for prices
at which houses are sold and future rent levels, let alone the
future of council housing, were not considered.

*Note
House of Commons, Environment Committee, 'Council House
Sales: Vol. 1 Report', HC366-I/1980-81. See also 'Vol. II Minutes
of Evidence', HC366-II (with memoranda from witnesses); and
'Vol. III Appendices', HC366-III (Comptroller and Auditor
General, 'Financial Consequences of the Sale of Council Houses';
D. Webster, 'The Redistribution of Wealth'; D. Webster, 'Loss
of Relets'; D. Webster, 'The Long Term Financial Effect of
Council House Sales on the Public Sector as a Whole'; J. Stevenson,
'An Analysis of the Short, Medium and Long Effects upon Private
Housing Finance, Output and Prices'; and A. Murie, 'A Short
History of Council Housing').

Notes on Contributors

<u>John English</u> Lecturer in Social Administration, Paisley College

<u>Ray Forrest</u> School for Advanced Urban Studies, University of Bristol

<u>Pam Gallagher</u> Director of Housing Administration Programmes, University of Stirling

<u>Colin Jones</u> Lecturer in Land Economics, Paisley College

<u>Valerie Karn</u> Centre for Urban and Regional Studies, University of Birmingham

<u>Bernard Kilroy</u> A London borough housing officer

<u>Alan Murie</u> School for Advanced Urban Studies, University of Bristol

<u>David Whitham</u> Joint Centre for Urban Design, Oxford Polytechnic

Index

(Note that references to the United States are all indexed under that heading)